First World War
and Army of Occupation
War Diary
France, Belgium and Germany

38 DIVISION
Divisional Troops
Machine Gun Corps
38 Battalion
2 March 1918 - 31 March 1919

WO95/2548/3

The Naval & Military Press Ltd
www.nmarchive.com
Published in association with The National Archives

Published by

The Naval & Military Press Ltd

Unit 10 Ridgewood Industrial Park,

Uckfield, East Sussex,

TN22 5QE England

Tel: +44 (0) 1825 749494

www.naval-military-press.com

www.nmarchive.com

This diary has been reprinted in facsimile from the original. Any imperfections are inevitably reproduced and the quality may fall short of modern type and cartographic standards.

© **Crown Copyright**
Images reproduced by permission of The National Archives, London, England, 2015.

Contents

Document type	Place/Title	Date From	Date To
Heading	WO95/2548/3		
Heading	38 Division 38 Bn Machine Gun Corps 1918 Mar-1919 Mar		
Heading	War Diary of the 38th Battalion M.G. Corps from 1.3.1918 to 31.3.1918 (Vol : I)		
War Diary	Armentieres	02/03/1918	31/03/1918
Miscellaneous	38th Battalion Machine Gun Corps	04/09/1918	04/09/1918
Miscellaneous	38th Battalion Machine Gun Corps.	28/09/1918	28/09/1918
Miscellaneous	38th Battalion Machine Gun Corps.	11/09/1918	11/09/1918
Operation(al) Order(s)	38th Battalion Machine Gun Corps. Order No. 51	17/09/1918	17/09/1918
Diagram etc	38th Batt. M.G.C.		
Operation(al) Order(s)	38th Battalion Machine Gun Corps Order No. 61	16/09/1918	16/09/1918
Diagram etc	38th Batt. M.G.C.		
Miscellaneous	Os.C., A.B.C. & D. Coys.	16/09/1918	16/09/1918
Operation(al) Order(s)	38th Battalion Machine Gun Corps. Order No. 62	17/09/1918	17/09/1918
Operation(al) Order(s)	38th Battalion Machine Gun Corps. Order No. 59	09/09/1918	09/09/1918
Operation(al) Order(s)	Administrative Instructions with Order No. 58	09/09/1918	09/09/1918
Miscellaneous	Os.C., A.B.C. & D. Coys.	14/09/1918	14/09/1918
Miscellaneous	Table of Calculations for S.C.S. Lines.		
Miscellaneous	A Form Messages And Signals		
Heading	38th Div. V. Corps. 38th Battalion, Machine Gun Corps. April 1918. Attached Appendices.		
War Diary	Merville Area	01/04/1918	01/04/1918
War Diary	Hedauville & Villers Bocage	02/04/1918	02/04/1918
War Diary	Puchevillers	03/04/1918	07/04/1918
War Diary	Rubempre	08/04/1918	10/04/1918
War Diary	Rubempre to Warloy	11/04/1918	13/04/1918
War Diary	Warloy	13/04/1918	30/04/1918
Miscellaneous	Appendices to accompany 38th Battalion Machine Gun Corps War Diary from 1/4/18 to 30/4/18. (Vol. 2)		
Miscellaneous	38th Battalion Machine Gun Corps.		
Miscellaneous	Train Arrangements	01/04/1918	01/04/1918
Operation(al) Order(s)	38th Battalion Machine Gun Corps. Battalion Order No. 1	31/03/1918	31/03/1918
Operation(al) Order(s)	38th Battalion Machine Gun Corps. Battalion Order No. 2	01/04/1918	01/04/1918
Miscellaneous	38th Divn. M.G.C.	03/04/1918	03/04/1918
Operation(al) Order(s)	C Company 38th Battn M.G.C Operation Order No. 18/18	04/04/1918	04/04/1918
Miscellaneous	Messages And Signals.		
Miscellaneous	C Form. Messages And Signals.		
Operation(al) Order(s)	38th Battalion Machine Gun Corps. Battalion Order No. 3	08/04/1918	08/04/1918
Operation(al) Order(s)	38th Battalion Machine Gun Corps. Battalion Order No. 4	10/04/1918	10/04/1918
Miscellaneous	Table of Reliefs and Moves to accompany 38th Battn. M.G.C. Order No. 4		
Operation(al) Order(s)	38th Battalion Machine Gun Corps. Operation Order No. 15	15/04/1918	15/04/1918

Operation(al) Order(s)	38th Battalion Machine Gun Corps. Operation Order No. 16	16/04/1918	16/04/1918
Operation(al) Order(s)	38th Battalion Machine Gun Corps. Operation Order No. 17	19/04/1918	19/04/1918
Operation(al) Order(s)	38th Battalion Machine Gun Corps. Operation Order No. 18	21/04/1918	21/04/1918
Operation(al) Order(s)	38th Battalion Machine Gun Corps. Order No. 19	22/04/1918	22/04/1918
Miscellaneous	O.C. "E" Coy. 38th Battn. M.G.C.	24/04/1918	24/04/1918
Miscellaneous	A Form Messages And Signals		
Operation(al) Order(s)	38th Battalion Machine Gun Corps. Order No. 20	24/04/1918	24/04/1918
Miscellaneous	Relief Table to accompany 38th Battn. M.G.C. Order No. 20		
Miscellaneous	A Form Messages And Signals		
Operation(al) Order(s)	Amendment to accompany 38th Battn. M.G.C. Order No. 20	02/08/1918	02/08/1918
Operation(al) Order(s)	38th Battalion Machine Gun Corps. Order No. 21	25/04/1918	25/04/1918
Operation(al) Order(s)	38th Battalion Machine Gun Corps. Order No. 22	26/04/1918	26/04/1918
Miscellaneous	Relief Table to accompany 38th Bn. M.G.C. Order No. 20		
Operation(al) Order(s)	Extract from 2nd Aust : Bn M.G.C. Order No. 13 (to accompany 38th Bn. M.G.C. Order 22.)	02/08/1918	02/08/1918
Miscellaneous	A Form Messages And Signals		
Heading	War Diary of 38th Battn M.G.C. from 1st May, 1918 to 31st May 18 (Vol. 3)		
War Diary	Warloy	01/05/1918	02/05/1918
War Diary	Contay	03/05/1918	05/05/1918
War Diary	Toutencourt	06/05/1918	31/05/1918
Operation(al) Order(s)	38th Battalion Machine Gun Corps. Order No. 23	30/04/1918	30/04/1918
Operation(al) Order(s)	38th Battalion Machine Gun Corps. Order No. 24	02/05/1918	02/05/1918
Operation(al) Order(s)	38th Battalion Machine Gun Corps. Operation No. 25	03/05/1918	03/05/1918
Miscellaneous	O.C., "A" Coy.	05/05/1918	05/05/1918
Operation(al) Order(s)	38th Battalion Machine Gun Corps. Order No. 26	07/05/1918	07/05/1918
Diagram etc	Taken from 57 DSE Scale : 1.20.000 Date 7.5.18		
Operation(al) Order(s)	Addendum To 38th Battn. M.G.C. Order No. 26	08/05/1918	08/05/1918
Diagram etc	Use with Artillery Maps.		
Operation(al) Order(s)	Amendment No. 1, to 38th Battn. M.G.C. Order No. 26	08/05/1918	08/05/1918
Miscellaneous	A Form Messages And Signals		
Operation(al) Order(s)	38th Battalion Machine Gun Corps. Order No. 27	10/05/1918	10/05/1918
Operation(al) Order(s)	38th Battalion Machine Gun Corps Amendment to Order No. 27	11/05/1918	11/05/1918
Operation(al) Order(s)	38th Battalion Machine Gun Corps. Order No. 28	17/05/1918	17/05/1918
Miscellaneous	Table to accompany 38th Battn. M.G.C. Order No. 28		
Operation(al) Order(s)	Administrative Instructions With Record To 38th Battn. M.G.C. Order No. 28	17/05/1918	17/05/1918
Operation(al) Order(s)	38th Battalion Machine Gun Corps. Order No. 29	17/05/1918	17/05/1918
Operation(al) Order(s)	38th Battalion Machine Gun Corps. Order No. 30	21/05/1918	21/05/1918
Miscellaneous	38th Battalion Machine Gun Corps. Administrative Instructions to Accompany Order No. 30	17/05/1918	17/05/1918
Miscellaneous	To 38th Battn M.G.C.	25/05/1918	25/05/1918
Miscellaneous	A Form Messages And Signals		
Heading	War Diary of 38th Battn M.G.C. from 1st June 18 to 30th June 18 (Vol. 4)		
War Diary	Toutencourt	01/06/1918	04/06/1918
War Diary	Forceville	05/06/1918	30/06/1918
Operation(al) Order(s)	38th Battalion Machine Gun Corps Order No. 31	01/06/1918	01/06/1918

Miscellaneous	Relief Table To Accompany 38th Battn. M.G.C. Order No. 31		
Operation(al) Order(s)	Administrative Arrangements with regard to 38th Battn. M.G.C. Order No. 31	02/06/1918	02/06/1918
Miscellaneous		02/06/1918	02/06/1918
Operation(al) Order(s)	38th Battalion Machine Gun Corps. Order No. 32	06/06/1918	06/06/1918
Operation(al) Order(s)	38th Battalion Machine Gun Corps. Order No. 33	06/06/1918	06/06/1918
Operation(al) Order(s)	38th Battalion Machine Gun Corps. Order No. 34	07/06/1918	07/06/1918
Miscellaneous	38th Battalion Machine Gun Corps.	06/06/1918	06/06/1918
Operation(al) Order(s)	38th Battalion Machine Gun Corps. Order No. 35	09/06/1918	09/06/1918
Operation(al) Order(s)	38th Battalion Machine Gun Corps. Order No. 36	12/06/1918	12/06/1918
Operation(al) Order(s)	Addendum No. 1 to 38th Battn. M.G.C. Order No. 37	19/06/1918	19/06/1918
Operation(al) Order(s)	Reference 38th Battn. M.G. Corps Order No. 57 of 17/6/18, Appendix	17/06/1918	17/06/1918
Operation(al) Order(s)	Amendment No. 1. to 38th Battn. M&G. C. Order No. 37	17/06/1918	17/06/1918
Miscellaneous	The Centre Group will consist of 4 eight gun Batteries and 1 four gun Battery under the Command of Major Adamson, 38th Battn. M.G. Corps, with Headquarters at Q.21.d.3.3		
Operation(al) Order(s)	38th Battalion Machine Gun Corps. Order No. 37	17/06/1918	17/06/1918
Map	Machine Gun Barrage Map.		
Operation(al) Order(s)	38th Battalion Machine Gun Corps. Order No. 38	19/06/1918	19/06/1918
Operation(al) Order(s)	38th Battalion Machine Gun Corps. Order No. 39	27/06/1918	27/06/1918
Miscellaneous	O.C., "B" Coy.	25/06/1918	25/06/1918
Operation(al) Order(s)	Amendment To 38th Battn. M.G.C. Order No. 38	19/06/1918	19/06/1918
Heading	War Diary of 38th Battn M.G. Corps from 1st July '18 to 31st July 18 (Vol. 5)		
War Diary	Forceville	01/07/1918	20/07/1918
War Diary	Camp Near Herissart	20/07/1918	29/07/1918
War Diary	Camp	22/07/1918	31/07/1918
Operation(al) Order(s)	38th Battalion Machine Gun Corps Order No. 40	01/07/1918	01/07/1918
Operation(al) Order(s)	38th Battalion Machine Gun Corps Order No. 41	08/07/1918	08/07/1918
Operation(al) Order(s)	38th Battalion Machine Gun Corps Order No. 42	08/07/1918	08/07/1918
Diagram etc	38th Batt. M.G.C.		
Miscellaneous	Reference 38th Battn. M.G.C. Order No. 42, dated 8th July, 1918	08/07/1918	08/07/1918
Operation(al) Order(s)	38th Battalion Machine Gun Corps. Order No. 43	11/07/1918	11/07/1918
Operation(al) Order(s)	Amendment No. 1, to Relief Table issued with 38th Battn. M.G.C. Order No. 44, dated 14th July, 1918	14/07/1918	14/07/1918
Operation(al) Order(s)	38th Battalion Machine Gun Corps Order No. 44	14/07/1918	14/07/1918
Miscellaneous	Table To Accompany 38th Battn. M.G.C. Order No. 44, dated 14th July, 1918	14/07/1918	14/07/1918
Diagram etc	38th Batt. M.G.C.		
Operation(al) Order(s)	Amendment No. 1, to 38th Battn. M.G.C. Order No. 45	17/07/1918	17/07/1918
Operation(al) Order(s)	38th Battalion Machine Gun Corps. Order No. 45	17/07/1918	17/07/1918
Miscellaneous	38th Battalion Machine Gun Corps. Order No. 46	17/07/1918	17/07/1918
Miscellaneous	Relief Table to accompany 38th Battn. M.G.C. Order No. 46		
Operation(al) Order(s)	38th Battalion Machine Gun Corps. Order No. 47	27/07/1918	27/07/1918
Heading	38 Bn M.G. Corps Vol 6		
Heading	D.A.G G.H.Q. 3rd Echelon Base.		
Heading	War Diary of 38th Battn M.G. Corps from 1st August '18 to 31st August '18 (Vol : 6)		
War Diary	Camp Near Herissart	01/08/1918	05/08/1918
War Diary	Forceville	06/08/1918	25/08/1918

War Diary	Contalmaison	26/08/1918	31/08/1918
Miscellaneous	Table to accompany 38th Battn. M.G.C. Order No. 48		
Operation(al) Order(s)	38th Battalion Machine Gun Corps. Order No. 48	03/08/1918	03/08/1918
Miscellaneous	Table to accompany 38th Battn. M.G.C. Order No. 49		
Operation(al) Order(s)	38th Battalion Machine Gun Corps. Order No. 49	11/08/1918	11/08/1918
Operation(al) Order(s)	38th Battalion Machine Gun Corps. Order No. 50	12/08/1918	12/08/1918
Diagram etc	Legend Each position Indicates Inc Ques.		
Operation(al) Order(s)	38th. Battalion Machine Gun Corps. Order No. 51	15/08/1918	15/08/1918
Diagram etc	Identification Trace for use with Artillery Maps.		
Operation(al) Order(s)	38th Battalion Machine Gun Corps Order No. 52	15/08/1918	15/08/1918
Operation(al) Order(s)	38th Battalion Machine Gun Corps Order No. 53	16/08/1918	16/08/1918
Operation(al) Order(s)	38th Battalion Machine Gun Corps Order No. 54	18/08/1918	18/08/1918
Operation(al) Order(s)	38th Battalion Machine Gun Corps Order No. 55	19/08/1918	19/08/1918
Operation(al) Order(s)	Amendment to 38th Battn. M.G.C. Order No. 55		
Operation(al) Order(s)	38th Battalion Machine Gun Corps Order No. 56	21/08/1918	21/08/1918
Miscellaneous	Os.C., B. & C. Coys.	21/08/1918	21/08/1918
Miscellaneous	Os.C. "B" & "C" Coys.	22/08/1918	22/08/1918
Miscellaneous	O.O., "B" Coy.	22/08/1918	22/08/1918
Miscellaneous	O.C., "C" Coy.	22/08/1918	22/08/1918
Operation(al) Order(s)	38th Battalion Machine Gun Corps Order No. 57	22/08/1918	22/08/1918
Miscellaneous	38th. Battalion Machine Gun Corps Warning Order	23/08/1918	23/08/1918
Operation(al) Order(s)	38th Battalion Machine Gun Corps Order No. 58	23/08/1918	23/08/1918
Diagram etc	Identification Trace for use with Artillery Maps.		
Miscellaneous	38th Battalion Machine Gun Corps	20/08/1918	20/08/1918
Operation(al) Order(s)	38th Battalion Machine Gun Corps Order No. 57	22/08/1918	22/08/1918
Map	38th Battn M.G.C.		
Operation(al) Order(s)	38th Battalion Machine Gun Corps Order No. 58	23/08/1918	23/08/1918
Miscellaneous	Herewith Tracing to accompany Order No. 50	12/08/1918	12/08/1918
Heading	War Diary of 38th Battn M.G. Corps from 1st to 30th September 1918 Vol: 7		
War Diary		01/09/1918	05/09/1918
War Diary	Les Boeufs	05/09/1918	09/09/1918
War Diary	Lechelle	10/09/1918	10/09/1918
War Diary	Etricourt	11/09/1918	18/09/1918
War Diary	Dessart Wood	18/09/1918	21/09/1918
War Diary	Beaulencourt	21/09/1918	30/09/1918
Operation(al) Order(s)	38th Battalion Machine Gun Corps. Order No. 62	17/09/1918	17/09/1918
War Diary	Sorel Le Grand	01/10/1918	02/10/1918
War Diary	Epehy	03/10/1918	06/10/1918
War Diary	Vendhuile	07/10/1918	07/10/1918
War Diary	Aubencheul	08/10/1918	09/10/1918
War Diary	Villers Outreaux	10/10/1918	10/10/1918
War Diary	Clary	11/10/1918	11/10/1918
War Diary	Bertry	12/10/1918	20/10/1918
War Diary	K 25 a 8.4	20/10/1918	23/10/1918
War Diary	Montay	24/10/1918	25/10/1918
War Diary	Herpies Mill	26/10/1918	26/10/1918
War Diary	Poix Du Nord	27/10/1918	31/10/1918
Operation(al) Order(s)	38th Battalion Machine Gun Corps Order No. 64	10/10/1918	10/10/1918
Operation(al) Order(s)	38th Battalion Machine Gun Corps Order No. 65	11/10/1918	11/10/1918
Operation(al) Order(s)	38th Battalion Machine Gun Corps Order No. 66	16/10/1918	16/10/1918
Operation(al) Order(s)	38th Battalion Machine Gun Corps Order No. 67	19/10/1918	19/10/1918
Miscellaneous	38th Battalion Machine Gun Corps.	19/10/1918	19/10/1918
Map	Tracing To Accompany 38th Battn. M.G.C. Order No. 67		
Miscellaneous	A.B.C.D. Coys Rear B.H.Q.	21/10/1918	21/10/1918

Miscellaneous	Reference W 17 Dated 21.10.18	21/10/1918	21/10/1918
Miscellaneous	38th Battalion Machine Gun Corps.	28/10/1918	28/10/1918
Diagram etc	Sheet 51A SE Sheet 51 SW		
Operation(al) Order(s)	38th Battalion Machine Gun Corps Order No. 67	19/10/1918	19/10/1918
Miscellaneous	38th Battalion Machine Gun Corps.	19/10/1918	19/10/1918
Operation(al) Order(s)	38th Battalion Machine Gun Corps. Order No. 68	11/11/1918	11/11/1918
Heading	War Diary Of 38th Battn M.G. Corps From 1st To 30th November 1918 Vol. 9 Despatched 7.11.18		
War Diary	Poix Du Nord	01/11/1918	03/11/1918
War Diary	Foret De Mormal	04/11/1918	06/11/1918
War Diary	Sartbaras & Aulnoye	07/11/1918	07/11/1918
War Diary	Aulnoye	08/11/1918	30/11/1918
Miscellaneous	38 Bn M.G.C.		
Miscellaneous	38 Bn M.G.C.	02/11/1918	02/11/1918
Miscellaneous	38 Bn M.G.C.		
Miscellaneous	38 Bn M.G.C.	02/11/1918	02/11/1918
Diagram etc	Identification Trace for use with Artillery Maps.		
Heading	War Diary of 38th Battn M.G. Corps From 1st To 31st December 1918 Vol 10		
War Diary	Aulnoye	01/12/1918	31/12/1918
Miscellaneous	Os. C., A.B.C. & D Coys.	02/12/1918	02/12/1918
Miscellaneous	Table Showing Staging Places, Routes, Accomodation and Destinations to accompany 38th Bn. M.G.C. Order No. 69		
Operation(al) Order(s)	38th Battalion Machine Gun Corps. Order No. 69	26/12/1918	26/12/1918
Heading	War Diary of 38th Battn M.G. Corps from 1st Jan. '19 to 31st Jan. '19 Vol : 11		
War Diary	Mehy	01/01/1919	01/01/1919
War Diary	Beaucourt	02/01/1919	31/01/1919
Heading	War Diary of 38th Battn M.G. Corps from 1st to 28th Feb 1919. (Vol : 12)		
War Diary	Beaucourt	01/02/1919	28/02/1919
Heading	War Diary Of The 38th Battn M.G. Corps From 1st to 31st March 1919 Volume 13		
War Diary	Beaucourt	01/03/1919	31/03/1919

WO 05/25483

38 DIVISION

38 BN MACHINE GUN CORPS

1918 MAR — 1919 MAR

Vol I

Confidential

War Diary

of the

38th Battalion M. G. Corps

From 1.3.1918 to 31.3.1918

(Vol. 1)

WAR DIARY
or
INTELLIGENCE SUMMARY.

Army Form C. 2118.

35th B- M.G.C.

Place	Date	Hour	Summary of Events and Information	Remarks and references to Appendices
	1/3			
	2/3	10pm	Bⁿ constituted as administrative & Tactical unit	
	3/3	11.50 pm	Bⁿ co-operated in raid by 17th R.W.F at 116d 59 as follows. A Battery 4 guns, B Battery 6 guns C. Co. C Battery 4 guns A Co. group commanded by Capt Taylor C. Co. Fire maintained at 100 r.p.m for 35 minutes. Box barrage fur-down. Ironed area heavy. Mud night firing by remainder of Bⁿ. Work continued on Railway	Op Order No 1
	4/3		E.Ross cut PANAMA CANAL & JAMES CORNER. Cos of Bⁿ Hqrs moved to ARMENTIERES. Work cont⁴ HOLENE ALLEY POSSE & DURHAM CASTLE Positions. Mand night firing	
ARMENTIERES	5/3		Battle position BREASTWORK complⁿ(W)	
	7/3		2nd Lts K.R.T. Low & J.W. Patchwick joined Bⁿ from GRANTHAM. 2nd Lt Low to C & 9th Bⁿ Coys respectively.	
	8/3 9/3		Re shuer usen in QUALITY ST. Reinforcements on & guns in accordance as unit Divisional Defence scheme. D.C.O in rearmed Study to LONE HOUSE sites & situation completed	Op Orders
	10/3	4.30 a.m	S.O.S. Signal. Opened fire from C.27. B.69 & ? + o.a.24	

WAR DIARY
or
INTELLIGENCE SUMMARY.

(Erase heading not required.)

Army Form C. 2118.

Place: ARMENTIERES

Date	Hour	Summary of Events and Information	Remarks and references to Appendices
10/3		3D-B-M G C Co-operated in raid by 13th W.War on CENTAUR TRENCH. C/4 R. Three 4-gun batteries. Group Commanded by Lieut WILKINSON B C/y	O/p Ord'rs III
12/3		Enemy raided opposite WEZ MACQUART 5.00 a.m. Guns opened fire on S.O.S signal. Enemy left a prisoner in our hands. LONE HOUSE destroyed by sand bagging	
13/3		B/y brought up to strength by addition of 130 infantry from disbanded 6th – opened school of instruction in École Professionelle in ARMENTIERES, under 2/Lt GRIFFITH & 2/Lt MATHESON. Contracted open implement at RAILWAY CROSS CUT	
14/3		Arm. Recens [built at?] FISHER'S HOLE, PANAMA CANAL. Began shelling & FLEURIE SWITCH	
15/3		Redistribut'n of guns in div's in accordance with Divl Defence Scheme Two Companys A B & E in line B in left Sector A in Centre, & to the right icon. B C/y withdrawn into reserve. A C/y relieved in centre by B "D" C/y	O/p Ord'rs IV
15/16 3	10.40pm	Co-operated in raid by 16/R W¹ on J11 a 5532. Three batteries, under 2/Lt FLETCHER A C/y	O/p Ord'rs V

Army Form C. 2118.

WAR DIARY
or
INTELLIGENCE SUMMARY.
(Erase heading not required.)

Instructions regarding War Diaries and Intelligence Summaries are contained in F. S. Regs., Part II. and the Staff Manual respectively. Title pages will be prepared in manuscript.

Place	Date	Hour	Summary of Events and Information	Remarks and references to Appendices
ARMENTIERES	15/16/3	11 p.m	Box Barrage was fired as follows:- A & B batteries 6 guns each from A Coy, & Battery (4 guns) from D Coy. H. & R. fired 52,500 r.p.s. RwD guns successful, Totalling 15 prisoners + 2 M.G. "B" were congratulated by G.O.C. 115 Bde on good work.	
	16/3		Repairs & improvements at Allan's Posse HELGNE Four guns here to be placed in full view of BUTERNE Post when complete.	
	17/3		Work carried out:- LONE Hse & BREASTWORK and:- SISTER Tree guns "b" Coy. Damaged by shellfire at LILLE GUARDIAN & released by 2 guns "B" Coy. d/o Order II Constructed shelters in FLEURIE SWITCH	
	18/3		RAILWAY Dugout improved. New night-firing pt constructed	
	20/21/3		2½ hours gas bombardment by heavy enemy position at FISHER's HOLE & Shelters in FLEURG SWITCH, night-firing positions on APPLE	
	23/3		"R" Coy returned left "B" in earlier Sector	d/o Order II
	26/3		Major MET EVANSON left "B" on appointment to XIX Corps	

WAR DIARY
or
INTELLIGENCE SUMMARY
(Erase heading not required.)

Army Form C. 2118.

Place	Date	Hour	Summary of Events and Information	Remarks and references to Appendices
38th Bn M.G.C.	26/5 17/5		Major T.J. Weir arrived to take over duties of 2nd in command. Cooperated in raid by 10/SWB, putting down box barrage. Three batteries as follows. Two 4-gun batteries from A Coy, one 6-gun battery of C & D Coys (left C & D. Jackson) A Coy from D Coy. 41,200 rds fired. Six prisoners captured. Commander's group.	op. order VIII
	15/5		Orders received to prepare for relief by 34th Div. Troops shewn to personnel sent to companies.	op order 9
		9.0 pm	Cloud 17 personnel sent to two raids J. 10 B.dr raids from his offt left seen. D Coy furnished a 4 gun battery firing on left but barraged 2nd Australian Bn provided remainder.	op order 10
		3.29 am	2nd R.W.F. raid from his offt right region. Two 4-gun batteries from D Coy (afsr Jackson) A Coy on 4-gun battery from D Coy fired. No prisoners Box barrage fired by three batteries. Command groups.	
	29/5		Cooperated in raid by 15th Welsh. Three 4-gun batteries under Lieut Wilkinson of order fired. Guns as follows. 1st Aust B= furnish 2nd Aust B= furnish covered a feint raid. Remainder B Coy furnished on batm B Coy remainder of barrage. D Coy furnished on batm B Coy remainder	op order 13

ARMENTIERES

Place	Date	Hour	Summary of Events and Information	Remarks and references to Appendices
Armentières	30/3		36th Bn- Bn- M.G.C. Bn- relieved by 34th Bn- & proceeded to billets as under. HQ LA VERTE RUE Bn- C.O. DOULIEU area. C. & D. Coys CAUDESCURE area. "A" Coy ARMENTIERES. Transport to STEENBECQUE	Orders 12 & 14
	31/3		"A" Coy proceeded by bus to STEENBECQUE. (Capt.) SMITH joined Bn.	

A.G. Lytton Lt-Col
Cmdg 36th Bn M.G.C.

SECRET.   M.G.B./S.927.

38th BATTALION MACHINE GUN CORPS.

WARNING ORDER.

1. 21st Division will probably relieve 38th Division to-morrow, 5th September. Advance Guard Brigade will be relieved to-morrow night, remainder as far as possible by daylight to-morrow. After relief, Brigades will withdraw to locations as follows :—
   - 113th Brigade........LE TRANSLOY.
   - 114th Brigade........BEAULENCOURT.
   - 115th Brigade........LES BOEUFS.

2. On relief, Machine Gun Companies will concentrate in vicinity of LES BOEUFS, T.4.a.O.5.
   Q.M's Stores, shops, and other Rear H.Q. details will join advanced Bn.H.Q. to-morrow.

3. Advance Billetting party will be sent by each Company and Rear H.Q. to report to Lieut. GRIFFITH at adv. Bn.H.Q. at 10-0 a.m. to-morrow, 5th.

4. Battle surplus personnel will join their respective Coys. after relief. 1 Senior Officer, 1 Subaltern, and 23 O.Rs. per Coy. will however be earmarked in case the Division resumes operations; in which event Battle Surplus will remain behind with Bn.H.Q. and await instructions. If the Division moves as Corps Reserve, Battle Surplus will move with their Coys.

5. Advanced Bn.H.Q. will remain at T.4.a.O.5.

                                                    Lieut-Colonel.
4th September, 1918.   Commanding, 38th Battn.M.G.C.
6-15 p.m.

Copy to/
   Os.C.
   A.B.C. & D. Coys.
   Rear H.Q.
   Bn.T.C.
   Q.M.
   Sigl.Offr.
   Intl.Offr.
   R.S.M.
   File.
   War Diary.

S E C R E T.

38th BATTALION MACHINE GUN CORPS.

ORDER NO.63.

28th September, 1918.

1. The Battalion will proceed to-day by route march with 115th Inf.Brigade Group to area V.24. and W.19. All Companies will be ready on their parade ground by 2-0 p.m. Battn. will march in order – H.Q., A, B, C, D, moving off 2-5 p.m. Company Transport will be ready to pull in behind its Company.

    Route –

    BEAULENCOURT – O.31.b.35.00 – ROCQUIGNY – MESNIL – HANANCOURT Bridge (V.13.d.4.2) – thence by track through V.14.b. V.16.c., V.17.

2. H.Q., and Coy.Guides will meet Battalion at X roads V.18.c.1.9.

3. Distances of 100 yards will be maintained between Coys. and 500 yards between Battalions.

4. There will be a halt from 4-30 p.m. to 5-0 p.m. in addition to the usual halts. H.Q., Cook will hand over sufficient tea to "A" Coy.) for H.Q. teas.
(cook

5. Bn.H.Q. will close at N.18.a.3.3. at 2-0 p.m. to-day. Reports to head of column.

Issued at 11-0 a.m.

L. Wright Capt. & Adjt,
38th Battn.,M.G.Corps,

Copy to all Coys.
    All H.Q. Staff.

38th BATTALION MACHINE GUN CORPS.

ORDER NO. 69.

11th September, 1918.   Copy No. _____

Ref: Map 1/40,000.
     Sheet 57.C.

1. To-night, the 38th Battn.M.G.C. relieves the 17th Battn.M.G.C. Details will be arranged by Company Commanders concerned.

    "A" and "C" Coys. are attached 113th Inf. Brigade.
    "B" Coy. is attached 115th Inf. Brigade.
    "D" Coy.   "   "   114th Inf. Brigade.

2. On completion of relief, Brigade H.Qrs. will be established as follows :-

    113th & 115th Bdes........Present H.Q. of 51st Bde.
                              in Huts. P.35.d.
    114th Bde.................Present H.Q. of 52nd Bde.
                              FOUR WINDS FARM, P.31.c.

3. Battn.H.Q. will close at P.26.b.50.15. at 3-0 p.m. to-day, and re-open at V.9.c.4.0., ETRICOURT, same hour.

4. Relief complete will be wired to Bn.H.Q. by Code Word "JOHN".

5. Addressees marked Ø to ACKNOWLEDGE.

                                          [signature] Capt. & Adjt.
                                          38th Battn.M.G.Corps.

Issued at 11-0 a.m.

Copy to/
    C.O.
    Ø A.B.C. & D. Coys.   38th Div. "G".
    Bn.T.O.   "   " "Q".
    Q.M.   "   " Train.
    Intl. Offr.   113th Bde.
    Sigl. Offr.   114th Bde.
    M.O.   115th Bde.
    Chaplain.   File.
    R.S.M.   War Diary.

SECRET.
****

38th BATTALION MACHINE GUN CORPS.

ORDER NO.61.

16th September, 1918.

Copy No. 8

Ref: Maps 1/40,000, Sheet 57.c.
     1/20,000. " 57.c.,S.E.

General Staff, 38th (Welsh) Div.
No. G.55.2/J
Date. 17.9.18.

ACTION OF NEIGHBOURING FORMATIONS.	1. At a date and hour to be notified later, the 5th Corps is attacking along the whole Corps front in conjunction with the Fourth Army and the French Army on their right. The 5th Division is making a simultaneous attack with the object of maintaining connection with our left.
OBJECTIVES.	2. Objectives and boundaries are shown on the attached tracing. The RED line shows the final objective (for the 17th and 21st Divisions only). The BLUE lines show areas of exploitation which will be mopped up but not held.
ACTION OF INFANTRY.	3. (a) The 38th Division is attacking with two Brigades, 114th Brigade on the right, 113th Bde. on the left. (b) The leading waves are detailed to take the farthest objective.
ACTION of MACHINE GUNS.	4. (a) From 9-0 p.m. 16th/17th and onwards, "B" Company is attached to 113th Brigade ; and "D" Coy. to 114th Brigade. (b) (i) "A" and "C" Coys. will each comprise a Sub-Group (A & C respectively) of 16 guns each, under command of respective Coy. Commanders. Their tasks, shown on attached tracing, are as under :-

Sub-Group Position.	No. of guns.	Section of guns.	Time.	Target.	Rate of fire.
"A" Sub-Group.	16	a	Z.to Z.plus 26 mins.	A.1. W.5.d.50.45. to W.6.a.25.55.	On each target CRASH at 250 R.P.M. for 2 mins ; afterwards at 100 R.P.M.
		b	Z.to Z.plus 21 mins.		
		c	Z.to Z.plus 16 mins.		
		d	Z.to Z.plus 10 mins.		
	16	a	Z.plus 28 to Z.plus 34	A.2. W.6.d.50.60. to W.6.a.70.99.	
		b	Z.plus 23 to Z.plus 36		
		c	Z.plus 18 to Z.plus 38		
		d	Z.plus 12 to Z.plus 40		
	16	-	-	S.O.S. Q.36.Central to Q.30.d.15.10	250 R.P.M. for 5 mins. Slow down with our Artillery.

G.S.O. 1	
G.S.O. 2	
G.S.O. 3	
G.S.O. 4	

4. (b) (i) continued –

Sub-Group Position	No. of guns	Section of guns	Time	Target	Rate of fire
"C" Sub-Group	16	a.... b.... c.... d....	Z.to Z.plus 18 mins. Z.to Z.plus 16 mins. Z.to Z.plus 14 mins. Z.to Z.plus 12 mins.	C.1. Q.35.d.40.85. to Q.29.d.70.20.	On each target CRASH at 250 R.P.M. for 2 mins afterwards 100 R.P.M.
	16	a.... b.... c.... d....	Z.plus 20 to Z.plus 24. Z.plus 18 to Z.plus 24. Z.plus 16 to Z.plus 30. Z.plus 14 to Z.plus 30.	C.2. left. Trenches Q.36.a.26.75. to Q.30.c.40.45. C.2. right. Trenches Q.36.c.00.55. to Q.36.a.15.15.	
	16	–	–	S.O.S. Q.36.Central to Q.36.d.99.20.	250 R.P.M. for 5 mins. Slow down with artillery.

NOTE: "a.b.c.d." represent Sections of 4 guns – "a" being the left section. of each Sub-Group.

(ii) General Report will be forwarded to Commanding Officer at W.3.a.3.1. as soon after the shoot as possible ; and a detailed report by noon following day.

(iii) Barrage done, Os.C. Coys. with two Section Officers will reconnoitre in Q.35.a. & c. with a view to putting a barrage on either sunken road.

Target A...Line .Q.30.b.0.8.
to
R.25.c.5.6.

or Target B...Line........R.25.d.0.2.
to
R.31.d.4.2.

"A" Coy. will in each case barrage the northern half. and
"C" Coy. the southern.half.

Companies will receive orders from Commanding Officer when to move forward.

HEADQUARTERS. 5. Sub-Group H.Q. "A" Coy.....W.4.a.10.98.
" " " " "C" Coy.....W.4.a.0.0.
Group Headquarters........W.3.a.3.1.

Signal Officer will connect these by wire. Two Runners per sub-group will report to W.3.a.3.1. at 8-0 p.m. "Y" day.

SYNCHRONISATION. 6. On Y day Lieut.F.S.GRIFFITH will synchronise watches with a Divisional Staff Officer at H.Q. in P.35.d. at 12-30 p.m. and again at W.3.a.3.1. at 6-30 p.m.
Os.C., Coys. will synchronise at 12-45 p.m. at "A" Coy. H.Q. and about 7-15 p.m. at their respective sub-group H.Qrs.

3.

SIGNALS.   7. The "Success" Signal will be the same as usual, i.e. A three white stars parachute Rifle Grenade Signal.

8. Os.C. "A" & "C" Coys. to ACKNOWLEDGE.

[signature] Capt and A/

Issued at 11-0 p.m.   38th Battn.M.G.Corps.

Copies to/
    Os.C.,
        A.B.C. & D.Coys.   38th Divn. "G".
        Sigl.Offr.   "   "   "Q".
        En.T.Q.   113th Brigade.
        Q.M.   114th Brigade.
        File.   115th Brigade.
        War Diary.   O.C., 5th Battn.M.G.C.
                              "   17th Battn.M.G.C.
                              C.M.G.O.

38th Batt. M.G.C.

Red Line = 1st Objective
Green " = 2nd & Final Objective
Purple " = Area of Exploitation by 17th Division

Taken from Sheet 57d N.E.
Scale 1:20,000

SECRET.
****

38th BATTALION MACHINE GUN CORPS.

ORDER NO.61.

13th September, 1918.

Copy No.

Ref: Maps 1/40,000, Sheet 57.c.
  1/" 1/20,000.   "   57.c., S.E.

ACTION OF NEIGHBOURING FORMATIONS.

1. At a date and hour to be notified later, the 5th Corps is attacking along the whole Corps front in conjunction with the Fourth Army and the French Army on their right.
The 5th Division is making a simultaneous attack with the object of maintaining connection with our left.

OBJECTIVES.

2. Objectives and boundaries are shown on the attached tracing.
The RED line shows the final objective (for the 17th and 21st Divisions only). The BLUE lines show areas of exploitation which will be mopped up but not held.

ACTION OF INFANTRY.

3. (a) The 38th Division is attacking with two Brigades, 114th Brigade on the right, 113th Bde. on the left.

(b) The leading waves are detailed to take the farthest objective.

ACTION of MACHINE GUNS.

4. (a) From 9-0 p.m. 16th/17th and onwards, "B" Company is attached to 113th Brigade ; and "D" Coy. to 114th Brigade.

(b) (i) "A" and "C" Coys. will each comprise a Sub-Group (A & C respectively) of 16 guns each, under command of respective Coy. Commanders.
Their tasks, shown on attached tracing, are as under :-

Sub-Group Position.	No. of guns.	Section of guns.	Time.	Target.	Rate of fire.
"A" Sub-Group.	16	a	Z.to Z.plus 26 mins.	A.1. W.5.d.50.45. to W.6.a.25.55.	On each target CRASH at 250 R.P.M. for 2 mins ; afterwards at 100 R.P.M.
		b	Z.to Z.plus 21 mins.		
		c	Z.to Z.plus 16 mins.		
		d	Z.to Z.plus 10 mins.		
	16	a	Z.plus 28 to Z.plus 34	A.2. W.6.d.50.60. to W.6.a.70.99.	
		b	Z.plus 23 to Z.plus 36		
		c	Z.plus 18 to Z.plus 38		
		d	Z.plus 12 to Z.plus 40		
	16	-	-	S.O.S. Q.36.Central to Q.30.d.15.10	250 R.P.M. for 5 mins. Slow down with our Artillery.

4. (b) (i) continued -

Sub-Group Position.	No. of guns.	Section of guns	Time.	Target.	Rate of fire.
"C" Sub-Group.	16.	a....	Z.to Z.plus 18 mins.	C.1. Q.35.d.40.85. to Q.29.d.70.20.	On each target CRASH at 250 R.P.M. for 2 mins. afterwards 100 R.P.M.
		b....	Z.to Z.plus 16 mins.		
		c....	Z.to Z.plus 14 mins.		
		d....	Z.to Z.plus 12 mins.		
	16	a....	Z.plus 20 to Z.plus 24.	C.2. left. Trenches Q.36.a.26.75. to Q.30.c.40.45.	
		b....	Z.plus 18 to Z.plus 24.		
		c....	Z.plus 16 to Z.plus 30.	C.2. right. Trenches Q.36.c.00.55. to Q.36.a.15.15.	
		d....	Z.plus 14 to Z.plus 30.		
	16	—	—	S.O.S. Q.36.Central to Q.36.d.99.20.	250 R.P.M. for 5 mins. Slow down with artillery.

NOTE: "a.b.c.d." represent Sections of 4 guns - "a" being the left section. of each Sub-Group.

(ii) General Report will be forwarded to Commanding Officer at W.3.a.3.1. as soon after the shoot as possible ; and a detailed report by noon following day.

(iii) Barrage done, Os.C. Coys. with two Section Officers will reconnoitre in Q.35.a. & c. with a view to putting a barrage on either sunken road.

    Target A....Line   .Q.30.b.0.8.
                          to
                          R.25.c.5.6.

   or Target B...Line........R.25.d.0.2.
                          to
                          R.31.d.4.2.

"A" Coy. will in each case barrage the northern half. and
"C" Coy. the southern.half.

Companies will receive orders from Commanding Officer when to move forward.

HEADQUARTERS. 5. Sub-Group H.Q. "A" Coy.....W.4.a.10.98.
                "   "   "   "   "C" Coy.....W.4.a.0.0.
                Group Headquarters.........W.3.a.3.1.

Signal Officer will connect these by wire. Two Runners per sub-group will report to W.3.a.3.1. at 8-0 p.m. "Y" day.

SYNCHRONISATION. 6. On Y day Lieut. F.S. GRIFFITH will synchronise watches with a Divisional Staff Officer at H.Q. in P.35.d. at 12-30 p.m. and again at W.3.a.3.1. at 6-30 p.m.
Os.C., Coys. will synchronise at 12-45 p.m. at "A" Coy. H.Q. and about 7-15 p.m. at their respective sub-group H.Qrs.

SIGNALS.   7. The "Success" Signal will be the same as usual, i.e. A three white stars parachute Rifle Grenade Signal.

8. Os.C. "A" & "C" Coys. to ACKNOWLEDGE.

W. Wright. Capt and A/
38th Battn.M.G.Corps.

Issued at 11-0 p.m.

Copies to/
    Os.C.,
        A.B.C. & D.Coys.   38th Divn. "G".
        Sigl.Offr.   "   " "Q".
        Bn.T.O.   113th Brigade.
        Q.M.   114th Brigade.
        File.   115th Brigade.
        War Diary.   O.C., 5th Battn.M.G.C.
                                "   17th Battn.M.G.C.
                              C.M.G.O.

38th Batt. M.G.C.

Red Line = 1st Objective
Green " = 2nd & Final Objective
Purple " = Area of Exploitation
 by 17th DIVISION

Taken from Sheet 57 SE
Scale 1: 20,000
Date 16/9/18

SECRET.

M.G.B./S.

O.s.C.,
   A.B.C. & D.Coys.

Reference M.G.B./S.979, dated 14th instant.

1.   At 9-0 p.m. 16th/17th Septr. Coys. will come under Commands as follows :-

   "A" & "C" Coys.........Officer Commanding 38th Bn.M.G.C.
   "B" Coy...............Brig-General Commdg.115th Inf.Bde.
   "D" Coy...............   "   "   "   114th   "   "

2.   "A" & "C" Coys. will prepare Battery positions as already detailed.
   On night 16th/17th, "A" & "C" Coys. dispositions will remain unaltered.
   They will move to Battery positions at 9-0 p.m. 17th/18th

3.   Please acknowledge.

                                          Capt. & Adjt.
16th Septr.1918.   38th Battn.M.G.Corps.
   12 noon.

Copy to/
   38th Divn. "G"

SECRET & URGENT.
✻✻✻✻✻✻✻✻✻✻✻✻✻✻✻✻✻✻✻✻✻✻

38th BATTALION MACHINE GUN CORPS.

ORDER NO.32.

17th September, 1918.

1. Bn.H.Q. closes present H.Q. at 6-30 p.m. today.
   Advanced H.Q. ("G") opens at V.3.a.3.1. same hour.
   Rear H.Q. ("A" & "Q" Branches) opens at O.36.c.5.6. (approx)
   at the same hour.
   All communications other than "G" Branch will be sent to
   Rear H.Q.

2. One cyclist runner per Company will report to rear H.Q.
   this evening and will be attached to Bn.H.Q. until further
   notice.

                                           Wright
                                        Capt. & Adjt.
                                     38th Battn.M.G.C.

Issued at 4-30 p.m.

Copy to/
    All M.G.Coys.
    Bn.T.O.
    Q.M.
    Sigl.Offr.
    Intl.Offr.
    R.S.M.
    File.
    War Diary.

38th BATTALION MACHINE GUN CORPS.

ORDER NO. 59.

Ref.Map: 1/40,000, Sheet 57.c., S.E.
" " " 57.c., S.W.

1. 38th Battn.M.G.C. will relieve 24th Battn.M.G.C. in the left Sector, 7 Corps front on 11th September, and night 11th/12th Septr. under orders being issued separately.

2. Moves will take place to-morrow in accordance with a movement table below.

3. Addressees marked Ø to ACKNOWLEDGE.

W. Wright Capt. & Adjt.
38th Battn.M.G.C.

9th Septr.1918.
Issued at 7-30 p.m.

Ser. No. 1.	Unit. 2.	Starting Point. 3.	Time to pass S.P. 4.	Destination. 5.	Route. 6.
1.	Bn.H.Q.	Cross Roads F.3.b.80.35.	2-15 p.m.	LECHELLE area. P.25.b. South of MESNIL - YTRES Rd.	LE TRANSLOY - ROCQUIGNY - BUS.
2.	A. Coy.	Ditto.	2-18 p.m.	Ditto.	Ditto.
3.	B. Coy.	Ditto.	2-22 p.m.	Ditto.	Ditto.
4.	C. Coy.	Ditto.	2-26 p.m.	Ditto.	Ditto.
5.	D. Coy.	Ditto.	2-30 p.m.	Ditto.	Ditto.

1. Transport will move behind its Company.
2. 100 yards interval will be maintained between Coys.
3. Halts will be made by Coys. at 10 minutes to each clock hour : and advances at each clock hour.

P.T.O.

M.G.B./S.948.

M.G.B./S.940.

ADMINISTRATIVE INSTRUCTIONS with ORDER No.58.

1. Advanced party of 1 Officer, and 15 O.Rs. per Coy. with day's Rations, will report at Bn.H.Q. at 9-15 a.m. to Capt.J.SMITH. 1 limber per Coy. with Coy's tentage, and any material, will accompany party. These limbers will return to Coy.H.Qrs. after delivering material.
2. Refuse waste paper will be buried and all refuse pits will be filled in before quitting Camp.

L.Wright. Capt. & Adjt.
38th Battn.M.G.C.

9th September, 1918.

Copy to/
    Os.C., A.B.C. & D. Coys.
    Bn.T.O.   Intl.Offr.   File.
    Q.M.   Sigl.Offr.   War Diary.
              R.S.M.
              Chaplain.

SECRET.   M.G.B./S.979.

O's.C.,
A., B., C., & D. Coys.

1. The following redistribution of Machine Guns will be completed by 8-0 a.m. 15th instant.

2. (a) "A" Coy. will be under the command of Front Brigade.
    3 Sections will be in the line, 1 in reserve.
    Guns will be sited so as to ensure :-
        (i)   Protection of front line by indirect fire.
        (ii) Harassing fire.
        (iii) Direct fire on our front line in event of enemy penetration.

    (b) "B", "C", & "D" Coys. will come under command of O.C., Battn.
    "B" Coy. less 1 Section, will take up positions in Q.32, Q.33.
    "C" Coy. less 1 Section, will take up positions in W.3.
    "D" Coy. less 1 Section, will take up positions in W.2.b. & d., W.3.c., and W.9.a.

    (c) The role of these Coys. is to ensure :-
        (i)   Harassing fire.
        (ii) S.O.S. Barrage in front of our front line.
        (iii) The protection of the system W.3., Q.32. by direct fire.

3. Harassing fire will be carried out by day and night, and will be especially vigorous at night. 1 Section per Coy. will be detailed for this duty at night, and will move forward to suitable positions where necessary.
    Special attention is to be paid to the sunken roads leading out of GOUZEAUCOURT on the West.

4. "D" Coy. is earmarked to accompany the Front Brigade in event of an advance.

5. Orders as to S.O.S. Barrages will be issued later.

6. Reserve Sections to be accommodated in vicinity of Coy.H.Q. Transport will remain as at present.

                                        W. Wright Capt-r.adjt
                                        Lieut-Colonel.
14th Septr. 1918.   Commanding, 38th Battn. M.G.C.

Copy to/
    38th Div. "G".   )
     "   "   "Q".) for information.
     "   "   Train.)
    113th Bde.   )
    114th Bde.   )
    115th Bde.   )

TABLE OF CALCULATIONS FOR S.C.S. LINES.

Sqn.	No. of guns.	Gun position.	Target position.	Altitude Gun	Altitude Target	V.I. metres	Range yards	Q.E.	Own troops range	Own troops Alt.	Own troops V.I. metres	Clearance metres	Traverso	Bearing (m)
A	4	Q.34.c.72.85	W.11.b.45.50	122m.	130m.	+8	2200	15°40'	1150	137m.	15	85	Nil.	140°
		Q.34.c.72.82		122m.	130m.	+8	2300	16°15'			15	75	Nil.	139°
		Q.34.c.72.80		123m.	130m.	+7	2375	16°40'			14	103	Nil.	139°
		Q.34.c.72.77		124m.	131m.	+9	2475	17°38'			13	101	Nil.	133°
A	2	W.10.b.80.90	Q.35.a.55.50	126m.	134m.	+8	1850	13°55'	525	135m.	9	26	Nil.	120°
				"	"	"	1900	14°00'		"	"	"	"	"
		W.11.a.05.42	Q.35.a.80.80	133m.	134m.	+1	2250	15°05'	700	137m.	4	56	10 r.	100°
					"	+1	2350	16°30'					30 r.	
		W.31d.55.40	Q.35.d.00.10	120m.	134m.	+14	1925	14°20'	1400	132m.	12	42	10 ea.	64°
C	2	W.3.d.56.35	W.5.b.25.90	120m.	135m.	+15	2000	14°45'	"	"	"	51	way.	66°
C	2	W.3.d.56.40	W.5.b.60.35	130m.	130m.	-	2475	17°20'	1800	135	5	110	10 ea.	91°
C	2	W.3.a.50.30	W.5.d.85.85	126m.	135m.	+9	2650	19°00'	1830	137	11	157	way.	95°
C	2	Q.33.c.12.83	Q.35.b.27.00	130m.	130m.	-	2540	18°10'	2050	133m.	6	136	10 ea.	80°
C	2	Q.33.a.12.80	Q.35.b.50.00	132m.	130m.	-2	2750	19°40'	2075	135m.	3	164	way.	78½°
B	2	Q.33.d.70.65	Q.35.c.00.52	130m.	125m.	-5	2150	15°00'	1250	133m.	3	65	75 ea.	85°
							2550	12°51'		"	"	95m.	way.	"
							2400	16°45'		"	"	100	20 L.	"
B	2	Q.33.d.70.00	Q.33.c.55.45	130m.	132m.	+2	2550	17°45'	"	"	"	125	"	"

"A" Form.
MESSAGES AND SIGNALS.

Army Form C. 2121.
(In pads of 100.)

TO:
A. B. C. D. Companies　　　38 Bn Rear HQ
113 Inf Bde　　115 Inf Bde
114 Inf Bde　　Div G"

Sender's Number: F 14　　Day of Month: 19

AAA

(1) The 17th Division is extending its present line to FINS - GOUZEACOURT ROAD, the 114 Inf Bde being withdrawn. The 115 Inf Bde is relieving 113 Inf Bde tonight.

(2)(a) D. Coy 38 Bn M.G.C. will be relieved by C Coy 17 Bn M.G.C. Arrangements made by Coy Commanders direct.

(b) B. Coy will pull out at 9.0pm tonight. B & D will stage the night at their transport lines and tomorrow move to Div Reception Camp N 18 B.

3. A & C Coys 38th Battn M.G.C. will tonight cover 115 Inf Bde as follows:—

A Coy 4 guns will form Machine Gun S.P. about F in AFRICAN Trench Q.35.A direct S.O.S fire will be put on fork Q.29.d.4.8 and on DEVILLERS Farm Q.36.A

"A" Form.
MESSAGES AND SIGNALS.

Army Form C. 2121.
(In pads of 100.)

(Cont'd) 8 guns at Q 34 c 4.4 and 2 guns at Q 34 d 15.20 will be ready on SOS lines Q 29 d central to the C in GOUZEAUCOURT 2 guns at Q 34 d 15.20 will be ready on SOS lines Q 29 c 75.00 to Q 29 d 0.5 These twelve guns tracked will be also ready for direct fire along AFRICAN Support Ridge

'C' Coy 16 guns on W 4 b will be laid on SOS line Q 36 a 6.6 to Q 36 d central

(4) B & D Coys will move wire Adv. B.H.Q. rely complet'd by word "LAURENCE" A & C Coys will phone B.H.Q. when guns as above are laid

(5) A B C & D Coys to acknowledge

Sd/ H. Wrigan Capt & Adjt
38th Bn M.G.C.

"A" Form.
MESSAGES AND SIGNALS.

Army Form C. 2121.
(In pads of 100.)

Secret

TO
A + C Coys
115 Inf Bde.
38 Bn Rear HQ
Div G

Sender's Number.	Day of Month.	In reply to Number.	
F 23	20		AAA

1. Remainder of 38th Division is being relieved tonight.

2. C Coy will pull out at 10.30 p.m. tonight.

3. A Coy will be relieved by a Coy (9 guns) of 17 Batt MGC. Most probably the 4 guns in AFRICAN Trench & 4 in Q 34 D 15 20 will be relieved. This will be confirmed. Guides from each battery position will be at X ROADS W 4 a 0 3 at 8.30 p.m.

4. A + C will stage tonight at their Transport lines and proceed BOUZENCOURT tomorrow afternoon.
Battle Surplus A + C have been instructed to move there today.

5. A + C Coys acknowledge

Capt & Adjt
38th Batt MGC

38th Div.
V.Corps.

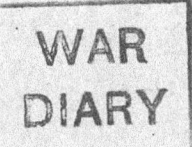

38th BATTALION, MACHINE GUN CORPS.

A P R I L

1 9 1 8

Attached:

Appendices.

WAR DIARY
or
INTELLIGENCE SUMMARY

Army Form C. 2118.

38ᵗʰ Bⁿ M.G.C.

Place	Date	Hour	Summary of Events and Information	Remarks and references to Appendices
MERVILLE AREA	1/4	5 a.m.	Bⁿ entrained for new area as follows: A Coy STEENBECQUE	Administrative Train Arrangement Apps 1 + 2
		6.30 a.m.	C Coy CALONNE	
		7.30 a.m.	B Coy MERVILLE	
		9.30 p.m.	B.H.Q. & Bⁿ ens } CALONNE	
			On reaching DOULLENS A.B.& C Companies detrained & marched to VILLERS BOCAGE	
HEDAUVILLE	2/4		A, B, & C Coys marched to HEDAUVILLE under orders F.O.C. 115 B⁄ᴱ B.H.Q. & B Coy had an accident on the line, one truck being derailed & upset. Total casualties 4 slight wounds. B detrained DOULLENS	
VILLERS BOCAGE		1.30 p.m.	& marched to VILLERS BOCAGE 12 miles	
PUCHEVILLERS	3/4		B.H.Q. "A" "B" & "D" Coys marched to PUCHEVILLERS with 3 day's rations. All in buses by 6.0 p.m. In 3ʳᵈ Army Reserve with remainder of 38ᵗʰ Div. "C" Coy remained at HEDAUVILLE under orders G.O.C. 115 B⁄ᴱ	
		5.0 p.m.	Orders received to proceed from G.S. V Corps for "C" Coy to entrain 63ʳᵈ Bⁿ in the Corps Area. Instructions to this officer under O.C.C. by	V Corps App 0-33
		6.30 p.m.	C Company	

Army Form 2118.

WAR DIARY
INTELLIGENCE SUMMARY

(Erase heading not required.)

Place: PUCHEVILLERS

Date	Hour	Summary of Events and Information	Remarks and references to Appendices
4/4		35th B" M.G.C.	
	5.0p	"C" Coy relieved "B" Coy 63rd B"	C.O's operation order
	5.0p	"D" Coy ordered to co-operate with 113 B⁴ in tactical scheme. Marched from to rendezvous at HÉRISSART. Information scheme postponed. Notification to that effect not received in time. Marched back to billets	
	5.0p	"C" Coy relieved "B" Coy 63rd B" in Corps line	C.O's operation order No 15/15
5/4	5.0am	Division at 1 hour's notice	35th Division 9.55
	11am	Orders received from 38th Div. — Relieving A & B Coys detailed position of readiness between WARLOY & VADENCOURT. 1 Coy to 114 B⁴ at HERISSART. A & B Coys moved off at 12.50pm & 12.45pm respectively. "D" in billet. Coys moved off at 12.50pm & 12.45pm respectively. 2 O.R. wounded "C" Coy 2 pairs & 2 limber rebounds in Jameago by shell fire	
6/4		Division no longer at 1 hours notice. "A" "B" "D" Coys move of 113 & 114 B⁴'s to billets under own command. "A" Coy PIERREGOT & MIRVAUX TALMAS	35th Div wire 5.52

WAR DIARY or INTELLIGENCE SUMMARY.

(Erase heading not required.)

38th Bn. M.G.C.

Place	Date	Hour	Summary of Events and Information	Remarks and references to Appendices
PUCHEVILLERS	7/4		"A" + "B" Coys rejoined HQrs	35 Div. WD G 2 5
RUBEMPRÉ	8/4	4.15pm	"A" + "B" marched to billets at RUBEMPRÉ. Village very crowded. B= accommodation bad.	B= orders no 3
RUBEMPRÉ	9/4		41st Div: HQrs moved out. Morning spent getting men into better billets.	
		9pm	Orders received to move one Cy to WARLOY in support of 12th Div. "B" Coy detailed. Move to be completed by 5 am 10/4	M.G. B= 10/4
RUBEMPRÉ	10/4		"A" + "B" Coys employed in training, washing etc. Arrangements made to carry out "short" programme of training. Orders received over Telephone to during morning to prepare to relieve 12th Div. in the late afternoon to move to ALBERT, i.e. the right sector. CO went to WARLOY in afternoon to arrange relief for night of 10/13	B= orders Nos 4 March Table

Army Form C. 2118.

WAR DIARY
or
INTELLIGENCE SUMMARY.
(Erase heading not required.)

35th Bn M.G.C.

Place	Date	Hour	Summary of Events and Information	Remarks and references to Appendices
RUBEMPRE to WARLOY	11/4		"B" Coy marched from WARLOY to HENENCOURT in relief of 1 coy 12th Bn "B" Coy	B.O. No 4. Main Table
			"A" " " " " RUBEMPRE to WARLOY " " " " "S" Coy	"
	12/4		"A" Coy arrived "C" Coy in Corps line	"
			"B" " marched from RUBEMPRE to HENENCOURT= relief of "D" Coy WARLOY	
	12/13		A. H.Q. "D" Coy relieved 1 coy 12th Bn in night sector	
	"		"C" " " " " " " left sector	
WARLOY	13/4		Relief completed by 2 a.m. C.O. reconnoitred positions of guns in afternoon. 2 O.R. wounded	
WARLOY	14/4		Reconnaissance of gun positions continued + minor read/ustments made	
WARLOY	15/4		to Bnture gun stuff "C" Coy Reconnaissance completed. 1 O.R. killed ("C" Coy)	

Army Form C. 2118.

WAR DIARY
or
INTELLIGENCE SUMMARY.
(Erase heading not required.)

35th Bn. M.G.C.

Place	Date	Hour	Summary of Events and Information	Remarks and references to Appendices
WARLOY	16/4		4 Reserve guns of "B" Coy placed in line in centre, 2 guns of "E" Coy Op. Order No. 16 transferred to left Section in front of BOUZINCOURT. SOS lines laid out for all available guns. "B" Coy relieves "C" Coy in left Section	Op. Order No. 15
WARLOY	17/4		Began construction of shelters for B.H.Q. outside village. Casualties wounded 1 O.R. "B" Coy	
WARLOY	18/4		Verbal instructions received from Div. HQ. that "B" Coy 12th E Bn is placed under command of O.C. 35th Bn. for tactical purposes. 8 guns to be placed in Reserve positions on ridge running N.E. from HENENCOURT. 6 guns to be kept in reserve in WARLOY. C.O. & O.C. "B" Coy 12th Bn. reconnoitred & chose all positions in morning Coy arrived in afternoon. 6 guns in position by nightfall.	

WAR DIARY
or
INTELLIGENCE SUMMARY.

(Erase heading not required.)

Army Form C. 2118.

Place	Date	Hour	Summary of Events and Information	Remarks and references to Appendices
Warloy	19/4		35th Bn. M.G.C. Conference at Div. HQ reference proposed minor operation to be carried out by 113 Bde with object of capturing high ground in W.15. T.M. gun barrage required. All initial arrangements begun. Battery positions reconnoitred in evening by C.O. 2i/c, 1/c & O.C. "A" Coy	
Warloy	20/4	9.00am 2.30pm	"C" Coy Rehearsal of attack attended by officers 2.Cor & nos 1 of "A" Coy. "C" Coy relieved "A" Coy in Corps Line	
	20/24/4		Casualties Killed: 1 O.R. "C" Coy Wounded 2/Lt H.H.W. Paull "C" Coy 1 O.R. (B" 3, " 1) Gassed 1 O.R. "B" Coy	Op order 17.

WAR DIARY or INTELLIGENCE SUMMARY

Army Form C. 2118.

38th B - M.G.C.

Place	Date	Hour	Summary of Events and Information	Remarks and references to Appendices
WARLOY	1/4		Coy/R's all preparations for support of attack by 112 B 35th.	Oper Order No. 15
WARLOY	2/4	7.30 p.m.	113 B⁻ attacked high ground W of B⁻ in conjunction with 2 Troops of 35th Div⁻ on left. 35th B⁻ supported attack with 16 guns. Used command of M⁻ E.A.H. Jauncey. 1st objective was 2nd commd (Ltd) M⁻ attack on second objective held up by enemy M.G. fire. 3 Officers & 5 O.R. 2 Lewis & 2 captured. 112,000 rounds in support of attack & harassing in action to annoy hostile coln. B Coy supplied 1 section to go forward & consolidate ground gained. Casualties. Killed 1 O.R. Wounded 1 Officer Lt J.N. Shaw 3 O.R. Three guns out of action - owing on case due to enemy shell fire & remaining cases seems to have been some neglect of parts during firing. Our fire unk. to be excellent	

Army Form C. 2118.

WAR DIARY
or
INTELLIGENCE SUMMARY.

(Erase heading not required.)

36=B? M.G.C.

Place	Date	Hour	Summary of Events and Information	Remarks and references to Appendices
WARLOY	23/4		"B" Coy were able to place 2 guns in position to cover & S.O.S. front of 19th Bn. Remaining 2 withdrawn to gb position	S/Bn10/0/35
WARLOY	24/4	7.30	Enemy endeavoured to counter-attack but were hit at 7.30 a.m. In answer to S.O.S. signal B Coys guns fired about 4 belts each, & Coy 25 belts. Germans beaten off leaving a prisoner in our hands. Casualties Wounded 2 O.R. A.& B.	
Warloy	25/4		Quiet day. 8 guns A Coy withdrawn into reserve in HENENCOURT during night 24/25. 6 left in position to cover new front line. Wood. Remaining 8 B Coy 2 O.R. "B" Coy Casualties Killed 2 O.R. B Coy Wounded 2/Lt W.B.Cleaver A Coy 4 O.R. B 3 A 1	9 A 24
WARLOY	26/4		8 guns "A" Coy withdrawn into reserve. "B" Coy arranged to fire down S.O.S barrage in their place. Casualties Wounded 2 O.R "A" & B	M.G.B. /S 237

Army Form C. 2118.

WAR DIARY
or
INTELLIGENCE SUMMARY.
(Erase heading not required.)

Place	Date	Hour	Summary of Events and Information	Remarks and references to Appendices
WARLOY	27/4		38th Bn M.G.C. 38th Bn relieved from Right Divl. boundary to W15 d 50 by 22 Aust. M.G.Bn. A & B Coys move to WARLOY. "B" Coy remained in Left Sector. "C" Coy to Reserve Positions & WARLOY 8 guns at each. Casualties Wounded 1 O.R - B Coy	Op order No 2.D " 21 " 22
WARLOY	28/4		"C" Coy withdrawn into reserve at WARLOY. A & B Coys marched to Billets at TOUTENCOURT. Casualties Wounded 2 O.R "C" Coy	11.9. W 35 Maps table sht 2 Op oran 20
WARLOY	29/4		Casualties Wounded 1 O.R. "C" Coy	
WARLOY	30/4		A & B Coys at training under O.C. Coys "C" Coy reconnoitred this W.L. by 35th Bn prior to relief.	

A.G. Lyttleton Lt. Col.
Commanding, 38th Bn M.G.C.

1/5/18.

A P P E N D I C E S to accompany 38th BATTALION MACHINE GUN CORPS WAR DIARY from 1/4/18 to 30/4/18. (Vol.2.)

38th BATTALION MACHINE GUN CORPS.

ADMINISTRATIVE ARRANGEMENTS.

1. Reference 38th Battn. O.O. No. 12. troops will entrain from STEENBECQUE, CALONNE and MERVILLE, in accordance with the TABLE attached.
The average interval between trains at each station will be 3 hours.

2. ARRANGEMENTS AT ENTRAINING STATIONS.

   The vehicles and horses of each train load will be at the station named three hours, and personnel one and a half hour, before departure of the train.

3. Entraining strengths, showing (a) Officers and O.Rs.
   (b) horses and mules.
   (c) vehicles and No. of wheels.
   will be handed to the R.T.O. or Officer detailed to assist at least two hours before departure of trains.

4. Units will not enter the station precincts previous to the three hours mentioned in para 2. Roads leading to the Station will not be blocked by Units, and to ensure this strict punctuality must be kept.

5. Each Brigade Group will detail one Company and one Cooker and team to be at their entraining station three and a half hours before departure of the first train, and report to the R.T.O. These will act as loading party for all Units. They will entrain on the last train and will be under the orders of the A.S.C. Officer detailed to superintend the entrainment.

6. BILLETING.

   Advance parties for Billeting will be sent on in the first train from each entraining station, under Staff Captains of Brigade Groups. Two days rations will be taken.

7. Entrainment will be completed half an hour before the departure of of the train.

8. Breast ropes for horses trucks must be provided by Units. Ropes for vehicles will be provided by the Railway.

9. All doors of covered trucks and carriages on the right hand side of the train when on the main line must be kept closed.

10. ARRANGEMENTS AT DETRAINING STATION.

    Staff Captains, with Billeting parties, will go by first train and will get into communication with the D.A.A.G., 38th Division, in charge at the most central station, as early as possible.

11. Each Infantry Brigade will detail one Company, and one Cooker and Team to go in the first train and to report to R.T.O. at each detraining Station. The Officer in command of this Company will act as detraining Officer.

12. GENERAL INSTRUCTIONS.

    Two blankets per man will be taken. All troops will move with the normal Field Service scale of transport. No extra transport will be provided, but arrangements will be made for the conveyance of extra blankets.

13. Rations. Rations to accompany troops will be (a) Iron ration.
    (b) Current day's ration.
    In addition, two days ration will be taken on trains, one in Unit transport and one in supply vehicles of the Divisional Train,

TRAIN ARRANGEMENTS.

APRIL 1st 1918.

STEENBECQUE.			CAJONNE.			EENVILLE.		
No. of Train.	Time.	113th Inf.Brigade Group.	No. of Train.	Time.	115th Infy.Brigade Group.	No. of Train.	Time.	114th Infy.Brigade Group.
1	5 a.m.	"A" Coy.	2.	6-30 a.m.	"C" Coy.	3.	7-30 a.m.	"B" Coy.
			17.	9-30 p.m.	Bn.H.Q. and "D" Coy.			

38th BATTALION MACHINE GUN CORPS.

BATTALION ORDER NO.1.

31st March 1918.

1. Reference Administrative Arrangements issued with Bn.O.O.14 of the 30th instant.

2. "C" Company move under own arrangements in accordance with above Administrative Arrangements, except that Train leaves CALONNE 6-10 a.m. and not 6-30 a.m.

3. O.C. "C" Company will detail 1 Officer and 1 N.C.O. to report to the Entraining Officer (Capt. — of the 2/R.W.F.) two hours before the departure of the train.
The above will travel with "C" Coy.

4. Reference para. 6. of Administrative Arrangements : Billeting parties are not required by 115th Infy. Brigade.

5. Reference para. 12 : The 2nd blanket will be dumped at the entraining station in bundles of 10. D.A.D.O.S. will arrange for a representative to be at each station to take over and check. Receipts for blankets will be taken and forwarded to this Office as soon as possible.

6. Reference para. 13 : Rations for those entraining on 1st April will be (a) Iron Ration. (biscuit portion to be issued before
(b) Current day's ration. entraining.)

7. Refilling for supply waggons will take place in the new area on the 2nd instant.

............Captain & Adjutant.
38th Battn.M.G.C.

Issued at 6-0 p.m.

Copies to/
"C" Coy.
Q.M.
Bn.T.O.
File.
War Diary.

War Diary

___ BATTALION MACHINE GUN CORPS.

BATTALION ORDER NO. 2.

1. Bn.H.Q. and "D" Company move today in accordance with Administrative and Training arrangements of 8-0 p.m. of the 30th-3-18.

2. All Transport will clear Oudezeele Church by 4-0 p.m. 1st April. Bn.H.Q. will be formed up at the Church by 4-45 p.m. Move off 5-0 p.m. followed by "D" Company.

3. 2nd Lieut. D. C. GRIFFITH will act as Entraining Officer. Entraining Strength showing (a) Officers and O.R.
   (b) Horses and Mules.
   (c) Vehicles and Wheels.
   will be handed to the R.T.O. or Officer detailed to assist him three hours before the departure of the train.

4. "D" Coy will detail 1 Officer and 1 N.C.O. to report to the Entraining Officer (Capt. ___ of the 2/R.W.F.) 2 hours before the departure of the train.
   The above will travel with their Unit.

5. Reference para. 6. of Administrative arrangements : Billeting parties are not required by the 115th Infy. Brigade : but one should be detailed ready to assist the Staff Captain of 115th Infy. Brigade, if required.

6. Reference para 12 : the 2nd blanket will be dumped at the Entraining Station in bundles of 5am. D.A.D.O.S. will arrange for a representative to be at the Station to take over and check. Receipts for blankets will be taken and forwarded to this Office as soon as possible.

7. Reference para. 13 : Rations for those entraining on the 1st April will be (a) Iron Ration (1 cwt. portion to be issued before entraining)
   (b) Current day's ration.
   (c) Tomorrow's ration.

8. ORDER of ENTRAINMENT.
   All vehicles will be drawn up on road G.2.b. CALOTTE sur in LYS. in following order :-
   255 Coy. A.S.C.
   Bn.H.Q. and "D" Coy. 34th M.G.Bath.
   1 Coy. and 1 Cooker 17th R.W.F.
   The head of the column will be the Railway Crossing at 6-0 p.m. the first April 1918.

   Troops of the Brigade Group will be drawn up on the above mentioned Road in the same order as the Vehicles. Head of the column to rest at Railway Crossing by 7-30 p.m. 1st April-1918.

9. ACKNOWLEDGE.

.... Captain & Adjt.
34th Batta. M.G.C.

1st April 1918.

Issued at 11-15 a.m.

Copies to/ "D" Coy.
O.R.
Bn.T.O.
R.S.M.
File
War Diary.

COPY.

V Corps.
C.M.G.O. - 33.
3rd. ~~dth~~ April 1918.

38th Divn. M.G.C.

The M.G. Coy. of the 38th Divn. at HEADAUVILLE will relieve the M.G.C. of the 63rd Divn. forthwith in the positions occupied in the Corps line between BOUZINCOURT and ENGELBELMER.

(Sgd.) J.M. BLAIR.
Lt.-Col.
Copy to C.M.G.O.   G.S. V. Corps.

SECRET.   "C" Company 38th Battn M.G.C   Copy No. 6

Operation Order No.18/18.

Ref. Sheet 57.D. S.E. 1/20,000.

1. "C" Coy 38th Battn M.G.C will relieve "D" Coy 63rd Battn M.G.C in the Corps Line between BOUZINCOURT and ENGELBELMER to-day. Opposite numbers will relieve.
2. Section Officers and the No's of each Section will be ready by 2.30pm to go on in advance. Guides from "D" Coy 63rd Battn M.G.C will report at "C" Coy H.Qrs at this hour.
3. Remainder of Sections for the Line will be ready by 5.0pm under Section Sergts to proceed to the Line. Guides from "D" Coy 63rd Battn M.G.C will report at "C" Coy H.Qrs at this hour.
4. All men proceeding to line will be in Fighting Order with one blanket per man, and water bottles filled.

   Packs of above men will be handed in to Coy Q.M.Stores as soon as possible.
5. Sections will take in all gun equipment, belt boxes, etc.
6. The Fighting Limbers of each Section will parade with their Sections at 5.0pm. These limbers, 4 animals, Transport N.C.O, and 1 driver per Section will remain with their Sections in the Line. Each Fighting Limber will take 5000 rounds S.A.A of the Mobile Reserve.
7. To-morrow's RATIONS rations and forage will go up with the Sections to-night.
   Water. No's 1&2 Sections –
   Drinking water will be sent up nightly in petrol tins, which must be returned when empty.
   No's 3&4 Sections will draw water from ENGELBELMER.
   Cooking.
   No's 1 &2 Sections will arrange to draw Tommy's Cookers from Coy Q.M. Stores before proceeding to Line.
   No's 3 & 4 Sections will cook in billets in ENGELBELMER.
8. One man per Section to be detailed by Section Officer will go up with the No's 1 at 2.30pm, and will return to Coy H.Q immediately he has been shewn his Section H.Qrs.
9. Aid Posts.
   No's 1 & 2 Sections HEDAUVILLE
   No's 3 & 4 Sections ENGELBELMER.
10. Company H.Qrs, surplus personnel, and remainder of transport will remain in present billets.
11. Relief complete will be reported to Coy H.Qrs by runner.

Issued at 1-40pm on 4.4.18.

Copies to:-
1. O's.C.Sections.
2. Transport Sergt.
3. O.C. "C" Coy.
4. C.S.M and C.Q.M.S.
5. 115 Inf.Bde.
6. C.O. 38th Battn M.G.C ✓
7. File.

Lieut
for O.C. "C" Coy

MESSAGES AND SIGNALS.

PRIORITY.

Lt. Col.
G.S.

Rec'd 12.15 p.m.

113th Brigade	C. R. E., 38th Divn.
114th Brigade	38th Div: "Q"
115th Brigade	
38th Bn. M.G.C.	(Copy to G.O.C.)
19th Welsh Regt.	

G. 55.   5th.

Hostile attack threatened from direction of ALBERT and MAROEUIL AAA.
113th Brigade will move to position of readiness between WARLOY and VARDINCOURT at once and on arrival there will reconnoitre country and defences between BAISIEUX and HENENCOURT AAA.
114th Brigade will move at once to position of readiness near HERISSART. AAA.
38th Bn.M.G.C. will send one company to join each of those Brigades at above places and to come under orders of Brigadier. AAA.
Brigades will report time first troops move and time when concentrated. AAA. After concentration they will be at half hours notice AAA.
115th Brigade and remainder Divisional Troops stand fast. AAA.

Addrd. 3 Bdes, M.G.Bn., Pnrs, C.R.E., "Q". Rep'td remainder of recipients of G. 49 of today
ACKNOWLEDGE by return.

38th Divn.

10-50.a.m.

J.E. Munby
Lieut. Colonel,
General Staff, 38th (Welsh) Divn.

MESSAGES AND SIGNALS

War Diary

PRIORITY & S.D.R.

Lt.Col.
G.S.

Rec'd 5·20 p.m.

38ᵈ Bn. M.G.C.

113th Bde.
114th Bde.
331st Coy. A.S.C.
332nd Coy. A.S.C.
129th Fd. Ambce.

G.82.   6th.

Following troops will march at 5 p.m. to billets as under AAA 113th Bde. and Sniping Section and "A" Coy. M.G.Bn. to RUBEMPRE, PIERREGOT and MIRVAUX AAA 114th Bde. and Sniping Section and "B" Coy. M.G.Bn. to TALMAS and LA VICOGNE AAA 331st Coy. A.S.C. and 129th Fd. Ambce to area RUBEMPRE, PIERREGOT, MIRVAUX to be billeted by 113th Bde. AAA 332nd Coy. A.S.C. to area TALMAS, LA VICOGNE to be billeted by 114th Bde. AAA Units of 38th Division are no longer required to be ready to move at one hour's notice AAA

"A" and "B" Coys. M.G.Bn. are still under orders of 113th and 114th Bdes. respectively and will move and be billeted under their orders AAA ACKNOWLEDGE Addsd 113th and 114th Bdes. 331st and 332nd Coys. A.S.C. and 129 Fd. Ambce Rptd all formations and units.

38th Division

3.   p.m.

To all Coys.
file
Qm
Bn T.O.

J. G. Munby
Lieut-Colonel,
General Staff, 38th (Welsh) Division.

38TH BATTALION,
MACHINE GUN
CORPS.
No. S.311
Date

"C" Form.   Army Form C. 2128.
MESSAGES AND SIGNALS.   (In books of 100.)
No. of Message

Prefix	Code	Words	Received.	Sent, or sent out.	Office Stamp.
		£ s. d.	From	At m.	
Charges to Collect			By	To	
Service Instructions				By	

Handed in at 9(11) 3.E. 9pm Office 12.45 pm Received 1. 6 m.

TO   38 M.G. Bn Puchevillers

*Sender's Number	Day of Month.	In reply to Number.	AAA
Lo 8	7		
order	m.g.	very	add
to	you	to	rejoin
m.g.	Bn	My	PUCHEVILLERS
today	by	any	route
and	any	time	desired
aaa	company	closes	to
be	under	your	command
from	time	of	departure
aaa	added	113	and
114	Bdes	rept-d	m.g
Bn	and	Q	Branch

[Stamp: 38TH BATTALION, MACHINE GUN CORPS. No. 537]

Rec'd 1.20 pm

FROM
TIME & PLACE   3.E. Bn   12.40 pm

*This line should be erased if not required.

(War Diary)

38th BATTALION MACHINE GUN CORPS.

BATTALION ORDER NO. 8.

RUBEMPRE

1. 38th Bn. M.G.C. less one Coy. will move to RUBEMPRE on 14th April, clearing Railway Crossing H.29.d.5.2. at times below :-

   No.10 .... 4-15 P.M.
   A. Coy .... 4-30 "
   B. " .... 4-45 "
   C. " .... 5- 0 "

2. Transport will move with Coy'ys.

3. Go parties will notify Bn. Orderly Room of exact location of Unit per M.G.Bn. as soon as possible on arrival at RUBEMPRE.

4. Quartermaster and stores will move with [illegible]

5. ACKNOWLEDGE.

14th April 1918.
Issued at 1-0 P.M.

Copies to:-
A. Coy.   B.M.
B. "   D.A.Q.
C. "   O.C.Coys. (for information).
T.   File.

.... Capt. & Adjt.
.... 38th Bn. M.G.C.

File War Diary

SECRET.

38th BATTALION MACHINE GUN CORPS.

BATTALION ORDER NO. 4.

10th April 1918.   Copy No........

Reference Maps, Sheet 11. 1/1000,000.
Sheet 57.D.1/40,000.

1. ~~Sub~~ The 38th Battalion Machine Gun Corps will relieve the 12th Battalion Machine Gun Corps in the line from N.2.Central to W.15.a.3.7. in accordance with attached table.

2. Os.C. Companies will make all details for relief with their opposite numbers of the 12th Battalion Machine Gun Corps. Any Defence Schemes, trench maps, &c. will be taken over.

3. Command of Machine Gun Companies will be exercised in the same manner as when the Battalion was last in the line, except that the Company stationed at HENENCOURT will be under the orders of the Brigadier-General Commanding the Reserve Brigade (i.e, 115th Brigade).

4. Copies of receipts for trench stores &c. will be sent to Bn.H.Q. as soon after relief as possible.

5. Relief complete will be sent by "B.A.B." Code.

6. Transport will be at CONTAY, with the exception of four fighting limbers at HENENCOURT (carrying all Reserve Company's guns).

7. Battle personnel stays at CONTAY, with Transport, under Major F.C.W. Taylor.

8. Bn.H.Q. will open at approximately fork roads, U.24.a.9.3. (exact location later) at 4-0 p.m. 12th instant.

9. ACKNOWLEDGE.

........Capt. & Adjt.
38th Battn.M.G.C.

Issued at 11-55 p.m.

Copies to/
O.C. "A" Coy.	38th Div. "G"
" "B" Coy.	12th Battn.M.G.C.
" "C" Coy.	113th Brigade.
" "D" Coy.	114th Brigade.
Bn.T.O.	115th Brigade.
Q.M.	File.
R.S.M.	War Diary.

APPENDIX to 2nd/5th BATTN.H.Q. ORDER NO.4.

TABLE of RELIEFS and MOVES.

Serial No.	Date.	Unit.	To.	In relief of.	Remarks.
	April.				
1.	11th.	"D" Coy.	HEBUTERNE.	One Coy. 12th Battn.M.G.C.	Will be under orders of Reserve Brigade.
2.	11th.	"A" Coy.	VARLEY.	"D" Coy. 24th Battn.M.G.C.	
3.	12th.	"A" Coy.	COUPE GORGE.	One Coy. 12th Battn.M.G.C.	Will be under orders of Reserve Brigade.
4.	12th.	"B" Coy.	HENNOCOURT.	"D" Coy. 24th Battn.M.G.C.	
5.	12th/13th.	"D" Coy.	LA__ (R...)	One Coy. 12th Battn.M.G.C.	
6.	12th/13th.	"C" Coy.	LA__ (L...).	One Coy. 12th Battn.M.G.C.	
7.	12th (afternoon)	Bn.H.Q.	VARLEY. (afternoon 12th).	H.Q. 12th Battn.M.G.C.	

NOTES.

O.C. "D" Coy. will be at Brigade H.q. (L.27.d.7.9.) at 9-0 a.m. 11th. to arrange details with Coy. Commander 12th Battn.M.G.C.
"D" Coy. will meet guides at V.27.b.1.9. at 10-30 a.m. 11th.
"D" Coy. will move at 200 yards interval, and do not close up on guides.
Section move at 200 yards interval. Relief after dusk.
Fix up Relief with O.C. "D" Coy. 12th Battn.M.G.C.

O.C. "A" Coy. to VARLEY to relieve "D" Coy. 24th Battn.M.G.C. at 8-0 a.m. 11th.
"D" - "A" Coy. 24th Battn.M.G.C. at SERRIS (V.12.d.6.5.) at 10 a.m. and arrange relief.

O.C. "B" Coy. 12th Inft. to HENNOCOURT. Relieving party arrive at HENNOCOURT on 12th. and take over from "B" Coy. (about VARLEY) at 7-0 p.m.)
Company march into HENNOCOURT after dusk.

O.C. "D" Coy. See O.C. "D" Coy. 12th Battn.M.G.C. at Chateau, SERRIS (V.12.c.2.2.) at 5-0 p.m. 12th inst. to arrange details of relief of relief of 12th/M.G.C.

See War Diary

S E C R E T

39th BATTALION MACHINE GUN CORPS

Copy No......10

OPERATION ORDER NO. 15

25th April 1918.

1. 'B' Coy. 39th Battn. M.G.C. will relieve 4 Coys. of the 49th Battery Machine Guns Corps 148th/APHQ Inf. Details will be arranged by Coy.Cdrs. concerned.

2. R.S.O. will arrange Transport.

3. All Trench Stores, Defence Schemes, etc. will be handed over, and receipts taken.

4. On completion of relief 'B' Company will move into billets and Bivouacs at present occupied by 'B' Company, and will not be in touch with Head-quarters 118th Inf. Brigade : also O.C. 'B' Coy. will be in touch with Head-quarters 148th Inf. Brigade.

5. Completion of relief will be wired to Batt. by "B.A.B.8 Code".

6. ACKNOWLEDGE.

.............(Sgd.) J. Kidd
                   39th Batt. M.G.C.

Issued at 12.15 P.M.

Copies to/
B Coy ...... 118th Inf.Bde.
C Coy ...... 148th Inf. Bde.
A Coy ...... 3rd Div. HQ.
D Coy ......
R.T.O......
Adjt ...... File.
O.C....... War Diary.

SECRET.

208th MACHINE GUN CORPS.

Attn War Diary

OPERATION ORDER No. 15.

Copy No. 8

7th April 1918.

1. The following alterations will be made in the positions of guns on the night of the 16th/17th.

2. The 2 guns of "B" Company now at W.20.c.8.4. will move to W.20.c.6.9.

3. The 4 Reserve guns of "B" Company will move as follows :-

   (a) 2 guns to relieve 2 guns of "C" Coy. at W.24.d.8.5.
   (b) 2 guns to W.24.B.5.0.

4. O.C. "B" Company will place 2 guns in position at W.14.a.3.5.
   O.C. "C" Company will arrange to have this position pointed out on relief by "B" Company.

5. ACKNOWLEDGE.

Issued at 11-15 p.m.

Copies to/
A. Coy. 113th Brigade.
B. Coy. 114th Brigade.
C. Coy. 38th Div.
D. Coy. M.G.#
        File.
        War Diary.

Lieut-Colonel.
Commandg. 38th Battn.M.G.C.

S E C R E T.

38th BATTALION MACHINE GUN CORPS.

Copy No. 12

See War Diary

OPERATION ORDER No. 17.

19th April 1918

1. On night 20th/21st. "C" Coy. will relieve "A" Coy. in the Corps Line: relief to be completed by 1.30 a.m. *Covering* parties before dawn.

2. B.M.O. will take transport arrangements.

3. Defence Schemes, Trench Maps or Tracings, stores, etc. will be handed over and accepted therein.

4. Relief complete – "A" Coy. will move into bivouacs vacated by "C" Coy. O.C. "A" Co. will get in touch with H.Q. 113th Inf. Brigade (Reserve Brigade). O.C. "C" Coy. will get in touch with 112th Inf. Brigade.

5. Relief complete will be rptd in "B.A.B." Code to this Office.

6. ACKNOWLEDGE.

Issued at 7.45 p.m.

C Wright
Capt. & Adjt.
38th Battn. M.G.C.

P.M.C.

SECRET.

38th. BATTALION MACHINE GUN CORPS.

OPERATION ORDER NO. 18.

21st April 1918.    Copy No ...7....

Reference Map. Sheet 57.D. S.E. 1/20,000.

1. On the evening of the 22nd instant the 38th and 35th Divisions will capture and consolidate the line W.21.b.central - 16.a.0.0. - 10.c.0.7. - 4.c.8.0. - 4.b.1.3.

2. The attack on that part of the objective allotted to the 38th Division will be carried out by the 113th Inf. Brigade.

3. The 38th Battn.M.G.C. and the 35th Battn.M.G.C. will co-operate in supporting the 113th Inf. Brigade as ~~follows~~ under :-

4. (i) O.C. "A" Coy. 38th Battn.M.G.C. will furnish three Batteries with tasks as follows :-

Battery positions.	Guns.	Time.	Target.	Rate of fire.	Remarks.
W.19.d.4.6. (4 Gun Battery).	2	Zero to Zero +10.	Communication trench, centre of sone to fall on a point W.15.d.7.2.	150 r.p.m.	Traverse 1° Left & 1° Right.
	2	Zero to Zero +5.	Point in Sunken Road W.9.d.35.35.	150 r.p.m.	Traverse 1° Left & 1° Right.
	4	Zero +10 to Zero +75.	Line W.22.a.4.0. - W.22.a.2.3.	50 r.p.m.	This line will be maintained as the S.O.S. line.
W.20.a.15.85. (8 Gun Battery).	12	Zero to Zero +15.	Line W.16.c.00.20. - W.15.b.95.30.	150 r.p.m.	50% frontage per gun except the two left guns which barrage on 25% front.
W.13.d.7.8. (4 Gun Battery).		Zero +15 to Zero +35.	Line W.16.d.0.2. - W.16.b.0.3.	150 r.p.m.	Ditto.
		Zero +35 to Zero +75.	Ditto.	50 r.p.m.	This final line to be the S.O.S. line.

(ii) O.C. 35th Battn.M.G.C. is furnishing two Batteries ~~113th Inf.~~ to support 113th Inf. Brigade, as follows :-

P.T.O.

4. (ii) contd.   2.

Battery positions.	Guns.	Time.	Target.	Rate of fire.	Remarks.
W.2.d.2.0. (approx).	2	Zero to Zero +8.	Sunken Rd. W.15.d.9.1. - W.15.d.6.6.	250 r.p.m.	
W.3.d.5.8. (approx)	4	Zero to Zero +15.	To fire direct on any target seen about sunken road, W.15.b.9.3. - W.15.b.9.9.		

5. MAJOR JACKSON, "A" Coy. 38th Battn.M.G.C. will act as GROUP COMMANDER, and will establish his headquarters at 113th Infantry Brigade Command Post at V.23.a.9.9.

6. Communications will be by telephone as already arranged. In case of this breaking down, Runners will be sent up with Batteries on night of 21st/22nd to reconnoitre the route. They will then return and remain with Group Commander.

7. Watches will be synchronised at Reserve Brigade Headquarters at 4-0 p.m. 21st, and again at Left Brigade Headquarters at 3-0 p.m. on the 22nd. Battery Commanders' watches will be ~~synchronised~~ checked over the telephone by O.C. Group.

8. O.C. Group will be responsible for the checking of all Battery Charts

9. S.A.A. arrangements will be made so that besides the expenditure of S.A.A. as per time table, each gun has 4,000 rounds for answering S.O.S. Calls.

10. The S.O.S. Signal will be as now existing, i.e. rifle grenade rocket bursting into GREEN - RED - GREEN. Each gun will, upon the S.O.S. Signal, fire 4 belts rapid, followed by slow fire, if necessary according to the situation.

11. All Batteries will be in position the night of 21st/22nd. so as to avoid movement during the 22nd April.

12. Medical Collecting Station for walking wounded located at Cross Roads, V.16.a.8.8., Regimental Aid Posts are located at W.13.a.8.3. W.19.b.4.7. and W.19.c.1.8.

13. The half of "B" Coy. 12th Battn.M.G.C. now at WARLOY will relieve "A" Coy. 38th Battn.M.G.C. on the afternoon of the 21st April, until 8-0 a.m. 23rd instant, when "A" Coy. 38th Battn.M.G.C. again comes under orders of Reserve Brigade. Relief to be arranged between Os.C. Companies concerned.

14. The Batteries of "A" Company will remain in position until 4-0 a.m. 23rd April, when they will be withdrawn again into reserve as above.

15. ZERO hour will be notified later.

16. ACKNOWLEDGE.

(Signed) A.G.LYTTELTON, Lieut-Colonel.
Commanding, 38th Battn.M.G.C.

Issued at 5-0 p.m.
(per Orderly).

Copies to/
O.C. "A" Coy.
35th Battn.M.G.C.
12th Battn.M.G.C. ("B" Coy.)
113th Brigade.
38th Div. "G"
File.
War Diary.

SECRET.   War Diary.

38th. BATTALION MACHINE GUN CORPS.

ORDER NO. 19.

22nd April 1918.   Copy No. 8

Ref. Map. Sheet 57.D. S.E. 1/20,000.

Reference my M.G.102 (sent to "B" & "D" Coys. only).

1. "B" Coy. will supply 1 Section (4 Guns) to consolidate the ground to be captured 22nd inst.

2. The positions at W.14.a.3.4. (L.15 & 16), W.20.c.2.4. (L.3 & 4), will be abandoned.

3. At dawn 23rd inst. the Section will move forward to a convenient central position approximately the Bank at W.14.b.7.7. ready to take up the selected positions.

4. O.C. "B" Company will arrange to have positions reconnoitred for these guns by 9-0 a.m. on the 23rd instant, when the guns will move as follows :-
   (a) One pair of guns to about W.15.a. to be sited to sweep the Eastern side of the ridge running N. & S. through W.10 central, as this ground cannot be kept under observation by the 35th Division, and also to fire up road running E. & W. through W.16a. & b.
   Suggested positions to reconnoitre : Bank at W.9.c.4.3. working down road to 15.central.
   (b) One pair of guns to about W.15.d. sited to fire down the road running S.E. by Brickworks, and also to fire to the East.
   Suggested positions to reconnoitre : shell holes about the Communication trench running from our present front line about W.15.c.8.0. to Sunken Road in 15.d.

5. The occupation of the above positions will be dependent upon the success of the attack. Our front line should run, if the attack is successful, W.21.central - 21.b.central - 16.c.0.0. - 16.a.0.0. - 10.c.6.7. - 4.c.8.0. - 4.b.1.3.

6. ACKNOWLEDGE.

                                                Lieut-Colonel.
                                      Commanding, 38th Battn. M.G.C.

Issued at 4-15 P.M.

Copies to/
    O.C. "B" Coy.
    " "A", "C", & "D" Coys.)
    38th Div. "G".   )
    113th Brigade.   ) for information.
    File.   )
    War Diary.

War Diary

SECRET.

Ref: Map 57^D S.E. 1/20,000

H.O.B./M.237.

O.C.
"B" Coy.
20th Battn. M.G.C.

1. From dawn 25th instant, you will attempt to barrage a line V.16.c.15.65. to V.16.a.15.50. in answer to the S.O.S. Signal.

2. The following guns will be employed, and will fire from their battle positions :-

   2 Guns at V.13.b.60.15.
   2 " " V.14.a.3.5.
   2 " " V.14.c.8.0.
   2 " " V.9.d.5.0.

   The two guns formerly at V.14.a.3.5. have been moved to a more forward position. These will return to V.14.a.3.5.

3. As most of these positions are under direct observation of the enemy, great care must be taken to arrange for screening the flash of the gun, where necessary.

4. The two most Northern guns will be laid on the Southern half of the barrage line, so as to give the maximum range for their task.

5. ACKNOWLEDGE.

(sgd) J.F.G. West Major
for Lieut-Colonel,
Commanding, 20th Battn. M.G.C.

24th April 1918.

Copy to/
O.C. "A" Coy.
119th Inf. Brigade.) For Information.
30th Div. "G"
File.
War Diary.

"A" Form.
MESSAGES AND SIGNALS.

Army Form C. 2121.
(In pads of 100.)

TO: M.G. Bn.
~~115 Bde~~
~~115 Bde~~

Sender's Number.	Day of Month.	In reply to Number.	AAA
* 6A 27	2		

Reference Division Order 171 eight of the twelve guns of A Co. 38 M.G. Bn. which have the bank in W16A and C for their second target will remain in action covering that target until the whole Division is relieved. The remaining guns of A Co. 38 M.G. Bn. will remain in action till 9 p.m. 23rd inst. and will then withdraw into Div. Reserve and come under the orders of 115 Bde.
Para 5 of Order 171 to be amended accordingly.

38TH BATTALION, MACHINE GUN CORPS.
S 278

From 38 Div
Place
Time 3 p.m.

(Z) J.E. Munby Lt. Col. G.S.

War Diary

SECRET.

38th. BATTALION MACHINE GUN CORPS.

ORDER NO. 20.

24th April 1918.   Copy No. 20

Ref: Sheets, 57 D., 1/40,000,
         62 D., 1/40,000.

1. The 38th Division will be relieved from the present Right Divisional Boundary to W.15.d.5.0. by the 2nd Australian Division on the 25th instant, and the Command will pass to the 2nd Aust: Division at 6-0 a.m. on that date.

2. All Machine Gun positions (less Reserve positions in front of MILLENCOURT) South of Grid running East through W.15.d.5.0. will be relieved by 2nd Battn. Aust: M.G.C. on night 25th/26th instant.

3. Trench tracings, Aeroplane Mosaic, Trench Stores, and Billet Stores, will be handed over and receipts taken. Copy of receipts will be forwarded to Bn.H.Q. by 9-0 p.m. 26th instant.

4. Bn.T.O. will arrange Transport.

5. Billets in WARLOY and TOUTENCOURT will be arranged by the Intelligence Officer : and Units will be advised directly by him.

6. All Tents in possession will be struck and dumped at U.27.a.8.8. and receipts obtained.

6.a. Amendment attached.

7. On completion of relief O.C. "B" Company will report to H.Q., 115th Infantry Brigade at V.15.a.5.0.

8. All completions of Company Reliefs will be wired to Bn.H.Q. in "B.A.B." Code.

9. ACKNOWLEDGE.

                                              ....Capt. & Adjt.
                                                    38th Battn.M.G.C.

Issued at 3-0 p.m.

Copies to/
       O.C.   Q.M.
       2nd i/c. Bn.T.O.
       Adjt.   Sigl.Offr.
       Int.Offr. R.S.M.
       O.C. "A" Coy.
       "   "B" Coy.
       "   "C" Coy.
       "   "D" Coy.
       38th Div. "G"
       "   " "Q"
       113th Brigade.
       114th Brigade.
       115th Brigade.
       2nd Aust:M.G.Battn.
       File.
       War Diary.

RELIEF TABLE to accompany 38th Battn. M.G.O. ORDER NO. 20.

Serial No.	Unit.	No. of Guns.	Position.	Date.	From.	To.	Relieved by.
1.	"D" Coy.	16	Right Sector.	Night 25/26th.	Right Sector.	WARLOY.	8 Guns of 22nd Aust: M.G.Coy. 4 " " 6th " " "
2.	"B" Coy.	2	S. of Grid line detailed above.	"	"	SENLIS MILL. W.3.d.9.2.	} 4 Guns of 22nd Aust. M.G.C.
		2	"	"	"	"	
3.	"C" Coy.	8		"	Corps line.	Reserve posns. MILLENCOURT. *	2 Guns of 22nd Aust: M.G.C. 2 " " 5th " " "
3.a.	"	4		"	"	WARLOY.	2 " " 6th " " "
4.	"C" Coy.	2	SENLIS MILL. W.3.d.9.2.	"	Corps line W.3.d.9.2.	WARLOY.	"B" Coy. 38th Battn. M.G.C.
4.a.	"	2	"	"	"	WARLOY.	"B" Coy. 38th Battn. M.G.C.
5.	"A" Coy.	8	HENENCOURT WOOD.	"	HENENCOURT WOOD.	WARLOY.	4 Guns of 5th Aust: M.G.Coy.

* Positions will be indicated by O.C., 38th Battn. M.G.C.

War Diary

6.a.   AMENDMENT to accompany 38th BATTN.M.G.C. ORDER NO.20.

EXTRACT from 2nd Aust: M.G.Bn. Order No. 13 :-

"A" Coy. 8 Guns in line. Remain pending further instructions.
          8 Guns, HENENCOURT WOOD, relieved by 4 Guns of the 5th Aust:MGC.

"B" Coy. 12 Guns left of dividing line remain at present.
          2 Guns at V.24.b.8.0.)
          2   "   " W.19.d.8.4.) relieved by 22nd Aust: M.G.Coy.

"C" Coy. 2 Guns at V.30.b.3.3. relieved by 22nd Aust: M.G.Coy.
          2   "   in V.23.b. relieved by 5th Aust:M.G.Coy.
          2   "   at D.6.a.3.2. relieved by 6th Aust: M.G.Coy. —*
          4   "   North of Grid running East through W.15.d.5.0. to be
                  relieved by "B" Coy. 38th Battn.M.G.C.
          8   "   if unrelieved, pull out at dusk 25th instant, to
                  Reserve positions to be detailed by O.C., 38th Bn.M.G.C.

"D" Coy. 2 Guns at W.26.a.1.1.)
          2   "   " W.20.c.7.9.) relieved by 22nd Aust: M.G.Coy.

* Reference the[se] … ordered
  O.C., 6th Aust[ralian] … [O]fficers
  in the line.

"A" Form — Army Form C.2121 (in pads of 100).
MESSAGES AND SIGNALS.

TO:
A/VKC	D/VKC	CUZ	2 Aus MGB
B/VKC	VKW-G	KAC	OC RSM
C/VKC	G	OXR	B/O Int Off

Sender's Number: MSW 3   Day of Month: 24th   In reply to Number: AAA

VKC Order No. 20
[Pos]tponed 24 hours aaa
[amend?] … aaa
… A/VKC rescinded all
[ref]... to … order No. 20.

From: VKC
Time: 7.20 hrs

6.a.   AMENDMENT to accompany 38th BATTN.M.G.C, ORDER NO.20.

EXTRACT from 2nd Aust: M.G.Bn. Order No. 13 :-

"A" Coy.   8 Guns in line. Remain pending further instructions.
           8 Guns, HENENCOURT WOOD, relieved by 4 Guns of the 5th Aust:MGC.

"B" Coy.   12 Guns left of dividing line remain at present.
           2 Guns at V.24.b.8.0.) relieved by 22nd Aust: M.G.Coy.
           2 "   " W.19.d.8.4.)

"C" Coy.   2 Guns at V.30.b.3.3. relieved by 22nd Aust: M.G.Coy.
           2 "   in V.23.b. relieved by 5th Aust:M.G.Coy.
           2 "   at D.6.a.3.2. relieved by 6th Aust: M.G.Coy. -*
           4 "   North of Grid running East through W.15.d.5.0. to be
                  relieved by "B" Coy. 38th Battn.M.G.C.
           8 "   if unrelieved, pull out at dusk 25th instant, to
                  Reserve positions to be detailed by O.C., 38th Bn.M.G.C.

"D" Coy.   2 Guns at W.26.a.1.1.)
           2 "   " W.20.c.7.9.) relieved by 22nd Aust: M.G.Coy.
           2 "   " W.19.c.3.4.)
           2 "   " W.25.a.3.2.)
           2 "   " E.2.a.1.3.)
           2 "   " D.6.a.9.2.) relieved by 6th Aust: M.G.Coy. *

           4 "   if unrelieved, pull out at dusk, 25th instant.

*Reference those guns : O.C., 2nd Aust: M.G.Battn. states he has ordered
 O.C., 6th Aust: M.G.Coy. to arrange relief direct with Section Officers
 in the line.

38th. BATTALION MACHINE GUN CORPS.

ORDER NO. 21.

25th April 1918. Copy No.......

1. 38th Battalion Machine Gun Corps Order No. 20 is cancelled.
2. ACKNOWLEDGE.

Issued at 4-0 P.M.

..........Capt. & Adjt.
38th Battn. M.G.C.

Copy to all recipients of Order No.20.

260
M.G.B.......

AMENDMEND to 38th Bn. M.G.C. ORDER NO. 20.

5,a, (Attached Amendment) :

        line II, ("C" Coy.)

                for "8 Guns" read "6 Guns".

25th April 1918.

..........Capt. & Adjt.
38th Battn. M.G.C.

Copies to all recipients of Order No. 20.

SECRET.

War Diary

38th. BATTALION MACHINE GUN CORPS.

ORDER NO. 22.

26th April 1918.   Copy No. 20

Ref : Sheets, 57 D., 1/40,000.
       62 D., 1/40,000.

1. The Division (less Artillery) will be relieved by troops of the 2nd Australian Division from the present Right Boundary to the Grid line running East and West through W.15.c.5.0.

2. Command of the above part will pass to G.O.C., 2nd Aust: Divn. at 6-0 a.m. on the 27th instant. The remainder of the present Division Front will remain under the Command of the G.O.C., 38th Divn.

3. Reliefs and moves will take place in accordance with attached table. Details will be arranged between Companies direct.
All trench tracings, Mosaics, trench stores, and S.A.A. in boxes, will be handed over, and receipts taken. Copy of receipts will be forwarded to this Office by 9-0 p.m. 28th instant.

4. Bn.T.O. will arrange Transport.

5. Billets in WARLOY and TOUTENCOURT will be arranged by Intelligence Officer : who will notify Companies direct.

6. All tents in possession will be struck and dumped at U.27.a.8.8. & receipts taken.

7. On completion of relief, Os.C. "A" & "B" Companies will get in touch with H.Q. 115th Inf. Brigade at V.15.c.5.0.

8. Completion of relief will be wired in "B.A.B." Code to Bn.H.Q.

9. Bn.H.Q., Q.M. Stores, and Transport lines (less Transport of "D" Coy. and of "A" Coy. which move with their Companies) will remain in their present positions.

10. ACKNOWLEDGE.

............Capt. & Adjt.
38th Battn. M.G.C.

Issued at 2-30 p.m.

Copies to/
    C.O.   Q.M.
    2nd i/c.   Bn.T.O.
    Adjt.   Sigl.Offr.
    Int. Offr. R.S.M.
    O.C. "A" Coy.
    "   "B" Coy.
    "   "C" Coy.
    "   "D" Coy.
    38th Div. "G"
    "   "Q"
    113th Brigade.
    114th   "
    115th   "
    2nd Aust: M.G.Battn.
    File.
    War Diary.

RELIEF TABLE to accompany 35th M.G.C.Order NO.20.

Serial No.	Unit.	No. of Guns	Position.	Date.	From.	To.	Relieved by.
1.	"D" Coy.	16	Right Sector.	Night 27/28th.	Right Sector. VARLOY.	VARLOY. TOUTENCOURT.	8 Guns of 22nd Aust:M.G.Coy. 4 " " 65th "
2.	"B" Coy.	2	S. of Grid line detailed overleaf.	Night 27/28th.	Right Sector.	SENLIS MILL V.3.d.9.2.	4 Guns of 22nd Aust:M.G.Coy.
	"	2	"	"	"	"	
3.	"C" Coy.	8	"	"	Corps line	Reserve posts MILLENCOURT. VARLOX.	2 Guns of 22nd Aust:M.G.Coy. 2 " " 5th " " 2 " " 65th " "
3.2	"	4	"	"	"	"	
4.	"B" Coy.	2	SENLIS MILL V.3.d.9.2.	"	Corps line V.3.d.9.2.	VARLOY.	"B" Coy. 35th Battn.M.G.C.
4.2	"	2	"	"	"	VARLOY.	"B" Coy. 25th Battn.M.G.C.
5.	"A" Coy.	8 }	HEBUCOURT WOOD.	28th	HEBUCOURT WOOD. VARLOY.	VARLOY. TOUTENCOURT.	4 Guns of 5th Aust:M.G.Coy.
5.2	"	8	VARLOY.	28th	VARLOY.	TOUTENCOURT.	

x Positions will be indicated by O.C., 35th Battn.M.G.C.

On completion of relief, location of H.Qs. will be :-

"B" Coy........SENLIS Chateau, V.11.a.10.15.
"C" Coy........VARLOY.

EXTRACT from 2nd: Aust: M.G.Bn.Order No.13. attached.

EXTRACT from 2nd Aust:Bn.M.G.C. Order No. 13.(to accompany 38th Bn.M.G.C. Order No.22).

"A" Coy. — 8 Guns in WARLOY.
            8 Guns, HENENCOURT WOOD, relieved by 4 Guns of the 5th Aust:MGC.

"B" Coy. — 12 Guns left of dividing line — remain at present.
            2 " at V.24.b.8.0.)
            2 " " W.19.d.8.4.) relieved by 22nd Aust:M.G.Coy.

"C" Coy.   2 Guns at V.30.b.3.3. — relieved by 22nd Aust: M.G.Coy.
            2 " in V.23.b. — relieved by 5th Aust: M.G.Coy.
            2 " at D.6.a.3.2. — relieved by 6th Aust:M.G.Coy. *
            4 " North of Grid running East through W.15.d.5.0. to be relieved by "B" Coy. 38th Battn.M.G.C.
            6 " if unrelieved, pull out at dusk, 27th instant. to Reserve positions to be detailed by O.C., 38th Battn.M.G.C.

"D" Coy.   2 Guns at W.26.a.1.1.)
            2 " " W.20.c.7.9.) relieved by 22nd Aust:M.G.Coy.
            2 " " W.19.c.3.4.)
            2 " " W.25.a.3.2.)
            2 " " E.2.a.1.3.) relieved by 6th Aust:M.G.Coy. *
            2 " " D.6.a.9.2.)

            4 " if unrelieved, pull out at dusk, 27th instant.

* Reference these guns : O.C., 2nd Aust:M.G.Battn. states he has ordered O.C., 6th Aust: M.G. Coy. to arrange relief direct with Section Officers in the line.

"A" Form
MESSAGES AND SIGNALS.
Army Form C. 2121 (in pads of 100).

TO: OC C Coy

Sender's Number: LyW35
Day of Month: 28

8 Guns at present in these positions will pull out tonight. Battalion will take over in a few days. Acknowledge.

War Diary

From: MC

(Z) W Wright Capt

Vol 3

War Diary
of
35th Bn. M.G.C.
from 1st May, 1918 to 31st May 18

(Vol. 3)

Confidential

Army Form C. 2118.

WAR DIARY
or
INTELLIGENCE SUMMARY.
(Erase heading not required.)

35th Bn M.G.C.

A.G.Lyttleton [?] Lt Col
O.C. 35th Bn M.G.C.

Place	Date	Hour	Summary of Events and Information	Remarks and references to Appendices
WARLOY	1/5		"C" Coy. entrained 16 guns of 35th Bn. in AVELUY WOOD sector	Order No 23
			"A" " marched from TOUTENCOURT to WARLOY	
"	2/5		"A" & "D" Coys. retained 35th Bn. in centre & Coy HQrs in WARLOY Transport, Q.M. Stores, Shops, Police etc. moved to HANGEN VILLE [?]	Order No. 24
CONTAY	3/5		B.H.Q. & Canteen & Coy HQ 22/5 ANC [?] Artillery (?) signal officer ! with the office staff moved to CONTAY & were attached to Div. HQrs Canadian Guard 2 O R "A" Coy	
"	4/5		"B" Coy relieved "B" Coy in Right Sector. 7 guns "B" Coy to Corps Div. remainder in reserve. Manned 10 O.R. "B" Coy	Order No 25

Army Form C. 2118.

WAR DIARY
or
INTELLIGENCE SUMMARY.
(Erase heading not required.)

Instructions regarding War Diaries and Intelligence Summaries are contained in F. S. Regs., Part II. and the Staff Manual respectively. Title pages will be prepared in manuscript.

Place	Date	Hour	Summary of Events and Information	Remarks and references to Appendices
CONTAY	5/5		38th B". M.G.C. All guns reorganised so as to distribute 3 Coys in Right Central & Left Sectors each Coy with 1 Section on Corps Line so as to allow inter Coy reliefs. The 4th Coy with 8 guns is in Corps Line without a fixed line of defence. The work of holding the line without a fixed Coy in reserve is with the Battle Surplus personnel assisted by this Coy in reserve on the men. Wounded 2 O.R. "C" + "D"	M.9. 13.S./38
Tentencourt	6/5		B.H.Q. & 4 guns moved back to TOTENCOURT with B.H.Q. Accommodation very limited. Wounded 1 O.R. "C" Coy.	
Totencourt	7.8.9 /5		Nothing of any interest	

Army Form C. 2118.

WAR DIARY
or
INTELLIGENCE SUMMARY.
(Erase heading not required.)

Place	Date	Hour	Summary of Events and Information	Remarks and references to Appendices
Tourmont	10/5	9.0 a.m	36th Bn M.G.C. Cooperated in attack by 114 Bde on S.W. corner of AVELUY WOOD. 3 Batteries of 8 guns each firing an enfilade creeping barrage, after winds lifting to a protective S.O.S. barrage. Two 8 gun batteries of 35th Bn also placed under command of C.O. for harassing fire throughout day on various areas. Group commander, Major Williamson. "B" Coy fired 115,000 rounds; no casualties; one gun damaged (infra side plates). Attack a failure & all guns withdrawn to normal positions at dusk. Casualties. Killed O.R. 2 "A"+"B" Coys. Wounded Lieut Brown "C" Coy "A" 3 "B" 2 "C" 3 "D" 1 (last July)	Order No. 6 attached. A/Dinton attached.
	11/5		Casualties Wounded 2 O.R. "A" 1 "B" 1	
	12/5		"B" Coy relieved "C" Coy in left sector; 8 guns "C" to Corps line remainder to reserve. Casualties Nil.	Order No. 7

WAR DIARY
or
INTELLIGENCE SUMMARY.

Army Form C. 2118.

Place	Date	Hour	Summary of Events and Information	Remarks and references to Appendices
Fonquevillers			36th Bn. M.G.C.	
	15/5		Casualties Killed 2 O.R. "B" Coy.	
"	16/5		Casualties Wounded 1 O.R. (self-inflicted) "C" Coy.	
"	17/5		Casualties Wounded 1 O.R. "A" Coy.	
"	18/5		Under orders of Corps Commander establishes system of night firing 4 gun battery, to fire 21,000 rounds nightly on selected targets. "B" Coy. did this duty in left section. Gunners apparently under impression that this was prelude to an attack, as their gas projector Order No. 29 drum barrage several times when battery opened.	
"	19/5		Nightfiring continued by "C" Coy. "B" & "D" Coys relieved # & ♦ in flank section by 35th Bn. Order No. 28	

WAR DIARY or INTELLIGENCE SUMMARY

Army Form C. 2118.

35th Bn M.G.C.

Place	Date	Hour	Summary of Events and Information	Remarks and references to Appendices
Toutencourt	20/5		"A" & "C" Coys relieved by 35th Bn. in enemy recon & reserve	Orders No. 5
			Casualties Killed 1 O.R. } "A" Coy Wounded 1 O.R. }	
"	21/5		Casualties Wounded 1 O.R. "C" Coy	
"	22/5		"B" & "D" Coys returned occupation of the Brown Line "A" & "C" under verbal instructions from V Corps M.G.O. proceeded to line to co-operate in raid by 63rd Div.	Orders No. 30
"	24/5		"A" & "B" Coys training. "A" & "C" covered raid. Weather very bad Casualties P.G. Bismark Wounded "C" & one or July 3 O.R. Wounded	Report of operation

Army Form C. 2118.

WAR DIARY
or
INTELLIGENCE SUMMARY.
(Erase heading not required.)

Place	Date	Hour	Summary of Events and Information	Remarks and references to Appendices
Tincourt	25/5		35th Bn 17 M.G.C.	
			Casualties Wounded O.R. 4 2 at July A + C	
"	26/5		C of E at Baths. Roman Catholic Church Parade	
"	27/5 28/5		Training Close Order Drill, Box respirator Drill, Section Tactical Schemes	
"	29/5		Inspection by G.O.C. V Corps. Companies turned out clean & were congratulated on handling of arms & smartness in marching past. Transport not so good	
	30/5		Training as above	
	31/5		C.O. inspected Transport. Considerable improvement. 1 Section "B" Coy proceeded to join (Night) (ca/tr) to co-operate with 35th Division	1(4)(b)

H.G. Lyttelton
Lieut Col
Commdg 35 Bn 17 C.C.
54/5

SECRET.   *War Diary*

38th. BATTALION MACHINE GUN CORPS.

ORDER NO. 23.

30th April 1918.   Copy No. 16

1.   "C" Company 38th Battn. M.G.C. will relieve –

        4 Guns of "A" Coy.) 35th Battn. M.G.C.
        8 "   " "C" Coy.)

        2 "   " "B" Coy, 38th Battn. M.G.C.

tomorrow night, 1st/2nd May, 1918. Details to be arranged by Company Commanders concerned.

    H.Q., "C" Coy, 35th Battn. M.G.C.....V.6.d.9.3.
    "   "A" Coy, "   "   "   near W.7.c.2.3. BOUZINCOURT.

2.   Bn. T.O. will arrange Transport.

3.   Copies of receipts of all stores taken over will be forwarded to this Office by 5-0 p.m. 2nd May.

4.   On completion of relief, O.C., "C" Coy. will get in touch with H.Q., 114th Inf. Brigade (Line Left).

5.   Positions to be relieved as per Notes in detail and tracing already issued, will be complied with.

6.   Relief complete will be wired in "B.A.B." Code.

7.   ACKNOWLEDGE.

                                                  Capt. & Adjt.
Issued at 2-30 p.m.   38th Battn. M.G.C.

Copies to/
    C.O.   Q.M.
    2nd i/c.   Bn. T.O.
    Adjt.   Sigl. Offr.
    Int. Offr.   R.S.M.

    O.C., "C" Coy.
     "   "B" Coy.
     "   35th Battn. M.G.C.
    38th Div. "G".
     "   "   "Q".
    114th Brigade.
    File.
    War Diary.

SECRET.

War Diary

38th. BATTALION MACHINE GUN CORPS.

ORDER NO. 24.

2nd May, 1918.   Copy No. 21.

1. "A" and "D" Companies will move to positions as shown on tracing issued yesterday, tonight 2nd/3rd instant. Details will be arranged by Company Commanders concerned. Number of filled belts in line to be taken over from 35th Battn.M.G.C. will be ascertained by Company Commanders and an equal number will be handed over.

2. "D" Company (less 1 Section) will occupy Billets vacated by "B" Company 35th Battn.M.G.C.; Headquarters at V.3.b.6.5.

3. Bn.T.O. will arrange Transport.

4. Q.M's Stores, Transport, Tradesmen's Shops, Armourer Sergeant, will move today to HARPONVILLE, and take over Billets and lines of 35th Battn.M.G.C. They will move under the orders of Q.M. and Bn.T.O. Medical Officer and Chaplain will move to HARPONVILLE on the 3rd inst.

5. Relief complete will be wired by Code word "HEN".

6. Copies of consolidated Trench Stores lists will be forwarded to Bn.H.Q. by 5-0 p.m. 3rd instant.

7. B.H.Q. will close at WARLOY at 2-0 p.m. 3rd instant, and open at Chateau, CONTAY, the same hour.

8. Communications - 1. Wires and D.R.L.S. messages through Brigades.

    2. 6 Emergency Runners will be attached to Right Line Coy.H.Q. SENLIS CHATEAU. They will be used only as Runners to and from Bn.H.Q. CONTAY.

9. ACKNOWLEDGE.

.......Capt. & Adjt.
38th Battn.M.G.C.

Issued at 9-0 a.m.

Copies to/

C.O.	Bn.T.O.	O.C., "A" Coy.	38th Div. "G".	
2nd i/c	M.O.	" "D" Coy.	" "Q".	
Adjt.	Chaplain.	" "C" Coy.	35th Battn.M.G.C.	
Int.Offr.	Sig.Offr.	" "B" Coy.	113th Brigade.	
Q.M.	R.S.M.		114th Brigade.	

File, War Diary.

SECRET.   *War Diary*

38th BATTALION MACHINE GUN CORPS

OPERATION NO. 25.

3rd May, 1918.   Copy No. 14

1.   Tomorrow night 4th/5th instant, "D" Company will relieve "B" Company, line Right ; Details to be arranged by Company Commanders concerned.

2.   Bn.T.O. will arrange Transport.

3.   Relief done, "B" Company will occupy positions, bivouacs, etc. vacated by "D" Company.

4.   Police and Guardroom will remain at HEDAUVILLE. R.S.M. will be attached to "B" Company for instructional purposes. The attached prisoners will be rationed by "B" Coy.

5.   O.C., "D" Company will get in touch with H.Q., 115th Inf. Brigade, V.15.a.5.0., after relief.

6.   Relief complete will be wired by Code word "DUKES".

7.   ACKNOWLEDGE.

                                        ....Capt. & Adjt.
                                            38th Battn.M.G.C.
Issued at 3-50 p.m.

Copies to/

C.O.	O.C., "D" Coy.	38th Div. "G".
2nd i/c.	" "B" Coy.	" "Q".
Adjt.	" "A" Coy.	115th Inf. Brigade.
Int.Offr.	" "C" Coy.	
Bn.T.O.	File.	
Q.M.	War Diary.	
Sigl.Offr.		
R.S.M.		

SECRET.

M.G.B./S.388.

War Diary

O.C., "A" Coy.
 "   "B" Coy.
 "   "C" Coy.

1. The following changes will take place in accordance with table below, tonight. Company Commanders will arrange details. Change should be complete by 1-0 a.m. tomorrow, 6th instant.

2. Companies will wire 'change complete' by Code word "TROY"

3. ACKNOWLEDGE.

Relieving Guns.	Position Relieved.	At present occupied by.
2 Guns, "D" Coy.	W.18.b.7.9.	2 Guns, "A" Coy.
2 Guns, "A" Coy.	W.7.b.7.6.	2 Guns, "D" Coy.
" "	W.9.a.1.8.	2 " "C" "
" "	W.9.a.1.0.	2 " " "
" "	W.8.a.6.0.	2 " " "
2 Guns, "C" Coy.	W.2.b.1.8.	2 Guns, "A" Coy.
" "	W.1.b.5.3.	2 " " "
" "	Q.31.c.5.5.	2 " " "

..........Capt. & Adjt.
38th Battn. M.G.C.

5th May, 1918.

Copy to/
 38th Div. "G".)
 113th Brigade.)
 114th   "   ) for information.
 115th   "   )
 O.C., "D" Coy.)

War Diary

SECRET.   *War Diary*

38th. BATTALION MACHINE GUN CORPS.

ORDER NO. 26.

7th May. 1918.   Copy No...9....

Reference Map. Sheet 57 D., S.E. 1/20,000.

1. On the morning of the 10th instant the 114th Inf. Brigade will capture and hold a line running from the South West Corner of AVELUY WOOD to the ride at W.4.c.8.0. and thence along the ride to our present front line at W.4.b.3.6.

2. The attack will be made from the North ; the Right flank of the attacking force will move along the Western edge of AVELUY WOOD.

3. The 38th Battn. M.G.C. will co-operate in supporting the attack with one Group consisting of 18 Guns.
   The guns will be supplied as follows :-

   "B" Coy. - 12 Guns ; 8 from Reserve and 4 from positions in the Corps line, W.1.b.7.0. and W.1.d.3.8.

   "C" Coy. - 6 Guns ; 4 from positions in the Corps line, Q.31.c.4.4. and W.1.b.5.5., and 2 guns from position at Q.33.c.15.95.

4. The Group will consist of three Batteries of 6 Guns each, lettered "A", "B", & "C", with tasks as follows :-

Battery position.	Guns.	Time.	Target.	Rate of fire.	Remarks.
"C" Battery. Q.32.d.15.38.	6	Zero to Zero+4.	Area enclosed in following co-ordinates: W.4.d.10.94.- b.20.15.- a.40.40.- a.35.20.	150 R.P.M.	To cover the areas of each Battery. Each area will be divided into three strips and two guns with combined sights will lay on the centre of each strip. Traversing ½° left and ½° Right
		Zero+6 to Zero+40.	Area enclosed in W.4.c.90.05 d.02.27. - c.30.70. - c.20.50.	75 R.P.M.	
		Zero+40 to Zero+60.	Ditto.	150 R.P.M.	
		Zero+60 cease fire.	Lay on S.O.S. line W.4.d.75.45. to d.90.90.		40 yds. per gun.
"B" Battery. Q.32.c.67.05.	6	Zero to Zero+4.	Area enclosed in W.4.d.05.70 -d.12.92. - a.30.15. - c.27.95.	75 R.P.M.	To cover the area of each Battery. Each battery will be divided into three strips, and two guns with combined sights will lay on the centre of each strip. Traversing ½° L. & R.
		Zero+4 to Zero+20.	Ditto.	150 R.P.M.	
		Zero+22 to Zero+60	Area enclosed in W.10.b.00.99 - a.96.80. - 4.c.35.35. - c.25.17.	75 R.P.M.	
		Zero+60 to Zero+85.	Ditto.	150 R.P.M.	
		Zero+85 cease fire.	Lay on S.O.S. line W.4.d.60.00. to d.75.45		40 yds. per gun.

P.T.O.

Battery position.	Guns.	Time.	Target.	Rate of Fire.	Remarks.
"A" Battery. W.2.a.95.85.	6	Zero to Zero +20.	Area enclosed in following co-ordinates: W.4.c.96.46. - d.05.70. - c.30.90. - c.22.70.	75 R.P.M.	To cover the area of each Battery. Each area will be divided into 3 strips, and two guns with combined sights will lay on the centre of each strip. Traversing ½° Left and ½° Right.
		Zero +20. to Zero + 40.	Ditto.	150 R.P.M.	
		Zero +42. to Zero +85.	Area enclosed in W.10.a.90.55 - b.00.75. - 4.c.30.10. - 10.a.25.92.	75 R.P.M.	
		Zero +85 to Zero 90.	Ditto.	150 R.P.M.	
		Zero +90. cease fire.	Lay on S.O.S. Lines. W.10.b.45.55. to W.4.c.60.00.		40 yds. per gun.

5. MAJOR WILLIAMSON, "B" Company, 38th Battn.M.G.C. will act as GROUP COMMANDER. He will establish his Headquarters with the Headquarters of the Infantry Battalion which will be in the Bank at Q.32.d.25.00. The Group Commander will appoint an Officer to act as Liasion Officer who will be at advanced Brigade Headquarters, Q.31.c.Central. The Headquarters of these two Officers may be inter-changed at the request of Brigade.

6. Communications will be by telephone to all Batteries through Inf.Battn. H.Q. at Q.32.d.25.00. and thence to Brigade.

7. Watches will be synchronised at Advanced Brigade Headquarters, 114th Inf. Brigade (Q.31.c.Central) at 6-0 p.m. on the 9th instant, and 6-0 a.m. on the 10th instant. A representative will be sent, detailed by Group Commander, with two watches. These watches should be Battery Commander's watches for preference.

8. O.C., Group will be responsible for the checking of all Battery Charts.

9. S.A.A. 80,000. rounds per Battery position to be dumped.

10. The S.O.S. Signal as now existing.

11. All Batteries will be in position the night of 9th/10th, and laid by 7-0 a.m. 10th instant.

12. Medical (to be notified later).

13. The Batteries will, after the attack, remain in position laid on their S.O.S. lines until further orders.

14. ZERO HOUR will be notified later.

15. Adjustment to existing S.O.S. lines : *but new line will necessitate the adjustment of 2 S.O.S. Barrages*
    (a) The four guns of "C" Company at Q.33.d.5.7.(approx.) will place their double enfilade barrage from W.10.c.85.40. to W.10.a.65.00.
    (b) The two guns of "C" Company at W.2.a.9.6. and the two guns of "A" Company at W.2.a.7.0. will barrage a line W.10.c.80.95. to W.10.b.00.25.
    The above alterations will take place after dawn, 10th instant.

16. ACKNOWLEDGE.

Lieut-Colonel.
Issued thro' Signals at 7-30 p.m.   Commanding, 38th Battn.M.G.C.

Copy to/ O.C., "B" Coy. O.C., "A" Coy. Bn.T.O.
         "C" Coy. "   "D" Coy. 114th Inf.Brigade) For information.
         File, War Diary.   38th Div. "G".

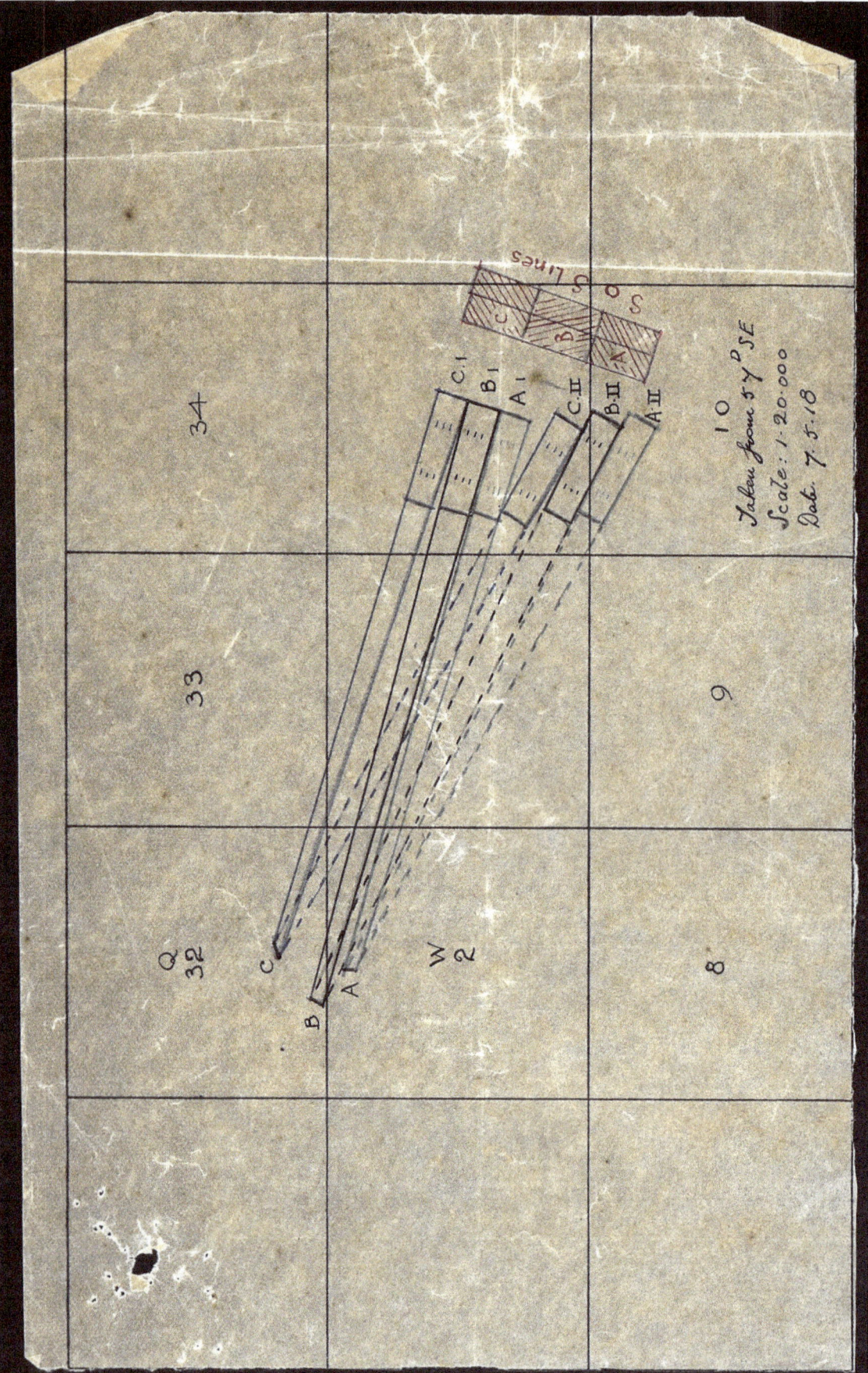

SECRET.

ADDENDUM to 38th BATTN.M.G.C. ORDER NO.26.

17. One Company 35th Battn.M.G.C. has been placed under orders of 38th Battn.M.G.C. for this operation.
    This Company will be formed into a Sub-Group of two Batteries of 8 Guns each under a Sub-Group Commander who will be situated at Inf. Battn.H.Q. in Bank at Q.32.d.25.00. and will be under O.C., Group, (see para.5.)

18. The two Batteries will be numbered "D" and "E" and will be in position as in para.11.
    "D" Battery at W.2.b.20.00. (Right Gun).
    "E" Battery at Q.32.d.25.85. (Right Gun).
    and will, (except see para.21) harass the numbered areas as per tracing attached, at the following times :-

Time.	D/Battery.	E/Battery.	Rate of fire.
Zero.	D.I.	E.II.	2 Belts per gun, rapid
" + 5.	—	E.VI.	" " " " "
" + 15.	D.IV.	—	" " " " "
" + 25.	—	E.V.	" " " " "
" + 35.	D.VI.	—	" " " " "
" + 45.	—	E.II.	" " " " "
" + 55.	D.I.	—	" " " " "
" + 65.	—	E.IV.	" " " " "
" + 75.	D.V.	E.VI.	" " " " "
" + 85.	D.I.	E.I.	1 Belt per Gun, rapid
" + 90.	D.I.	E.II.	1 " " " " "
" + 100.	D.II.	E.II.	1 " " " " "
" + 105.	D.I.	E.I.	1 " " " " "
" + 110.	D.II.	E.II.	1 " " " " "
" + 115.	D.I.	E.I.	1 " " " " "
" + 2 hrs.	D.III.	—	2 Belts per gun, rapid
" + 2½ "	D.V.	E.VI.	" " " " "
" + 3 "	D.VI.	E.IV.	" " " " "
" + 4 "	D.V.	E.V.	" " " " "
" + 6 "	D.VI.	E.IV.	" " " " "
" + 8 "	D.V.	E.VI.	" " " " "
" + 10 "	D.IV.	E.V.	" " " " "
" + 11 "	D.III.	E.III.	" " " " "
" + 11½ "	D.V.	E.VI.	" " " " "
" + 12 "	D.II.	E.V.	" " " " "
" + 12¼ "	D.VI.	E.V.	" " " " "

19. The Batteries will be connected up to Group Commander by telephone.

20. O.C., "D" Battery will arrange to establish an O.P. in W.2.d.

21. In the event of an enemy target presenting itself or at the request of O.C. Operations, these Batteries may be switched and used as the situation requires, the time table only being adhered to when there is no other call upon the Batteries.

J H Jessy Weiss
Lieut-Colonel,
Commanding, 38th Battn.M.G.C.

May 8th, 1918.
Issued thro' Signals at 11-55 p.m.

Copies to all recipients of Order No.26, & 35th Battn.M.G.C. (to acknowledge

Q			
32 "E" Battery	33	34	35
W "D" Battery	3	4 E VI	D VI 5
			E V
		E IV	D V
8	9 E II E I	E III 10 D II	D IV
		D I D III	

Taken from Sheet 57° SE
Scale: 1/20,000
9-5-18

use with Artillery Maps.

S E C R E T.

A M E N D M E N T NO. 1, to 35th BATTN.M.G.C. ORDER NO.26.

3. Owing to amendment to Artillery Creeping Barrage, the times of lifting in para. 4, will now read :-

"C" Battery. Zero + 40 to Zero + 55 (instead of Z.+ 40 to Z.+ 60.)
Zero + 55 cease fire (instead of Z.+ 60.)

"B" Battery. Zero + 60 to Zero + 75 (instead of Z.+ 60 to Z.+ 85.)
Zero + 75 cease fire (instead of Z.+ 85.)

"A" Battery. Zero + 20 to Zero + 35 (instead of Z.+ 20 to Z.+ 40.)
Zero + 37 to Zero + 80 (instead of Z.+ 42 to Z.+ 85.)
Zero + 80 to Zero + 85 (instead of Z.+ 85 to Z.+ 90.)
Zero + 85 cease fire (instead of Z.+ 90.)

Lieut-Colonel,
Commanding, 35th Battn.M.G.C.

May 8th, 1918.
Issued thro' Signals at 11-55 p.m.

Copies to all recipients of Order 26.
and 35th Battn.M.G.C.)
"B" Coy. (35th)) to acknowledge.

"A" Form
MESSAGES AND SIGNALS.
Army Form C. 2121 (in pads of 100).

TO: B Coy 38th Bn 44th MGC
    "   "   35th   "   "

Sender's Number.	Day of Month.	In reply to Number.	AAA
FL.197	9th		

Reference Order 26 Medical arrangements are as follows. Walking wounded Collecting Station will be established near V.5.c.6.4. A track will be marked out labelled Walking Wounded Track A. Head of Track is at W.2.a.8.4 Beaver Aid Posts &

	Q 31 b	9 9
	Q 32 c	8 9
	Q 32 c	7 6

From: 38th Bn MG Corps

(Z) (Sgd) L.F.R. Dees

SECRET.

War Diary

38th. BATTALION MACHINE GUN CORPS.

ORDER NO. 27.

10th May, 1918.   Copy No. 17

1. On night 12th/13th instant, "B" Company will relieve "C" Company, line left ; all details to be arranged by Company Commanders.

2. Trench Store receipts will be taken and a copy sent to this Office by 1st D.R. 14th instant.

3. Bn.T.O. will arrange Transport.

4. Relief done, "C" Company will occupy positions, bivouacs, etc. vacated by "B" Company.

5. O.C., "B" Company will get in touch with H.Q., 114th Inf. Brigade.

6. 'Relief complete' will be wired by Code word "CAT".

7. ACKNOWLEDGE.

                                            ....Capt. & Adjt.
Issued thro' Signals at 9-0 p.m.   38th Battn.M.G.C.

Copies to/
C.O.	Sigl.Offr.	38th Div. "G".
2nd i/c	R.S.M.	" " "Q".
Adjt.	O.C., "B" Coy.	114th Inf.Brigade.
Int.Offr.	" "C" Coy.	File.
Q.M.	" "A" Coy.	War Diary.
Bn.T.O.	" "D" Coy.	

M.G.B./S.472.

38th BATTALION MACHINE GUN CORPS.

AMENDMENT to ORDER NO.27.

For night "12th/13th"

        read

           "night 13th/14th".

                    ....Capt. & Adjt.
11th May, 1918.   38th Batth.M.G.C.
  6-0 p.m.

Copies to all recipients of Order No.27.
    O.C. "C" & "B" Coys. to acknowledge.

War Diary

SECRET.

38th BATTALION MACHINE GUN CORPS.

ORDER NO.26.

17th Mar. 1918.   Copy No.......

1. The 39th Battn.M.G.C. will be relieved by the 38th Battn.M.G.C. in accordance with attached Table and tracing.

2. Company Commanders concerned will arrange details with their opposite numbers.
   Bn.T.O. will arrange Transport.

3. Defence Schemes, details of work in-hand, trench tracings, trench stores, S.A.A. in boxes, aerial photographs will be handed over. Receipts will be taken and copies of all sent to Bn.H.Q. by noon the day following relief.

4. Command will pass to O.C., 38th Battn.M.G.C. at 10-0 a.m. 21st instant at which hour Bn.H.Q. closes at U.1.b.60.10. and re-opens at U.1.d.1.2.

5. Q.M. Stores and H.Q. Transport will move to TOUTENCOURT and occupy lines and billets of 38th Battn.M.G.C.
   Representatives will report to 2nd/Lt.F.S.GRIFFITH, Bn.H.Q. at 10-0 a.m. 21st instant to take over Billets etc.

6. 1 Officer and batman per Company will meet 2nd/Lt.F.S.GRIFFITH,Bn.H.Q. at 10-0 a.m. 19th instant and take over Billets for their Companies.

7. Relief complete will be wired Code Word "SINK".

8. ACKNOWLEDGE.

2.a. In case of "C" Coy : Pos. Positions 1,2,3 & 4, will be relieved by
                          "B" Coy. 38th Battn.M.G.C.
                          Pos. positions 13, 14, 15 & 16 will be relieved
                          by "D" Coy. 38th Battn.M.G.C.

   The following positions will not be taken over :

        Nos.5 to 12 inclusive.
        L.13 & 14, L.5,6,7, & 8.
        R. 13 & 14.
        & 2 Guns W.14.b.7.0. & V.14.b.75.00.

   Trench Stores of these positions will be taken to the nearest Section or Company H.Q. which is to be relieved ; and handed over to 38th Battn.M.G.C.

5.a. All details at HARPONVILLE not included in above will move to TOUTENCOURT on 21st instant.

                                                    ....Capt. & Adjt.
                                                         39th Battn.M.G.C.

Issued thro' Signals at 10-0 p.m.

Copies to/
            C.O.   O.C., "A" Coy.   39th Div. "G".
            2nd i/c.   "   "B" Coy.   "   "   "Q".
            Adjt.   "   "C" Coy.   O.C., 38th Battn.M.G.C.
            Int.Offr.   "   "D" Coy.   113th Inf.Brigade.
            Sigl.Offr.   " Battle Surplus   114th "   "
            Q.M.   Details.   115th "   "
            Bn.T.O.   File.
            R.S.M.   War Diary.

TABLE to accompany 56th Battn.H.Q.O.ORDER NO.29.

1. Serial No.	2. Unit.	3. Date. (Hour)	4. From.	5. To.	6. Relieved by.
1.	"B" Coy. (Left)	19th/20th.	LINE.	TRENCHOUTER.	"B" Coy. 25th Battn.N.Z.C.
2.	"D" Coy. (Right)	19th/20th.	"	"	"D" Coy. " " "
3.	"A" Coy. (Centre)	20th/21st.	"	"	"A" Coy. " " "
4.	"C" Coy. (Reserve)	20th/21st.	"	"	"C" Coy. " " "

NOTE: Transport will move with Companies.

SECRET.

ADMINISTRATIVE INSTRUCTIONS WITH REGARD TO
59th DIVNL.R.G.O. ORDER NO.29.
————oOo————

1. **TENTS & SHELTERS** will be left in "SITU" by outgoing units, handed over, and receipts obtained which will be forwarded to Bn.H.Q.

2. **SUPPLIES.** On and after the 21st instant, Railhead will be the.ROMM. The second days supplies will be delivered at the Transport Lines of the new locations. Refilling Points will be notified later.

   to Q.M

3. **HOT FOOD CONTAINERS** will be handed over and receipts obtained. The remainder will be handed into D.A.D.O.S.
   by him

4. **BATHS.** will be established on the 20th instant at -

   ...., ... & ....
   Applications to Bn.H.Q.

5. **SOCKS.** Additional socks in possession, issued for duty in the line, will be handed in to the Divisional Clothing Depot, Billet 54, ..., and receipts obtained.

6. **PRESENT RAILHEAD** - BAINGHEVAL.

7. **CANTEENS.** (X Regt) Divisional Canteens will be arranged for at .... In addition the 2 Carts will be available as desired.

————————————

.........Capt. & Adjt.
59th Battn.R.C.R.

15th May, 1916.

SECRET.

38th BATTALION MACHINE GUN CORPS.

ORDER NO. 28.

HARASSING FIRE.

1. Whilst the Division is holding the line not less than 21,000 rounds will be fired nightly in Harassing Fire.

2. This night firing will be undertaken by Machine Gun Companies in the line in rotation.

3. Harassing Fire will be in the form of 'CRASHES' and will be in co-operation with the night firing of the Artillery.
The Artillery programme will be sent to the Company concerned as soon as received by this Office, and O.C., Company will arrange to Crash, as far as possible, the same areas as the Artillery, during the intervals between Artillery Shoots.

4. The remaining period the Division is holding the line will only necessitate two nights harassing fire.
This fire will be undertaken on the night 18th/19th by "B" Coy. On the night 19th/20th by "A" Company.
"B" Company will prepare and fire from a position approximately W.2.b.5.8.
"A" Company from a position approximately W.2.b.2.0.
On each night a battery of 4 Guns will be used ; Guns on "S.O.S." lines will not be used.

5. To carry out this Harassing Fire 84 Belts in Belt Boxes will be required. The Bn.T.O. will collect this number from the existing stock held by Companies at the Transport lines, and will send them up filled to a rendezvous selected by O.C., Company concerned.
A second limber will at the same time be detailed to carry the guns to be used for this fire from their positions to the Battery position under orders to be issued by O.C., Company concerned.

6. One hour before dawn on the morning of the 19th instant and 20th instant, two limbers will be at the respective Battery positions, one to move the guns back to their Battle positions, and one to take the empty 84 belts, boxes and empty cases to "C" Coy's bivouacs.

7. By 10-0 a.m. on the 19th and 20th instant, Bn.T.O. will arrange to deliver 21,000 rounds to "C" Coy's bivouacs.

8. The empty belts will be refilled under direction of O.C. "C" Company

9. On the night of the 19th/20th the ammunition limber will load up at "C" Company's bivouacs and proceed to rendezvous as in para. 5 above

10. If there are not 84 belt boxes ready filled, Bn.T.O. will on receipt of this order send them to "C" Company's bivouacs with the necessary S.A.A. and they will be filled forthwith.

11. ACKNOWLEDGE.

17th May, 1918.

Lieut-Colonel.
Commanding, 38th Battn.M.G.C.

Copies to/
O.C.
A. B. & "C" Coys.
Bn.T.O. (Q.M. to see).
"D" Coy. for information.
File.

SECRET.

38th BATTALION MACHINE GUN CORPS.

ORDER NO. 30.

21st May, 1918.   Copy No. 9

Reference "Instructions for Defence, No.7." (38t Divn.GSS.5/64/9.)

1. In the event of it being necessary to occupy the BROWN LINE, "B" & "D" Companies will come under the orders of 114th Inf.Brigade. They will move in accordance with 114th Inf.Brigade Order No.178. "B" Company passing the road junction U.2.c.10.75. at Zero, and "D" Company at Zero plus 10 minutes.

2. "B" Company will occupy the following positions as already reconnoitred :-

   No.1. Section.
         2 Guns.........V.7.a.50.55.
         2 Guns.........V.7.b.10.55.
   No.2. Section.
         2 Guns.........V.8.b.50.70.
         2 Guns.........V.2.d.15.50.
   No.3. Section.
         2 Guns.........V.2.a.70.00.
         2 Guns.........V.2.b.10.30.
   No.4. Section.
         2 Guns.........P.33.a.40.45.
         2 Guns.........P.27.c.75.60.

Company Headquarters with Headquarters, "B" Battalion, 114th Inf.Bde. at V.2.b.70.60.

"D" Company will occupy the following positions as already reconnoitred

   No.1. Section.
         1 Gun..........V.7.c.40.85.
         1 Gun..........V.7.c.30.75.
         2 Guns.........V.13.b.50.60.
   No.2. Section.
         2 Guns.........V.14.d.25.60.
         2 Guns.........V.14.b.75.20.
   No.3. Section.
         2 Guns.........V.8.d.20.90.
         2 Guns.........V.8.d.15.75.
   No.4. Section.
         2 Guns.........V.13.b.75.30.
         2 Guns.........V.13.c.80.30.

Company Headquarters will be with "A" Battn., 114th Inf. Brigade at V.2.b.20.45.

3. In the event of an order to regain any part of the PURPLE LINE, Battalion Headquarters (as laid down in Administrative Instructions issued herewith) and "A" and "C" Companies will fall in on alarm posts on order "prepare to move". On the order "move" they will march in order of march as above to U.5.d.8.7. starting point road junction U.2.a.7.4. (1/20,000 Map).

4. The Division may be ordered to occupy the RED LINE and Companies will reconnoitre this line by the 23rd instant, "A" and "B" Companies paying special attention to the Northern half of the Divisional area. "C" and "D" Companies to the Southern half. Any Company may however be ordered to occupy any part of this line. Tracing herewith (to Coy

5. Until further orders, all Companies will, between the hours of 6-0 a.m. and 10-0 a.m., be on one hour's notice to move.

P.T.O.

6. Communications between Companies and Battalion Headquarters will be through Infantry Brigade Headquarters and Divisional advanced Headquarter.

21st May, 1918.

Lieut-Colonel.
Commanding, 38th Battn. M.G.C.

Copies to/
    Os.C.
To acknowledge
    ("A" Coy.   38th Div. "G". (2 Copies)
    ("B" Coy.   113th Inf. Brigade.
    ("C" Coy.   114th "   "
    ("D" Coy.   115th "   "
    Q.M.
    Bn.T.O.
    Sigl. Offr.
    File.
    War Diary.

38th BATTALION MACHINE GUN CORPS.

ADMINISTRATIVE INSTRUCTIONS to accompany ORDER NO.30.

Reference para.2, of 38th Division No.GSS.5/64/10, dated 17th May, 1918.

1. On receipt of movement orders, First line Transport (less Bn.H.Q. limber and Mess Cart) will move with Companies.

2. Advanced Headquarters and Water Carts, and 3 mounted orderlies move to U.5.d.8.7.

3. Standing Orders to ensure a state of readiness are :-

   1. Limbers will be kept packed ready for action by night.
   2. Water carts will always be kept full.
   3. Water bottles will be kept full by night, and as far as possible, always.
   4. Fighting order will be kept ready by night.
   5. Iron rations will always be kept in haversacks.
   6. Arrangements for issuing unconsumed portion of the day's ration to their men by Company Commanders.

4. In the event of move forward being ordered : O.C., Battle Surplus will be in Command of all details left behind.
Company Q.M. Stores, and Company Orderly Rooms will remain at TOUTENCOURT.

5. All packs, blankets, Officers Kits, will be dumped at C.Q.M.Stores. Those of Bn.H.Q. personnel at Q.M. Stores.

6. System of runners to be detailed by Signalling Officer :-

   7 to move with advanced H.Q. personnel.
   4 at rear H.Q., TOUTENCOURT.
   1 with Quartermaster.
   1 with Bn.T.O.

                                              Lieut-Colonel.

21st May, 1918.   Commanding, 38th Battn.M.G.C.

Copies to all recipients of Order No.30.

SECRET.

C.69.
25.5.18.

To 38th Battn M.G.C.

Barrage Fire night 24th/25th May

1. 16 Guns of this Company helped to put down a M.G. Box Barrage to support raids by the 63rd (R.N.) Division.
2. Each battery of 8 guns barraged a line as per instructions of the 63rd Battn M.G.C. and searched 500x.
   In addition 21 crashes of 125 rounds were put down on the same target at intervals of 3 or 4 minutes until Zero plus 120.
3. Each battery fired 200 belts.
   The following breakages or losses occurred:-

Lock Springs	11.
Fusee Springs	3.
Firing Pins	8.
Roller Collar Split Pins	4.
Rollers + Collars	4.
Screw Plug & Cork Plug	1.
Condenser Screw Protector Boss	1.
Condenser Tube	2.
Crank Handle Fixing Pin	2.
Tumbler Axis Pin	1.
Extractor	1.
Trigger	1.
Muzzle Cup Attachment	2.
Gib Spring	1.
Top Lever Feed Block	1.

4. The guns were withdrawn at Zero plus 3 hours (2.15am 25th inst)
5. Casualties to Personnel -
   Wounded Lieut. P. Godsmark.
   " 51461 Pte. Edmonds.H.T.
   " 148099 Pte. Jones.H.
   " 7566 L/c Blake.R. (remained at duty)
   " 54314 Pte. Jones.W. (wounded and remained at duty)
   " 130650 Pte. Bradley.J.J. (remained at duty).

   F.W.Doyle Major
   O.C. "C" Coy 38th Bn. M.G.C.

25.5.18

"A" Form
MESSAGES AND SIGNALS.

Army Form C. 2121
(in pads of 100).

Prefix....Code....m.	Words.	Charge.	This message is on a/c of:	Recd. at....m.
Office of Origin and Service Instructions.	Sent			Date
	At....m.		....................Service.	From
	To......			
	By......		(Signature of "Franking Officer.")	By

TO	OC ~~[crossed out]~~			
	D Coy			

Sender's Number.	Day of Month.	In reply to Number.	AAA
MG/W 54	31		

Please detail 1 Section Officer & Personnel ~~and~~ (only 16 belt boxes per gun) to be ready by 2.0 pm to proceed if necessary to Hedauville today. Details will follow when available.

From: 38 Bn MGC

The above may be forwarded as now corrected. (Z)

Censor. Signature of Addressee or person authorised to telegraph in his name: Wright Capt

"A" Form
MESSAGES AND SIGNALS.

TO OC D Company

Sender's Number: M Gr 56
Day of Month: 31

Reference M Gr 54. The section detailed will proceed to HEDAUVILLE on receipt of this, & report to A Coy 35th Battⁿ MGC at V.3.6. 50.30 at 5.0 pm for barrage work. Acknowledge.

From
Place: 38th Battⁿ MGC
Time:

Signature: B Griffith Lt

Vol 4

Confidential

War Diary
of
38th Battn. M.G.C.
from 1st June '18 to 30th June '18
(Vol. 4)

WAR DIARY
or
INTELLIGENCE SUMMARY

Army Form C. 2118.

Place	Date	Hour	Summary of Events and Information	Remarks and references to Appendices
Toutencourt	1/6		36th B - M.G.C. Inspection of Transport by G.O.C. 38th Div. Great improvement	
"	2/6		Transport Competition. God turn out. "C" Coy winners	
"	3/6		Shooting Competition. Each company entered a 4-gun battery for a barrage shoot on 30" target. Standard of battery work low. "D" "A" Coys winners	
"	4/6		Began relief of 63rd Bn - in MESNIL sector. B + C Coys to right & left of front. 2/Lt CRUSE joined. Posted to "A" Coy	Order No 31 table
Toutencourt	5/6		Completed relief of 63rd Bn. Hqrs established in bank just south of TOUTENCOURT. Transport & Baggage Sub-Sn near VARENNES	"
"	6/6		Reorganised gun positions so as to get one Coy complete out of the line. Wounded 1.O.R. Lieut. Shaw rejoined from Hospital	Order No 32
			Casualties	

Place	Date	Hour	Summary of Events and Information	Remarks and references to Appendices
FOREVILLE	7/6		3rd Bn M.G.C. Sector reorganised on a two Brigade frontage. M.G. Defence reorganised accordingly with two groups in front, one group in Purple line + one in Reserve	Order no 33
"	8/6		Raid by 17th Division in left Sector. B Coy cooperated with an 8-gun battery which carried on an area shoot + 5 guns of left group firing overhead. Barrage (A) Coy harassed the batting. Raid very successful, over 30 prisoners + 4 m.g. captured	Warning order + very order no 34
"	9/6		Reserve Coy brought back to P 22 b 24. Casualties Wounded 1 OR. 'C' Coy draft of 29 OR joined B. About half were old machine gunners + remainder transferred infantry with 2 months training in m.g. "C" 2/Lt V.G. Back] joined B. "B" Lt. Richards] joined B.	

WAR DIARY
INTELLIGENCE SUMMARY
(Erase heading not required.)

Army Form C. 2118.

Place	Date	Hour	Summary of Events and Information	Remarks and references to Appendices
Acheville	10/6		36th Bn M.G.C. Following Officers joined B Co. 2/Lt. C.H. Hands to "A" Co. 2/Lt. A.F. Allen to "C" "	Orders Nos 35 & 18
"	11/6		All preparations completed for attack on AVELUY Sector by 35th & 18th Divisions. B" furnished 1 6-gun & 1 4-gun battery. Operation cancelled at last minute	
"	12/6		9.3 position in Right sector badly shelled. Guns moved 100 & 200 yds. Casualties Killed 1 O.R. Missing believed killed 1 O.R. Wounded 7 O.R.	
"	13/6		Draft of 20 men joined B" 5 O.R. machine gunners remainder were transferred infantry about half of whom had not been overseas before. B" now up to strength	

Army Form C. 2118.

WAR DIARY
or
INTELLIGENCE SUMMARY.
(Erase heading not required.)

Instructions regarding War Diaries and Intelligence Summaries are contained in F. S. Regs., Part II. and the Staff Manual respectively. Title pages will be prepared in manuscript.

38th Bn M.G.C.

Place	Date	Hour	Summary of Events and Information	Remarks and references to Appendices
Jocourt	13/6		"A" Coy. relieves "B" in Left Sector	Order No. 36
"	14/6		Casualties Wounded (at duty) 1 O.R.	
"	15/6		2/Lt Holloid to Army School of Signalling for course. 2/Lt Farlow joined "B" temporarily as signal officer	
"	16/6			
"	17/6		Casualties Killed 1 O.R. "B" Coy. Two forward guns in left sector moved back to position behind Intermediate line covering left flank	

Army Form C. 2118.

WAR DIARY
or
INTELLIGENCE SUMMARY
(Erase heading not required.)

Instructions regarding War Diaries and Intelligence Summaries are contained in F. S. Regs., Part II. and the Staff Manual respectively. Title pages will be prepared in manuscript.

Place	Date	Hour	Summary of Events and Information	Remarks and references to Appendices
Meaulte	18/6		35th Bn M.G.C. Nothing of interest	
"	19/6		Feint attack on AVELUY WOOD. "B" Coy cooperated with an 8-gun battery firing on target as for raid on following night.	Appendix 6 O.O. No 37
"	20/6 21/6	2.50 am	35th Bn "B" Coy cooperated in raid on enemy lines north of AVELUY WOOD) in conjunction with following units 35th Bn. M.G.C. 12th Can. M.G. Squadron 17th Bn. M.G.C. furnished 5-gun battery. Total 11.6 guns Result of raid 1 m.g. captured. No garrison in position raided. M.G. barrage effectually neutralised hostile m.g. fire. Casualties Wounded 2 O.R. (1 at duty) B Killed #1 O.R. "B"	O.O No 37

Army Form C. 2118.

WAR DIARY
or
INTELLIGENCE SUMMARY.
(Erase heading not required.)

35th Bn. M.G.C.

Place	Date	Hour	Summary of Events and Information	Remarks and references to Appendices
Acheville	22/6		"B" Coy relieved "B" in right sector. These 3 positions for other Coys mind. Dug outs in conjunction with R.E. Casualties Wounded 1 O.R. "B" Coy	
"	23.24/6		Nothing of interest	
"	25/6		8 guns of Reserve Coy replaced in Purple line by order of 1 M.G.B. V. Corps. Positions in Brown line for remaining 8 reconstructed. $441	
"	26/6		Construction of Brown line Positions begun. New positions for 4 of Coy Hqrs in Reserve begun. Casualties Wounded 2 O.R. "C" Coy 3 O.R. "A" Coy while standing to by 9.1.1 shell	

Army Form C. 2118.

"WAR" DIARY
or
INTELLIGENCE SUMMARY.
(Erase heading not required.)

Place	Date	Hour	Summary of Events and Information	Remarks and references to Appendices
Yvrencourt	27/6		35th Bn. M.G.C. 2/Lt. W.A. White reported to Bn. 2/Lt. & Q.M. F. Findlay evacuated to Base sick.	
"	28/6		Lt. Col. A.G. Lyttelton to Paris on leave. Major J.F.T. wce assumed command. Quiet & of interest.	
"	29/6			
"	30/6		8 guns of 'B' Coy co-operated in a minor operation east side of attack. Result objectives gained. 20 prisoners. no	39

J.H. Davies Major
Maj. 38th Bn. R.G.C. M.G.C.
30/6/18

SECRET.

38th. BATTALION MACHINE GUN CORPS.

ORDER No. 31.

1st June 1918.

Copy No. 9

1. The 38th Battn.M.G.C. will relieve the 63rd Battn.M.G.C. in MESNIL SECTOR, in accordance with table on reverse.

2. Trench and Fighting Maps, Defence Schemes, Work in progress, Trench Stores, Positions as on attached tracing (to Companies and Div. "G") will be taken over.
(Defence Schemes for Right Supporting Division in V Corps Reserve will be handed over.)

3. Details will be arranged by Company Commanders concerned.

4. Bn.T.O. will arrange Transport.

5. Command will pass on completion of relief.

6. Relief complete will be wired by Code Word "CEASE".

7. Movement :-
   (a) East of Coy.H.Q. will be by gun teams, at 50 yards distance.
   (b) Between the line mentioned in sub-para (a) and East of the line ACHEUX - VARENNES, by Sections at 200 yards distance.

8. M.G.Coys. Bn.T.O., and 63rd M.G.Bn. to acknowledge.

Issued at 8-0 p.m.

..................Lieut-Colonel.
Commanding 38th Battn.M.G.C.

Copies to/
O.C. "A" Coy.   C.O.   38th Div. "G"
 "   "B" "   2nd i/c.   "   "   "G"
 "   "C" "   Adjt.   115th Inf.Bde.
 "   "D" "   Int.Offr.   114th "   "
Bn.T.O.   R.S.M.   115th "   "
Q.M.   M.O.   63rd M.G.Bn.
Sigl.Offr.
File
War Diary.

RELIEF TABLE to accompany 39th Battn. M.G.C. ORDER NO.31.

Serial No.	Date 1918.	Unit.	From.	To.	Unit to be relieved.	Relief to be complete by.	H.Q.
1.	4/5 June.	"B" Coy.	TOUTENCOURT.	LINE (Right).	"C" Coy.62nd Bn.M.G.C.	12 midnight.	P.25.b.9.5.
2.	4/5 June.	"D" Coy.	"	LINE (Left).	"D" Coy. " "	"	P.24.c.1.2.
3.	5th June.	2 Sections "A" Coy.	"	Reserve.	2 Sections "B" Coy.	6-0 p.m.	P.36.a.1.9.
4.	5/6 June.	2 Sections "A" Coy.	"	Reserve (P.1.a. & P.5.a.)	2 Sections "D" Coy.	12 midnight.	"
5.	5/6 June.	"C" Coy.	"	LINE (Centre)	"A" Coy.	"	P.24.A.3.3.
6.	5th June.	H.Qrs.	"	P.27.b.3.2. (adv.) O.36.b.4.2. (rear)	H.Q.	7-0 p.m.	

ADMINISTRATIVE ARRANGEMENTS with regard to 38th Battn.M.G.C. ORDER No.31.

1. **LOCATIONS.-** Q.M. Stores, Transport Lines, and Battle Surplus Details will be in O.36.b. near Fork Roads.

2. **BILLETS.-** Quartermaster will take over all Billets, tents and shelters. Q.M. & Bn.T.O. will go over to VARENNES to see lines and billets to-morrow 3rd inst.

3. **BATTLE SURPLUS.-** Personnel will move with their Company Transport.

4. **SUPPLIES.-** Supplies for the 2nd day's consumption will be delivered at Transport lines of new locations. Refilling points will be notified later.

5. **AMMUNITION.-** The supply will be normal, i.e. Mobile Reserve will be maintained full. A Divisional Ammunition Dump will be established, the location of which will be notified later.

6. **BATHS.-** A bath will be established on June 5th, at Billet No.64, FORCEVILLE. It is hoped to complete another shortly in the neighbourhood of CLAIRFAYE. Applications to Bn.H.Q.

7. **GAS CHANGING CENTRE.-** The Gas Changing Centre is at the Bath at here FORCEVILLE. A supply of Service Dress and Underclothing will be kept / for a change for men whose clothing have been affected by Mustard Gas. Priority to men affected will be given for bathing.

8. **SOCKS.-** The usual supply of 2,000 pairs per Brigade for men in the Forward Line is available on application to the Officer i/c Baths. Whale oil, if required, can be supplied on demand.

9. **CANTEENS.-** Divl.Canteens will be established on June 5th, at LEALVILLERS, VARENNES and FORCEVILLE. In addition 2 carts will be disposed according to requirements. Bn.Canteen will be at Transport Lines.

10. **CEMETERIES.-** Cemeteries will be located as follows : Q.25.a.1.7., P.34.a.2.3., P.21.a.1.2., P.25.a.3.2.

11. **PERSONNEL RAILHEAD.-** Personnel Railhead will be at RAINCHEVAL. All ranks arriving or departing will report to the Divl.Railhead Officer there.

12. **WATER TROUGHS** are at : FORCEVILLE,P.21.d.3.1. - VARENNES,O.36.d. - CLAIRFAYE,O.23.d.9.2.
    Water Cart points at : FORCEVILLE,P.21.c.9.6. - VARENNES,P.31.a.8.8.

13. **R.E.MATERIAL.-** Dump is at O.30.b.8.4.

14. **CLEAN CLOTHING.-** The Divisional Clothing Exchange will remain at Billet 34, TOUTENCOURT, where the "Foden" will also be located.

15. **SALVAGE.-** Main Dump will be LEALVILLERS, Billet No.47. Subsidiary Dump at VARENNES, Billet No.10.

16. **SOLDER.-** The Kiln is at N.12.d.1.8. All tins collected will be sent to one of the two Salvage Dumps at LEALVILLERS or VARENNES, where the Salvage Officer will arrange Transport to the Kiln.

2nd.June 1918.

.... Lieut-Colonel.
Commanding 38th Battn.M.G.C.

Copies to all recipients of Order No.31.

12. of MTRO "C.N." 14th Feb. of passed thro' STEENKERQUE INTERMEDIATE.

1. "SCAVENGER". – C. stokes, Passed thro' Lundi, six passing engines between York & ...? speed ... 35.0 in C. & LTD.

2. BILLITE. – Passed thro' Lillie, took over day all Lille repairmachshops. Switch and rail 100 S.R. "C." Lille to cars of STEENRAY to 300 times and slight
   ...

3. SANTARA BILLERY – Personnel with some more whirl Combat Preparatory.

4. SIDERIES – T. supplied at Lille speed ... new locomotors, petrolled stores with ... Northern ...
   ... locations of Lille speed of man locomotory.

5. STATURIAN – The supply of Lille an portery. L.C. Morrill Present with be ... regulatored by Lille dump Petroleum Temperature. With something the ... positioned by Lille mobil takes.

6. BRAND – A man with be substituted on some Sou. Billie 10.6°A
   TONGUE Shell in the Aurther superior efficient always in the nor ...borry...
   Looped to STATURIA, Application to L.M.C.

7. ONE STEERING CLOSED. – The man Operated control is at the mark of 1905.
   TONGUE A supply of powder passed are in...decoration by hassay one to look be Littlebettamentoned. And some may whose atackhary here been expedited to a chaser for ...
   Surfaced has said to Lille repeater now of airposito.

8. DUES. – The matter suppose of 2,000 depts per singular for non in the Rossary line unfold wis antighthera on unsquirtment of the effects cuff wise. Sum.
   Jineks or Postitu Can use suppose on domary.

9. SNARRAS. – LML canneurs with be eshbuitrabe on Sum Sub So ERALTINCS. In ...
   STATURAS see PORELTTICS in etchinger a copy over of ElMLSTOR and SNARRAS Tongyrytoy to reportedwere. Capscleion with be of primrosofi rebels.

10. CHANNELS. – Genereques will be poisson as torogot: C.25S,6,7,T,A." "L,T.R.9,P,T,S,J." B.32S,6,7." ...

11. SEROUX TRAILOVENT. – Personnel mobiler with be pastory temporary to SERESHE. Lile dany desseting or separary will pepdyr to the Distributory office ...

12. ...RA WHOSES ON of SSELLEMN, F.21, p.T,S,7,G,T. – AUREDUGS, C, 25,9,7." ...
   Hour east poled of: PUCKDUHOM, F.21,9,0.6.0." – AUREDURS, T,9,0,0,7."
   CAVERLRY, C,0,0,0,0."

13. P.TATMIN – Dump it at C,20,9,0."

14. GRAND ELONTHIO. – The historrical sitesail besotved with some of Bulle
    BELLE TO REPEATE BURNOURS, where the "Popor Lills site to locator."

15. AVATAR – rear Dump with be LISTELTO, BRILE 10.76."
    Supplies will be AUREDUGS, as Dump Apenyaars.

16. LEDUS – his M.L.D.C.L.R.T.S. All type perlies will be cosnd thar 10 of the obers SREDER or AUREDUS, where the serve stages will positing ebser.

...gont-calves
Gonvaletts took Bullet, C.G. ......
....

.... date Iril.

Copes to all recipitent ths of ORSS to.21.

8th BATTALION MACHINE GUN CORPS.

ORDER NO. 32.

6th June, 1917.   Copy No. 10

1. The following alterations in gun positions will take place to-night, June 6th.

   (a) O.C., Reserve Group ("A" Coy.) will withdraw guns at R.1.a. and R.5. into Reserve.

   (b) O.C., Right Group ("B" Coy.) will send two guns from R.2. to take over two of the positions at R.6.R.1.a.

   (c) O.C., Left Group ("D" Coy.) will send two guns from R.6. to take over two of the positions at R.5.

2. In event of hostile attack, the Reserve Group will man the unoccupied positions at R.1.a, R.2, R.5.a, and R.6, sending two guns to each.

3. Move will be complete by dawn June 7th. Details will be arranged by Group Commanders concerned.

4. ACKNOWLEDGE.

                                        .... Lieut-Colonel,
                                        Commanding, 8th Bgtn. M.G.C.

Copies to/
   O.C., "A" Coy.
    "   "B" Coy.
    "   "C" Coy.
    "   "D" Coy.
   118th Brigade.
   114th   "
   115th   "
   34th Div. "G"
   File.
   War Diary.

S E C R E T.   COPY.

38th BATTALION MACHINE GUN CORPS.

ORDER NO. 33.

6th June, 1918.   Copy No. 10.

1. THE MESNIL SECTOR will in future be held by two Brigades in the Line, and one in Reserve.

2. The M.G. Defence will accordingly be reorganised on a frontage of two Groups in line, 1 Group in the PURPLE LINE, and one in Reserve.

3. The following exchanges of gun positions will be completed by 3-0 a.m., June 8th :-

Guns.	From.	Exchange with.	At.
2 Guns, "D" Coy.	R.5.a.	2 Guns, "C" Coy.	I.7.
2 Guns, "D" Coy.	R.6.	2 Guns, "C" Coy.	I.8.
4 Guns, "B" Coy.	R.3.	4 Guns, "C" Coy.	(I.5. & (I.6.
2 Guns, "B" Coy.	R.1.a.	2 Guns, "C" Coy.	I.4.
2 Guns, "B" Coy.	R.1.	2 Guns, "C" Coy.	F.1.

4. Trench and fighting maps, defence schemes, work in progress, trench stores, will be taken over.

5. Details will be arranged by Company Commanders concerned.

6. ACKNOWLEDGE.

                                       (Sgd.) A.G. LYTTELTON,
                                                 ....Lieut-Colonel.

Issued at 11-15 p.m.   Commanding, 38th Battn. M.G.C.

Copies to/
     O.C., "A" Coy.   38th Div. "G".
     "   "B" Coy.   File.
     "   "C" Coy.   War Diary.
     "   "D" Coy.   Q.M.
     113th Brigade.
     114th   "
     115th   "

SECRET.

38th BATTALION MACHINE GUN CORPS.

ORDER No. 34.

7th June 1918.   Copy No ..6...

1. Reference Warning Order dated 6th June, re co-operation in 17th Divisional Raid.

2. This Order stands with the following amendments.

   Para.1. Zero hour will probably be 3-0 a.m. and not 9-40 p.m.

   Para.3. Cancel times and rates of fire and substitute :-

   Zero to Zero plus 30...................125 r.p.m.
   Zero plus 30 to Zero plus 50.......... 60 r.p.m.
   Zero plus 50 to Zero plus 65..........125 r.p.m.
   Zero plus 65 to Zero plus 70.......... 60 r.p.m.
   Zero plus 70 to Zero plus 90..........125 r.p.m.

3. **Synchronisation of watches.**
   A synchronised watch will be sent to O.C., "A" Coy's H.Q.

4. Guns specially moved for this operation may be withdrawn at Zero plus 90.

                                           .... Lieut-Colonel.
Issued at 12-30 p.m.   Commanding 38th Battn.M.G.C.

Copies to/
   Os.C. "A" & "D" Coys. (to acknowledge).
     "   "B" & "C"   " } for information.
     38th Div, "G".   }
   file - War Diary.

SECRET.

38th BATTALION MACHINE GUN CORPS.

WARNING ORDER.

Map Reference. 57.D. S.E. 1/20,000.

1. The 17th Division are carrying out a Raid by two Battalions on the night 8th/9th June, in Q.10.b., Q.11.a. & c. at about 9-40 p.m. Exact time will be notified later.

2. The 38th Division is co-operating by M.G., L.G., and rifle fire, and T.M. and rifle grenade activity along the whole of the 38th Divisional front.

3. The 38th Battn.M.G.C. will co-operate as follows :-

O.C., "A" Coy will place one 8 gun battery in position in or about RIDGE SUPPORT (Q.22.) and will fire on the area enclosed in the following co-ordinates : Q.17.b.0.0. - Q.17.b.00.45 - Q.18.a.0.0. - Q.18.a.00.45, at the following times and rates of fire :-

        Zero to Zero plus 30................100 r.p.m.
        Zero plus 30 to Zero plus 60....... 60 r.p.m.
        Zero plus 60 to Zero plus 75.......100 r.p.m.
        Zero plus 75 to Zero plus 90....... 60 r.p.m.
        Zero plus 90 to Zero plus 100......100 r.p.m.

4. O.C., "D" Coy will also, during this operation, co-operate by firing CRASHES in Q.18.c. with all available guns from their existing positions.

5. O.C., "A" Coy will arange to move the 8 gun battery into position night of 7th/8th.

.... Lieut-Colonel.
6th June 1918.   Commanding 38th Battn.M.G.C.

Copies to/
    Os.C., "A" & "D" Coys.
         " "C" & "B" "   (for information).
    38th Div. "G".
    File
    War Diary.

SECRET.

38th. BATTALION MACHINE GUN CORPS.

ORDER NO. 35.

8th June, 1918.   Copy No. 7

1. On the night of the 11th/12th instant, the 105th Brigade of 35th Division will capture and hold the line W.15.d.8.2. to W.15.c.8.4. at the same time raiding the trenches and sunken road South of the Cross Roads at W.15.b.98.25. to W.15.d.98.25 ; M.Gs. near the Nissen Huts in W.15.b.1.7 ; M.Gs. and trenches about W.15.b.8.7.

2. The 38th Battn.M.G.Corps will co-operate with 12 guns, eight of which will be found by the Reserve Company ("A" Coy.) four by the Right Group ("B" Coy.)

3. The tasks for these guns will be as follows :-

Position.	Found by	Target	Times	Rate of fire.
8 gun Battery O.32.b.6.5.	Reserve Coy.	Barrage a line W.9.b.80.80. to W.10.a.15.70.	Zero to Z.plus 10.	200 r.p.m.
			Z.plus 10 to Z.plus 30.	100 r.p.m.
4 Gun Battery O.33.b.1.4.	R.Group guns at I.1. & I.1.a. to be used.	Barrage a line W.10.a.30.55. to W.10.a.40.60.	Z.plus 30 to Z. plus 90.	75 r.p.m.
			Followed by irregular bursts of one belt each gun until guns are withdrawn.	

4. O.C., Reserve Guns will move his 8 guns into position the night of 10th/11th instant.

5. Synchronisation.
A watch will be sent from each Battery and synchronised with the 35th Battn.M.G.Corps, Left Group Commander, at 6-0 p.m. 11th instant, at his Headquarters V.6.d.9.8.

6. Guns will be withdrawn at dawn to their normal positions.

7. ZERO HOUR will be notified later.

.... Lieut-Colonel.
Commanding, 38th Battn.M.G.C.

Issued at 8-0 p.m.

Copies to/
    O.C., Reserve Group.) to acknowledge.
    " Right Group.)
    " Left Group.)
    " Support Group.) for information.
    38th Div. "Q".
    35th Battn.M.G.C.
    War Diary (2).
    File.
    CMGO.

SECRET.

38th BATTALION MACHINE GUN CORPS.

ORDER NO. 36.

12th June, 1918.   Copy No. 14

1. During night 13th/14th instant, Reserve Group ("A" Coy.) will relieve Left Group ("D" Coy.), relief to be complete by 12 mid-night.

2. Details of relief will be arranged between Company Commanders concerned.

3. Bn.T.O. will arrange Transport.

4. Defence Schemes, trench tracings, trench stores, aeroplane photographs will be handed over and receipts taken. Copy of receipts to reach this Office by 5-0 p.m. 14th instant.

5. Completion of relief to be reported by code word "WHEAT"

6. On relief, "D" Coy. will occupy shelters and lines vacated by "A" Coy. in P.22.d.

.... Lieut-Colonel.
Issued at 12 noon.   Commanding, 38th Battn.M.G.C.

Copies to/
O.C., Reserve Gp. ("A" Coy.)
 "   Left Gp.   ("D" Coy.) } to acknowledge.
Bn.T.O.

O.C., Support Gp. ("C" Coy.)   }
 "   Right Gp.   ("B" Coy.)   }
Q.M.   }
Sigl.Offr.   Res.Brigade (114th.)   }
M.O.   Left Brigade (113th.)   } for information.
38th Div."G".   File.   }
 "   " "Q".   War Diary. — (3)   }

SECRET.
※※※※※※※※※※※

H.G.B./S.970.

ADDENDUM NO.1 to 38th BATTN.M.G.C.ORDER NO.37.

17. If it should be found necessary to postpone the operation, the code word "BLUE" will be used and will mean "The Operation ordered in 38th Bn.M.G.C.Order No.37 is postponed".

18. The 16 Guns of "D" Company, 38th Battn.M.G.C. will on the night 20th/21st remain in action till 3-30 a.m., when in conjunction with the Field Artillery, they will fire two belts rapid per gun on the following targets :-

   The 8 guns at Q.21.d.4.0.

   (A) 4 guns on a line Q.24.a.1.8. to Q.24.a.3.5.
   (B) 4 guns on a line Q.35.d.4.7. to Q.35.b.3.2.

   The 8 guns at Q.21.d.7.3. -

   (A) 4 guns on a line Q.24.c.7.8. to Q.24.a.5.2.
   (B) 4 guns on a line Q.30.c.5.7. to Q.30.a.3.1.

19. The usual harassing fire by Machine Guns, 38th Battn.H.G.C. will be continued up to Zero on night 20th/21st with all available guns.

19th June, 1918.
3-45 p.m.

Lieut-Colonel.
Commanding, 38th Battn.M.G.C.

Copies to/
    O=C.,
    A.B.C. & D. Coys.
    Left & Right Gp.Commdrs., 38th Battn.M.G.C.) to acknowledge.

    38th Div. "G".)
    Left Brigade..) for information.
    ~~Right Brigade.~~)
    Reserve

SECRET.
****

M.G.B./S.962
----

1. Reference 38th Battn.M.G.Corps Order No.37 of 17/3/18, APPENDIX.

   (a) The ZERO HOUR for the Feint attack will be 2-0 a.m. 19th/20th.

   (b) The Corps heavy Artillery will commence a bombardment of the enemy's lines at Zero minus 2 hours until Zero minus 5 minutes. At Zero to Zero plus 50 minutes the Field Artillery will fire a Creeping Barrage.
   The Machine Guns will take their time by the Field Artillery.

   (c) Reference Appendix, para 2 (b), to targets already allotted Right and Left Companies, add the Village of AUTHUILLE.

2. Reference Order No.37, para.13 :-

   (a) The Artillery is to fire a Crash for 5 minutes at Zero plus 3 hours, 50 minutes, on the night 19th/20th.
   Teams should avoid movement in the open during this Crash.

   (b) Amend para.4, Right Group, "D" Battery :-
   This Battery will fire on a line Q.30.c.95.45. to Q.30.b.15.20. and not as stated.

   (c) Para.12. 2nd line : for "1-0 a.m." read "12 mid-night".

3. ACKNOWLEDGE.

                                         J. J. Weir, Major
                                         for Lieut-Colonel.
18th June, 1918.   Commanding, 38th Battn.M.G.C.
   8-0 p.m.

SECRET.   M.G.B/S.946.

AMENDMENT NO. 1. to 38th BATTN.M&G.C.ORDER NO.37.

Para.13 :-

    For "1-0 a.m. 19th/20th"

               read

                      "12 mid-night 19th/20th".

                W. Wright Capt & adjt for
                        Lieut-Colonel.
17th June, 1918.   Commanding, 38th Battn.M.G.C.
  8-0 p.m.

Copies to all recipients of Order No.37.

4. (contd.)

THE CENTRE GROUP will consist of 4 eight gun Batteries and 1 four gun Battery under the Command of Major ADAMSON, 38th Battn. M.G. Corps, with Headquarters at Q.21.d.3.3.

Battery position.	Guns.	Time.	Target.	Rate of fire.	Remarks.
"A" Battery. ø (Q.21.d.65.15.) approx.	Two lots of 8.	Zero plus 1 to Zero plus 40 mins.	'A' on map. a line Q.35.a.83.71. to Q.35.b.17.13.	100 rounds per minute.	38th Battn. Guns.
"I" Battery. ø (Q.21.a.45.70.)	8		'I' on map. a line Q.23.c.80.98. to Q.23.a.78.00.		
"F" Battery. (Q.21.d.30.25.)	4		'F' on map. a line Q.23.a.70.40. to Q.23.d.70.70.		Cavalry Squadron guns.
"J" Battery. (Q.22.c.1.5.)	8		'J' on map. a line Q.24.a.20.30. to Q.24.a.00.90.		

ø AVELUY WOOD Outposts and CRAB TRENCH are specially being cleared to allow these Batteries to fire as shewn.

LEFT GROUP will consist of 4 eight Gun Batteries under the Command of Major TROUP, 35th Battn. M.G.C. with Headquarters at Q.22.c.1.8.

Battery Position.	Guns.	Time.	Target.	Rate of fire.	Remarks.
"E" Battery. (Q.22.b.1.1.)	8	Zero plus 1 to Zero plus 40 mins.	'E' on map. a line Q.30.b.10.25. to Q.30.b.30.85.	100 rounds per minute.	35th Battn. Guns.
"G" Battery. (Q.22.a.1.7.)	8		'G' on map. a line Q.24.c.70.20. to Q.24.c.85.85.		
"H" Battery. (Q.22.b.1.9.)	8		'H' on map. a line Q.24.d.47.12. to Q.24.d.65.75.		
"M" Battery. (Q.22.c.1.8.)	8		'M' on map. a line Q.18.c.05.23. to Q.18.c.40.80.		

P.T.O.

SECRET.

38th. BATTALION MACHINE GUN CORPS.

ORDER NO. 37.

17th June, 1918.   Copy No. 21

Reference Map. 57 D.S.E. 1/20,000.

1. On the night 20th/21st June, the 115th and 113th Infantry Brigades are carrying out a raid employing one Battalion each.

2. The objective will be the enemy's dug-outs, emplacements and trenches on the line Q.35.b.55.50. to Q.23.d.55.00.

3. The following Machine Gun Units will co-operate :-

    38th Battn. M.G. Corps.
    "D" Coy ...... 16 guns.
    "C" Coy ...... 8 guns. (Taken from most convenient positions in PURPLE LINE).

    35th Battn. M.G. Corps.
    64 Guns.

    17th Battn. M.G. Corps.
    16 guns.

    12th Cavalry M.G. Squadron.
    12 Guns.

                                        Total ... 116 guns.

4. The above, with the exception of the 17th Battn. M.G. Corps' guns which will co-operate from their own area, will be formed into three Groups and will have tasks as follows :-

    THE RIGHT GROUP will consist of 4 eight gun Batteries under the Command of Major NAYLOR, 35th Battn. M.G. Corps, with Headquarters at Q.22.c.6.2.

Battery position.	Guns.	Time.	Target.	Rate of fire.	Remarks.
"B" Battery. (Q.28.b.3.3.)	8	Zero plus 1 to Zero plus 40 mins.	"B" on map. A line Q.36.c.60.65. to Q.36.b.00.20.	100 rounds per minute.	All guns from 35th Battn.
"C" Battery. (Q.22.d.3.4.)	8		"C" on map. A line Q.36.b.10.40. to Q.36.b.50.90.		
"D" Battery. (Q.28.b.2.9.)	8		"D" on map. A line 4 guns barrage a line Q.30.c.97.10. to Q.30.d.10.30. 4 guns barrage a line Q.30.b.42.90. to Q.30.d.50.10.		
"N" Battery. (Q.23.c.6.2.) 22	8		"N" on map. A line Q.17.b.75.05. to Q.17.b.25.45.		

4.

14. All movement near the Battery positions must be kept down to a minimum during the hours of daylight.

15. <u>Medical</u>. R.A.P. at Q.28.c.6.2. for stretcher cases. Walking wounded will proceed by CUTHBERT AVENUE thence up the MARTINSART – ENGLEBELMER Road, where they will be directed.

16. ZERO hour will be notified later.

J. F. Jessop W... Major
for ———— Lieut-Colonel.
Commanding, 38th Battn. M.G.C.

<u>Issued at 3-0 p.m.</u>

Copies to :-

O.C., "A" Coy.
  "   "C" Coy.
  "   "D" Coy.
  "   35th Battn. M.G.C. (5 copies)
  "   12th Cavalry Squadron.
  "   17th Battn. M.G.C.
} With Maps.
TO ACKNOWLEDGE.

38th Div. "G".
113th Brigade.
115th Brigade.
C.M.G.C.
2nd i/c.
2nd/Lt. Griffith.
Bn. T.C.
} For information.
(without maps).

File.
War Diary (3).

APPENDIX.

1. On the night 19th/20th, not before 1-0 a.m. the R.A. is to carry out a feint bombardment of AVELUY WOOD.

2. To co-operate with this :-

   (a) 8 Guns of "A" Battery ("D" Coy.) will fire on their target as for the night of 20th/21st from Zero plus 1 minute to Zero plus 40 minutes. 100 rounds per gun per minute. The line of fire for these guns must be staked out on the 19th, so that the guns need not then be brought up before the night of the 19th/20th.

   (b) Harassing Fire by Right and Left Companies, 38th Battn. M.G.C. will not begin till Zero and will be directed on targets East of the ANCRE shown on attached Map.

   (c) O.C., 17th Battn. M.G.C. will co-operate firing on targets as for night of 20th/21st.

3. ZERO hour will be notified later.

J. F. J. W... Major
for ———— Lieut-Colonel.
Commanding, 38th Battn. M.G.C.

17th June, 1918.

4./contd.

17th Battn. M.G. Corps.

Battery position.	Guns.	Time.	Target.	Rate of fire.	Remarks.
"K" Battery.	8	Zero plus 1 to Zero plus 40 mins.	'K' on map. a line Q.23.b.20.60. to Q.17.d.40.20.	100 rounds per minute.	C.O., 17th Battn.M.G.C. will decide as to how near the barrage lines he can fire according to the extent the front line in 17th Divn. area is vacated.
"L" Battery.	8		'L' on map. 4 guns - Q.17.d.15.57. to Q.17.d.25.85. 4 guns - Q.17.d.80.33. to Q.17.d.88.60.		

5. COMMUNICATIONS. Major ADAMSON will act as Senior Group Commander, and all messages will be sent through his Headquarters at Q.21.d.3.3. by Runner. He will establish communications by runner and telephone from P.24.c.1.1. (PURPLE LINE M.G.Coy.H.Q.) to M.G.Battn.H.Q. O.C., "D" Coy. will detail an Officer to report to Right Raiding Battn.H.Q. at Q.34.b.2.7 2nd/Lieut. GRIFFITH will be at Left Raiding Battn.H.Q. at Q.28.a.9.8. These Officers will act as liaison Officers and will report to the respective Battn.H.Qrs. with two runners each at Zero - 3 hours.

6. Synchronisation of watches. The Officer supplied by "D" Coy. (see para.5) will report to Left Brigade H.Q., Q.24.d.3.3. at 12 hours and 6 hours before Zero, and will take the synchronised time to Group Commanders.

7. All Machine Gun fire will commence at Zero plus 1 minute, and the time will be taken from the commencement of the Field Artillery Barrage. All artillery and T.M.Fire will cease at Zero plus 30, and all M.G. fire will cease at Zero plus 40 minutes.

8. Group Commanders are responsible for the checking of all calculations.

9. The near Danger area of Batteries must be picketed if firing over Tracks &c.

10. Each gun will have 16 filled Belt Boxes.

11. At Zero plus 40 Batteries will be withdrawn under Company arrangements.

12. All guns will be brought in on the night 19th/20th. Limbers must be clear of ENGLEBELMER by 1-0 a.m.
    O.C., "A" Coy. 38th Battn.M.G.C. will supply 9 Guides who will meet 2nd/Lieut GRIFFITH at the corner of the Wood at P.23.d.85.85. at 8-45 p.m 19th instant. This point will be the rendezvous for the 35th Battn. M.G.Coys' guns, and the 12th Cavalry Squadron. They will then be guided to the Prisoners Cage, Q.21.c.9.4., by Batteries at suitable intervals, from which point Battery Commanders will be responsible for conducting their Batteries to their positions.

13. Owing to the Dummy Raid which is to take place on the night 19th/20th as per Appendix, Group Commanders should, after the guns are dumped in their Battery positions, withdraw their men to the PURPLE LINE in Q.20.a. & c. by 1-0 a.m. 19th/20th. They must return at dawn.

P.T.O.

SECRET.
✱✱✱✱✱✱✱✱✱✱✱✱

58th BATTALION MACHINE GUN CORPS.

ORDER NO.38.

June 19th, 1918.   Copy No. 18

1. "D" Company (Reserve Coy.) will relieve "B" Company (Right Coy.) during the night 21st/22nd instant, relief to be complete by 12 mid-night.

2. All details will be arranged by Company Commanders concerned.

3. Bn.T.O. will arrange Transport.

4. Trench Tracings, trench stores, defence Schemes, aero-photos, work in hand, will be handed over and receipts taken. Copy of receipts to reach this Office by 12 noon, 22nd instant.

5. "B" Company will take over all dug-outs and bivvy shelters at present occupied by "D" Company.

6. Relief complete will be wired to Bn.H.Q. by Code Word "NERVE".

7. O.C., "D" Coy. will advise H.Q., 114th Inf.Brigade of completion of relief.

                                        W. Wright Capt & Adjt
                                             58th Battn.M.G.C.

Issued at 12-30 p.m.
Copies to/
O.C., Reserve Coy. ("D")
 "   Right Coy.   ("B") } to ACKNOWLEDGE.
Bn.T.O.

O.C., Support Coy. ("C")   )
 "   Left Coy.   ("A")   )
Q.M.   58th Div."G".)
Int.Offr.   "   " "Q".)
Sigl.Offr.   Right Bde. (114th).) for information.
M.O.   Reserve Bde.(115th).)
O.C. Rear H.Q. File. War Diary.)

War Diary

SECRET.

58th BATTALION MACHINE GUN CORPS.

ORDER NO. 39.

27th June, 1918.   Copy No. 11

Map reference, Sheet 57D., S.E.

1. The 12th Division proposes to carry out a minor operation on the 30th June, 1918, (Zero hour will probably be about dusk) with a view to capturing and consolidating the ridge W.15.a.8.4. - W.15.d.8.2.

2. The 58th Battn. M.G. Corps will co-operate with 8 guns. These guns will be found by "B" Company, the 8 guns being taken from the PURPLE LINE.

Battery position.	Target.	Time.	Rate of fire.
8 guns at Q.32.b.0.3.	Barrage a line W.10.a.30.60. to W.4.c.75.15.	Zero to Zero plus 20.	100 R.P.M.
		Zero plus 20 to Zero plus 70.	50 R.P.M.

O.C., "B" Coy. will make the necessary arrangements, and will be responsible for checking all calculations.

3. Guns will be moved to their position on the night 29th/30th.

4. ZERO HOUR will be taken from the opening of the Artillery Barrage.

5. Upon completion of the shoot, guns will be withdrawn to their Battle positions.

6. ZERO HOUR will be notified later.

J.J.J. Weiss, Major
for Lieut-Colonel.
Commanding, 58th Battn. M.G.C.

Issued at 4-0 p.m.

Copies to/
    O.C., "B" Coy. - to acknowledge.

    38th Div. "G".   )
    C.M.G.O.   )
    12th Battn. M.G.C.   ) for information.
    Os.C.,   )
      "A", "C", & "D" Coys.)

    File.
    War Diary (3).

SECRET.

H.Q.S./S.41.

War Diary

O.C., "B" Coy.
"   "C" Coy.

1. To-night, 25th/26th instant, the following changes will take place ; details to be arranged by Company Commanders concerned :-

   (a) "C" Coy. will put two extra guns in R.5.a., and R.1.a., vacating R.1. and R.6.

   (b) "B" Coy. will put 2 guns in R.1 ; 2 in Reserve position alongside R.1 ; and 4 in R.6.

2. Alteration will be complete by 12 mid-night.

3. Completion will be wired by Code Word "JOCELYN".

4. "B" and "C" Coys. to acknowledge.

Lieut-Colonel.
Commanding, 38th Battn.M.G.C.

25th June, 1918.
12-30 P.M.

Copies to/
    38th Divn. "G")
    113th Brigade.)
    114th Brigade.)
    115th Brigade.) for information.
    O.C., "A" Coy.)
    "   "D" Coy.)

SECRET.

H.Q.S./S.971.

AMENDMENT TO 38th BATTN. M.G.C. ORDER NO. 38.

Para. 1 :-

For "night 21st/22nd"

read

"night 22nd/23rd".

19th June, 1918.
6-0 p.m.

_____
Capt. & Adjt.
38th Battn. M.G.C.

Copy to all recipients of Order No. 38.
O.s.C., "B" & "D" Coys. to acknowledge.

Vol 5

War Diary
of
38th Battn. M.G. Corps.
from 1st July '18 to 31st July '18.

(Vol. 5)

Confidential

WAR DIARY

INTELLIGENCE SUMMARY

36th Bn M.G.C.

Place	Date	Hour	Summary of Events and Information	Remarks and references to Appendices
Foncille	1/7/18		nil	order no 40
	2/7/18		"B" Coy relieved "C" in the Purple Line. Casualties 2 O.R wounded	
	3/7		Casualties 3. O.R. wounded	
	6/7		Commanding returned from leave & took over command of Bn. from Major Weiss. Casualties 1 O.R. wounded	
	9/7		"C" Coy relieved "A" in the Left Sector. Began construction of Dummy Mine Areas, in two from 1 & 5 Mon Pattern hill 151 C⁰ R.E. Total of 80 men engaged on the above both men & working on mine gallery under 145 Tunnelling Coy R.E.	order no 41

Army Form C. 2118.

WAR DIARY
or
INTELLIGENCE SUMMARY.
(Erase heading not required.)

Instructions regarding War Diaries and Intelligence Summaries are contained in F. S. Regs., Part II. and the Staff Manual respectively. Title pages will be prepared in manuscript.

Place	Date	Hour	Summary of Events and Information	Remarks and references to Appendices
Foncville	10/4		36th B: M.G.C.	
			Nil.	
	11/4		Co/operated in raid by 2/R.W.F. in Left section 9 & gun employed.	Order 42
			Raid a great success 20 prisoners 1 M.g. no casualties to	
			36th B: 2/5 B: who were co-operating lost an officer & 2	
			men killed by chance shell.	
	14/4		Draft of 10 men inspected by C.O. All o/b machine gunners	
			Casualties Wounded 2.O.R. "A" C".	
			"B" C" furnished 6 gun battery to co/operate in raid by	Order 43
			6" Div". in Left Section. Raid a great success, 20 prisoners	
			2 m.g. + hardly any casualties.	
			C.O. + Officer of 21st B: up to arrange relief.	
	15/.		Nil.	

Army Form C. 2118.

WAR DIARY
or
INTELLIGENCE SUMMARY.

(Erase heading not required.)

Place	Date	Hour	Summary of Events and Information	Remarks and references to Appendices
Forceville			35th Bn M.G.C.	
	15/7		Casualties. Killed 1 O.R. (accidentally) "D" Coy	
			Lieut Pugh joined Bn. Posted to "B" x "C" Coy	
	16/7		Relief by 21st cancelled. 1 O.R. joined Bn.	
	17/7		Casualties wounded O.R. 2 "B"+"D"	
	18/7		Casualties wounded 1 (on duty) "C" Coy	
	19/20		Bn. relieved in Right subsection by 14th Bn.	
			" " " Left " " 63rd Bn.	
			This gave to reorganisation of IV Corps with 2 Divisions in line & two in support. Bn withdrawn to camp near HERISSART as Right supporting Bn. Bn. bivouacked	
			Cooperated in raid on left sector by 63rd Bn. B. furnished guns & two t-guns featherista under Major Jackson A Coy to 45.	

A.3093. Wt. W728 9/M1293. 750,000. 1/17. D. D & L. Ltd. Forms/C2118/14.

WAR DIARY or INTELLIGENCE SUMMARY

Army Form C. 2118.

Place	Date	Hour	Summary of Events and Information	Remarks and references to Appendices
Camp nr Herissart	20/7		36th Bn M.G.C. B⁹ less "A" Coy in camp T.S.a. "A" Coy in bivouacs near Brown Line under orders of 113 B⁹⁴	
	21/7		Capt Norris posted to B⁹ for 2 months instruction. Attached to "C" Coy	
	22/7 to		Began by training. 5 hours daily spent in Sec Lewis gun, musketry, Range practices with M.G. Section schemes, Standards of Drill much improved by work done by Staffs at Rear H.Q's during past B⁹ was in line. All Companies busy night & day at everything the + no advanced tactical training possible in consequence. Large numbers of men have made M.G. shooting moderate 6-8 weight training + all shooting in the line being confined to good habits & observation of fire. Fusions of fire from 75's Lt.M.G. have been neglected with a rifle. Just a short course on I.M. 110 R.I.R. wind untrained. 5° + range	
	29/7			

WAR DIARY
INTELLIGENCE SUMMARY

Place	Date	Hour	Summary of Events and Information	Remarks and references to Appendices
Camp	22/7 – 28/7		38th B= M.G.C. Wks musketry (bad shots) & short courses in smoke funking etc. Barn & Strond in afternoon.	
	29/7		2/Lt WILLIAMS 15/ Welch attached to B= for family July. Posted to B= Coy. Coy. completed plans to take part of 10 men from B= 7 coy. completed plans to take part in Brig. 3rd Army manoeuvres to which during opposite have been allowed to continue their lines— harassing fire etc.	
			"C" Coy relieved "A" Coy in Brown line. Owing to withdrawal of left supporting division 38th Division responsible for support of whole Corps front.	D) N to L7
	31/7		B= sports. Championship won by "A" Coy with 45 points. B= Coy (coal) 2nd with 33½ points.	

A.G. Lyttelton Lt Col
38th B= M.G.C.

SECRET.
****

38th BATTALION MACHINE GUN CORPS.

ORDER NO. 40.

1st July, 1918.   Copy No. 14

1. "B" Company (Reserve) will relieve "C" Company (Support) during the night 2nd/3rd inst., relief to be complete by 12 mid-night.

2. All details will be arranged by Company Commanders concerned.

3. Bn.T.O. will arrange Transport.

4. Trench Tracings, trench stores, Defence Schemes, aero-photos, work in hand, will be handed over and receipts taken. Copy of receipts to reach this Office by 12 noon, 3rd instant.

5. "C" Company will take over all dug-outs and bivvy shelters at present occupied by "B" Company.

6. 'Relief complete' will be wired to Bn.H.Q. by Code word "DIBACH".

7. O.C., "B" Company will advise H.Q., Support Brigade (114th) of completion of relief.

W. Wright. Capt. & Adjt.
38th Battn.M.G.C.

Issued at 3-30 p.m.

Copies to/
    O.C., Reserve Coy. ("B")
     "   Support Coy. ("C")   } to ACKNOWLEDGE.
    Bn.T.O.   )

    O.C., Right Coy. ("D")
     "   Left Coy. ("A")
    Int.Officer.
    Sigl.Offr.   38th Divn. "G".)
    M.O.   113th Brigade.   )
    R.Q.M.S.   114th Brigade.   ) for information.
    O.C., Rear H.Q.   )
    File. War Diary.   )

THE CENTRE GROUP will consist of 2 eight gun Batteries under the Command of Captain WILKINSON, 38th Battn.M.G.C., with Headquarters at Q.21.d.2.4.

Battery Position.	Guns.	Time.	Target.	Rate of fire.	Remarks.
"L" Battery. (Q.22.c.5.2.)	8	Zero plus 3 to Zero plus 70	'L' on map. a line Q.17.b.65.05. to Q.17.b.15.45.	100 R.P.M. for first 10 mins. 75 R.P.M. for remainder.	All guns from 38th Battn. M.G.C. 'L' supplied by "A" Coy
"G" Battery. (Q.21.a.45.70.)	8	Zero plus 3 to Zero plus 4.	'G.1.' on map. a line Q.23.a.80.30. to Q.23.a.80.95.	250 R.P.M.	'G' supplied by "E" Coy.
		Zero plus 6 to Zero plus 70	'G.2.' on map. a line Q.17.d.75.05. to Q.17.d.70.70.	75 R.P.M.	

* CRAB TRENCH is being cleared of troops from Q.23.a.1.0. to Q.17.c.5.0.

THE LEFT GROUP will consist of 4 eight gun batteries under the Command of a Company Commander of Corps Reserve M.G.Battn. with Headquarters at Q.22.c.1.8. (same as Right Group Commander).

Battery position.	guns.	Time.	Target.	Rate of fire.	Remarks
"A" Battery. (Q.22.b.1.1.)	8.	Zero plus 3 to Zero plus 70.	'A' on map. a line Q.30.c.75.60. to Q.30.b.05.15.	100 R.P.M. for first 10 mins.	All guns from Corps Reserve M.G.Batt
"F" Battery. (Q.22.b.0.4.)	8		'F' on map. a line Q.24.b.35.25. to Q.24.b.35.90.	75 R.P.M. remainder.	
"J" Battery. (Q.22.c.1.8.)	8		'J' on map. a line Q.18.c.85.40. to Q.18.a.60.00.		
"E" Battery. (Q.22.a.1.7.)	8		'E' on map. a line Q.24.c.85.55. to Q.24.a.90.20.		

63rd (RN) Battn.M.G.C.

Position.	Guns.	Time.	Target.	Remarks.
"E" Battery.*	8	Zero plus 3 to Zero plus 70.	'I' on map. a line Q.17.d.20.10. to Q.17.d.40.70.	O.C., 63rd Battn.M.G. will in the case of 'I' target decide as to how near the barrage line he can fire according to the position of the Battery in 63rd Divn. area.
"H" Battery.*	8		'H' on map. a line Q.23.b.95.75. to Q.18.c.15.40.	

* These Batteries are putting down a flank barrage 200 yards North of the furthermost Raiders.

Communications. Capt. WILKINSON will act as Senior GROUP COMMANDER, and all messages will be sent through his Headquarters at Q.21.d.2.4. by Runner, thence by wire.

Capt. Wilkinson will detail an Officer as liaison Officer to report to Raid Battn.Headquarters at Q.22.d.5.0. (Left Forward Inf.Battn.H.Q.) at Zero minus 2 hours.

2.

6. Synchronization of watches. The liaison Officer (see para.5) will report to 115th Brigade H.Q. P.24.d.3.5. at 10-0 a.m. and at 5-0 p.m. on the 11th, and will take synchronised time to Group Commanders.

7. All Machine Gun fire will commence at Zero plus 3 minutes, and the time will be taken from the commencement of the Field Artillery Barrage. Artillery fire ceases at Zero plus 60, Machine Gun fire at Zero plus 70.

8. Group Commanders are responsible for the checking of all calculations.

9. The near danger area of Batteries must be picketed if firing over trenche tracks, etc.

10. Each gun will have 24 filled belts.

11. At Zero plus 70, Batteries will be withdrawn under Company arrangements.

12. All guns will be brought in on the night 10th/11th.
O.C., "A" Company, 38th Battn.M.G.C. will supply 3 Guides to be at the corner of the wood P.23.d.85.95. at 9-0 p.m. 10th instant. This point will be the rendezvous for the Corps Reserve M.G.Battn. who will be guided to the Prisoners Cage Q.21.c.9.4. by batteries, from which point Battery Commanders will be responsible for conducting their batteries to their positions. O.C., "C" Company, 38th Battn.M.G.C. will send an Officer to the rendezvous to see that guides turn up, and that suitable intervals are maintained.

13. Medical. R.A.P..C.29.c.6.2. for Stretcher cases. Walking wounded will proceed by CUTHBERT AVENUE, thence up the MARTINSART - ENGLEBELMER Road, where they will be directed.

14. ZERO Hour will be notified later.

Issued at 11-55 p.m.

Lieut-Colonel.
Commanding, 38th Battn.M.G.C.

Copies to/
O.C., "A" Coy.
 "   "B" Coy. (2 copies)   } With maps.
 "   "C" Coy.   } to ACKNOWLEDGE.
 "   63rd Battn.M.G.C.   }
 "   31st Battn.M.G.C. (7 copies - 3 with maps.)

O.C., "D" Coy.   }
     115th Brigade.   } for information.
     C.M.G.O.   } (without maps).
     Bn.I.O.   }
     38th Divn. "G".   }
           "   "Q".

File.
War Diary (3).

SECRET.
****

38th BATTALION MACHINE GUN CORPS.

ORDER NO. 41.

8th July, 1918.   Copy No 11

1. "C" Company (Reserve) will relieve "A" Company (Left) during the night 9th/10th instant, relief to be complete by 12 mid-night.

2. All details will be arranged by Company Commanders concerned.

3. Bn.T.O. will arrange Transport.

4. Trench tracings, trench stores, Defence Schemes, aero-photos, work in hand, will be handed over, and receipts taken. Copy of receipts to reach this Office by 12 noon, 10th instant.

5. "A" Company will take over all dug-outs and bivvy shelters at present occupied by "C" Company.

6. 'Relief complete' will be wired to Bn.H.Q. by Code Word "BELWARD".

7. O.C., "C" Company will advise H.Q., Front Brigade (115th) of completion of relief.

                                             W. Wright Capt. & Adjt.
                                                        38th Battn. M.G.C.

Issued at 2-0 p.m.

Copies to/
    O.C., Left Coy. ("A")
     "   Reserve Coy. ("C") } to ACKNOWLEDGE.
    Bn.T.O.

    O.C., Right Coy. (B)
     "   Support Coy. (E)
    Sigl.Offr.
    M.O.   38th Divn. "G".)
    O.C., Rear H.Q.   115th Brigade.) for information.
    R.Q.M.S.   113th Brigade.)
    File.
    War Diary (3)

SECRET.

38th. BATTALION MACHINE GUN CORPS.

ORDER NO. 42.

8th July, 1918.   Copy No. 21

Reference Map, 57 D., S.E. 1/20,000.

1. On the night 11th/12th inst. the 2nd R.W.F. (115th Inf. Brigade) is carrying out a Raid (Zero hour probably 11 p.m.).

2. The objective will be the Village of HAMEL. The limits of the Raid will be approximately :-

   To the East. - The Railway Line running through Q.23.b. and d.

   To the North. - A line drawn through Q.24.a.0.5. and Q.23.b.0.8.

   The Raiding Battalion is forming up outside HAMEL OUTPOSTS and advancing in a North Easterly direction.

3. The following Machine Gun Units will co-operate :-

   38th Battn. M.G.Corps.

   "A" Company...8 guns (from the BROWN LINE).
   "B" Company...8 guns (from the PURPLE LINE).

   From Corps Reserve.

       64 Guns.

   63rd (RN) Battn.M.G.Corps.

       16 guns.

   Total 96 guns.

4. The above, with the exception of the 63rd (RN) Battn.M.G.C. guns, which will co-operate from their own area, will be formed into THREE GROUPS, and will have tasks as follows :-

   THE RIGHT GROUP will consist of 4 eight gun Batteries, under the Command of a Company Commander of Corps Reserve M.G. Battn. with Headquarters at Q.22.c.1.8.

Battery position.	Guns.	Time.	Target.	Rate of fire.	Remarks.
"B" Battery. (Q.28.b.2.3.)	8	Zero plus 3 to Zero plus 70.	'B' on map. A line Q.30.b.30.15. to Q.30.b.30.80.	100 R.P.M. for first 10 mins. 75 R.P.M. remainder.	All guns Corps Re M.G.Batt
"K" Battery. (Q.28.b.3.9.)	8		'K' on map. a line Q.18.c.30.65. to Q.17.b.80.10.		
"D" Battery. (Q.22.d.4.4.)	8		'D' on map. a line Q.24.d.50.40. to Q.24.b.50.00.		
"C" Battery. (Q.22.c.1.5.)	8		'C' on map. a line Q.30.b.00.80. to Q.24.d.05.45.		

G.S.G.S. 2023.

NOTE.—(1). These traces are intended to facilitate the communication of information as to the position of targets, which have be
(2). The squares on this trace are 500 yards in length on the 1/10,000 scale, 1,000 yards in length on the 1/20,000 sc
can be used for the 1/10,000, 1/20,000, or 1/40,000 scale.
(3). The squares on the trace are fitted to the squares of the map showing the targets, which are then drawn
letters and numbers must also be added to enable the recipient to place the trace in the correct position on his
may also be traced, but this is not essential. The name and scale of the map to which the trace refers must b

38th Batt M.G.C
Legend: Red = 38th Divnl Targets
Purple = 63rd " "
Black = Suppting " "
Each lettered area represents the
E.B.Z. of One 8 gun battery

Taken from Sheet 57½R. 28
Scale 1:20,000
Date. 9.7.18.

SECRET.

M.G.B./S.255.

Reference 38th Battn.M.G.C.Order No.42, dated 8th July, 1918.

para.14. — ZERO HOUR will be 11 p.m.

Please acknowledge by wire.

11/7/18.

Lieut-Colonel.
Commanding, 38th Battn.M.G.C.

Copy to all recipients if Order No.42.

SECRET.

38th. BATTALION MACHINE GUN CORPS.

ORDER NO. 43.

11th July, 1918.   Copy No. 7

Map reference, 57 D., S.E.

1. On the 12th/13th instant the 33rd Division is carrying out a raid with objectives as follows :-

    (a) <u>First Objective</u> - Enemy's Trench "LUSTRE SUPPORT", from Q.17.d.20.77. to Q.17.central.

    (b) <u>Second Objective</u> - Clearing up "LOUNGE TRENCH" from Q.17.d.42.77. to Q.17.b.12.18.

    The raiding party will form up on Track Q.17.c.75.55. to Q.17.a.3.0.

2. The 38th Battn. M.G. Corps will co-operate with two four-gun Batteries found by "B" Company, with the following tasks :-

Battery position.	Guns.	Time.	Target.	Rate of Fire.	Remarks.
Q.21.d.20.30.	4	Zero to 'Cease fire' signal.	2 guns a line - Q.23.b.95.90. to Q.17.d.85.15.	Zero to Zero plus 5, 100 R.P.M.	
			2 guns a line - Q.23.b.70.75. to Q.23.b.60.95.	Z.plus 5 to Z.plus 15, 75 R.P.M. Z.plus 15 onwards, 100 R.P.M.	
Q.21.d.30.20.	4	Ditto.	2 guns a line - Q.17.d.35.00. to Q.17.d.50.20.	Ditto.	
			2 guns a line - Q.23.b.40.80. to Q.17.d.25.00.		

3. O.C., "B" Company will be held responsible for the checking of all calculations.

4. 20 filled belts will be with each gun.

5. Synchronised time will be sent to "B" Coy's Headquarters at 6-30 p.m. 12th instant.

6. On completion of the shoot guns will be withdrawn to battle positions.

7. 'Cease fire' signal and ZERO HOUR will be notified later.

                                                                    Lieut-Colonel,
                                                        Commanding, 38th Battn.M.G.C.

Issued at 9-0 p.m.

Copy to/
    O.C., "B" Coy, - to acknowledge.
    Os.C., A.C. & D. Coys.   33rd (RN) M.G.C.)
    Bn.T.O.   38th Divn. "G".) for information.
    File.   )
    War Diary (2)

S E C R E T.
****

H.G.B./S.354.

AMENDMENT NO.1, to RELIEF TABLE issued with
58th BATTN.M.G.C.ORDER NO.44, dated 14th July, 1918.

Serial Nos. 1 & 2, Column 6. — For "D" Coy. 21st Battn. M.G.C."
                                   read
                                         "C" Coy. 21st Battn.M.G.C."

Serial No.3, Column 6. — For "C" Coy. 21st Battn.M.G.C."
                                   read
                                        "D" Coy. 21st Battn.M.G.C."

                                                  W. Wright Capt. & Adjt.
                                                        58th Battn.M.G.C.

15th July, 1918.

Copy to all recipients of Order No.44.

SECRET.
****

38th. BATTALION MACHINE GUN CORPS.

ORDER NO. 44.

14th July, 1918.

Copy No. 13

Reference Map, Sheet 57.D.

1. 38th Battn.M.G.C. will be relieved by 21st Battn.M.G.C. in the MESNIL Sector, V Corps front in accordance with attached Table.

2. Details of work in hand, aeroplane photographs, Defence Schemes, trench stores will be handed over. (Gas Rattles are **not** trench stores).

3. Details of relief will be arranged directly by Company Commanders concerned.

4. Company Commanders will report relief complete by Code Word "JESSOP".

5. Command will pass to O.C., 21st Battn.M.G.C. on completion of relief ; at which time Bn.H.Q. will close at P.27.b.1.2. and re-open at N.35.b.2.8. On night 18th/19th there will be representatives at both places.

6. Regulation intervals will be maintained on the march.

7. On relief the 38th Division will become V Corps Left Supporting Division and will be at the following hours notice to move :-

        Mid-night to 5-0 a.m................One hour.
        Remainder of day and night.........24 hours.

                                  W. Wright Capt. & Adjt.
                                        38th Battn.M.G.C.

Issued at 9-30 p.m.

Copies to :-

    All M.G.Coys.   )
    Bn.T.O.   )
    O.C., Details.) to ACKNOWLEDGE.
    R.Q.M.S.   )
    R.S.M.   )

    Intl.Offr.   38th Divn. "G".   )
    Sigl.Offr.   "   "   "Q".   )
    M.O.   113th Inf.Brigade.)
    File.   114th Inf.Brigade.) for information.
    War Diary.   115th Inf.Brigade.)
                     21st Battn.M.G.C.)
                     17th Battn.M.G.C.)
                     63rd Battn.M.G.C.)

SECRET.

TABLE TO ACCOMPANY 58th BATTN.H.Q.ORDER NO.44, dated 14th July, 1918.

1. Ser: No.	2. UNIT.	3. Date JULY.	4. From.	5. To.	6. Relieved by.	7. Instructions.
1.	2 Sections (BROWN LINE)	17th	Line.	QUESNOYE	"D" Coy. 21st Bn. H.G.C.	Route. If tracks are open - Track to LEALVILLERS, V. thro' 0.20. - HANDLEY CROSS - CANDLE PIG X Roads. If tracks closed - VARENNES - HARPONVILLE - TOUTENCOURT.
2.	"A" Coy. (less 2 Sectns.)	17th/18th.	"	QUESNOYE	"D" Coy. 21st Bn.	
3.	"B" Coy.	17th/18th	PURPLE LINE.	"	"C" Coy. " "	
4.	"C" Coy.	18th/19th	Line.	"	"A" Coy. " "	
5.	"D" Coy.	18th/19th	Line.	"	"B" Coy. " "	
6	Headquarters. Day 18th.		P.27.b.1.2.	E.55.b.6.8.	H.Q., 21st Bn.M.G.C.	Advanced H.Q. will remain at P.27.b.1.2. until completion of relief on 18th/19th inst.

Notes :-

1. Company Transport and Battle Surplus will move with Coys.
2. Hot drinks should be given somewhere en route from Line to QUESNOYE.

Q		
6	12	*Taken from Sheet 57^d S.E.* *Scale 1/20,000* *Date: 17.7.18*
5	J K	
4	10	
3	9	

38th BATT. M.G.C.

Tracing taken from Sheet ....

of the 1: .... map of ....

Signature .... Date ....

S E C R E T.   M.G.B./S.373.

AMENDMENT NO.1, to 38th BATTN.M.G.C.ORDER NO.45.

Reference para.1.   – The Raid will take place on the night
                       19th/20th July, 1918.

Reference para.2.   – Cancel all reference to ZERO plus
                       50 in Time and Rate of Fire columns,
                       and substitute "to 'Cease fire' Signal"
                       (Note. The 'Cease fire' signal – color
                        to be notified later – will be a
                       rifle grenade fired 3 times in
                       succession from our front line trench
                       opposite the point raided. On the
                       last of these grenades being fired,
                       the M.G.Barrage will die down).

Reference para.5.   – Cancel, and insert "If the situation
                       is clear at 10 minutes after the
                       'cease fire' signal, Batteries will
                       rejoin their Units.

Reference para.6.   – O.C., "A" Company will have a Runner
                       with a watch at Bn.H.Q. at 5-30 p.m.,
                       19th instant.

                                           [signature]
17th July, 1918.   Lieut-Colonel.
  9-20 p.m.   Commanding, 38th Battn.M.G.C.

Copy to all recipients of Order No.45.
  O.C., "A" Coy. to acknowledge.

SECRET.

58th. BATTALION MACHINE GUN CORPS.

ORDER NO. 45.

17th July, 1918.

Copy No 10

Ref. Map 57 D., S.E.

1. At a time and date to be notified later the 188 Infantry Brigade will raid the trenches marked red in attached tracing. Eight guns of this Battalion will co-operate with some of the 63rd (RN) M.G.C.Battn. and 42nd Battn.M.G.C.

2. Tasks as under :-

Battery position.	Guns.	Time.	Target.	Rate of Fire.	Remarks.
"J" Battery.	4	Zero to Zero plus 50.	Q.11.a.95.60 to Q.11.a.75.65. Searching 250 yards N.E.	100 r.p.m. for first 5 mins. 75 r.p.m. for next 30 mins. 100 r.p.m. from Z. plus 35 to Z. plus 50.	Found by "A" Coy. from R.6. position.
"K" Battery.	4	As for "J" Battery.	Q.11.a.95.05. to Q.11.d.2.0.	As for "J" Battery.	Found by "B" Coy. from R.5.a. position.

3. O.C., "A" Company will be GROUP COMMANDER ; and responsible for siting the Battery Positions and checking all calculations.

4. 4 guns from R.6. and 4 guns from R.5.a. will move forward to Battery positions to-morrow night. One N.C.O. will be left at each position to hand over Trench stores, and all details of the emplacements to 63rd (RN) Battn.M.G.C. on the 19th/20th instant. Everything, less Trench Stores and material for the Barrage, will be brought out to-night.

5. At Zero plus 60 if the situation is clear, Batteries will rejoin their Units.

6. Synchronisation orders will be issued later.

Issued at 5-30 p.m.

Lieut-Colonel.
Commanding, 58th Battn.M.G.C.

Copies to/
Major Jackson (3) - to ACKNOWLEDGE.
O.C., "B" Coy.
63rd (RN) Battn.M.G.C. - to Acknowledge.
58th Divn "G".
File.
War Diary (3)

SECRET.

38th. BATTALION MACHINE GUN CORPS:

ORDER NO.46.

17th July, 1918.   Copy No. 13

Ref: Map 57 D., 1/40,000.

1. On night 19th/20th 38th Battn.M.G.C. will be relieved by 63rd (RN) Battn.M.G.C. in the Left half of the Divisional Sector ; and by 17th Battn.M.G.C. in the Right half Divisional Sector : The dividing line is grid due West through Q.28.Central.

2. All details will be arranged by Company Commanders concerned. Relief will take place in accordance with Table overleaf.

3. All trench Stores (in all positions occupied by Battn.) Defence Schemes, aeroplane photographs, details of work in hand will be handed over and receipts taken. Copies will be sent to Bn.H.Q. by noon 21st instant.

4. Command will pass on completion of relief. Bn.H.Q. will close on completion at P.27.b.1.2. and re-open at T.5.a.7.5. Representatives will be at both places on night 19th/20th instant. Completion will be wired by Code Word "JESSOP".

5. Relief done, "A" Company will be attached to 113th Inf.Brigade (H.Q.P.27.b.2.2.)

6. On completion 38th Divn. will be in G.H.Q. Reserve (V Corps Right Supporting Division).
   The Battalion will be at following notice to move :-

   Midnight to 5-0 a.m.............1 hour.
   Remainder of day & night........24 hours.

                                              W. Wright Capt. & Adjt.
                                                         38th Battn.M.G.C.

Issued at 11-55 p.m.

Copies to/
   All M.G.Coys.   )
   Bn.T.O.   ) to ACKNOWLEDGE.
   R.Q.M.S.   )
   O.C., Details.   )
   Sigl.Offr.   )
   M.O.   )
   17th Battn.M.G.C.) to ACKNOWLEDGE.
   63rd Battn.M.G.C.)
   38th Divn. "G"   )
   3 Brigades.   )
   38th Divn. "Q"   ) for information.
   File.   )
   War Diary.   )

RELIEF TABLE to accompany 38th BATTN. M.G.C. ORDER NO.43.

1 Ser. No.	2 Date July	3 Unit	4 No. of Guns.	5 From	6 To	7 Relieved by	8 No. of Guns.	9 Remarks.
1	19th.	"A" Coy.	8 (BROWN Line)	Line	Engineer Valley V.8-b. V.2.d.8.8	—	1	Take over billets from 77th Field Coy.R.E. Detailed instructions from 113th Inf.Brigade.
2	19/20	"A" Coy.	4 (R.0.)	Line	Ditto (after the shoot)	"A" Coy. 33rd Bn.M.G.C.	2	M.G.O. will hand over as in Order No.45.
3	19/20	"A" Coy.	2 (R.1.)	Line	Ditto.	"A" Coy. 17th Bn.M.G.C.	1	
4	19/20	"A" Coy.	2 (R.2.a.)	Line	Ditto.	"D" Coy. 17th Bn.M.G.C.	1	
5	19/20	"B" Coy.	6 (R.4.& R.5.a.)	Line	T.5.a.2.7.5.	"A" Coy. 33rd Bn.M.G.C.	4	R.5.a. M.G.O. will hand over as in Order No.45.
6	19/20	"B" Coy.	4 (R.3.)	Line	T.5.a.2.7.5.	"D" Coy. 17th Bn.M.G.C.	1	
7	19/20	"B" Coy.	4 (R.1.a.)	Line	T.5.a.2.7.5.	"A" Coy. 17th Bn.M.G.C.	1	
8	19/20	"C" Coy.	13	Line	T.5.a.2.7.5.	"D" Coy. 17th & 18 Bn.M.G.C.		
9	19/20	"D" Coy.	13	Line	T.5.a.2.7.5.	"D" Coy. 17th Bn.M.G.C.	12	

Note.

A. (1) Relief in Left Sector to be complete (i) INTERMEDIATE Guns by 12 mid-night 19th/20th instant
   (ii) PURPLE Line by 10-30 p.m. 19th/20th instant.

(2) Relief in Right Sector to be complete by 1-0 a.m., 19th/20th instant.

B. Following guns will not be relieved at all :—
   6 BROWN Line....(A).
   R.5..............(B).
   R.1. & R.3......(B).

SECRET.

58th BATTALION MACHINE GUN CORPS.

ORDER NO. 47.

27th July, 1918.   Copy No. _____

1. On the 29th instant, "A" and "C" Companies inter-change billets. "C" Company to clear Camp T.5a. by 9-0 a.m. Arrival at V.2.d.8.8. will be wired by Code Word "COOPER".

2. Machine Gun Defence Schemes will **not** be handed over. "C" Coy. will take over BROWN LINE Brigade Defence Scheme, targets, and billet stores. "A" Company will take over HERISSART Brigade Defence Scheme. Copy of receipts to be sent to Bn.H.Q. by noon 30th.

3. "A" Company on completion occupy present lines of "C" Company. Details will be arranged by Os.C. "A" and "C" Companies.

4. Reference M.G.B./S.458 : "C" Company will be BROWN Line M.G.Coy. from 12 noon, 29th instant, and "A" Company will be HERISSART Brigade M.G.Coy.

                                              W. Wright Capt. Adjt.
                                                   58th Battn. M.G.C.

Issued at 1-0 p.m.

Copy to/
    Os.C.
      "A" and "C" Coys.
      Bn.T.O.   } to
      113th Brigade. ACKNOWLEDGE.
      115th Brigade. }

    Os.C.
      "B" and "D" Coys.   58th Divn. "G".   }
      Intl. Offr.   "   "   "Q". } for
      Sigl. Offr.   O.C., 58th Divn. Train} information.
      M.O.   114th Brigade.   }
      R.S.M.   File.
      R.Q.M.S.   War Diary.

38. Bn. M.G. Corps
9516

On His Majesty's Service.

Registered

Capt G Wyethen
3rd Echelon
Base

M4/3393

Confidential

WAR DIARY
of
38th Batt: M.G. Corps.
from 1st August '18 to 31st August '18

(Vol: 6.)

Army Form C. 2118.

WAR DIARY
or
INTELLIGENCE SUMMARY

(Erase heading not required.)

35th Bn M.G.C.

A.G. Ley Hulton
35 Bn M.G.C.

Place	Date	Hour	Summary of Events and Information	Remarks and references to Appendices
Camps near HERISSART	Aug 1st		Training continued. Tactical exercise for officers of B Coy.	
	2nd		"B" Coy cooperated in Tactical scheme with 1 & 2 Lts 118 Bde. Rehearsal of counter-attack on Brown line. Two Lts on trips independently, & not much value gained by M.G.	
	3rd		Div. Sports. 2/Lt E.R. PROBERT attached for duty as Ts. officer. "E" Coy.	
	4th		Div. Horse Show. Staff lectures. Capt A.D.E. W. WRIGHT on month's leave. Relief of 17th Bn in Right Sector began. "A" & "B" Coys to relieve VARENNES "D" Coy to Purple Line. "C" Coy from REHEUX to line (L.P.).	
YZEEVILLE	6th		Relief continued. "A" & "B" Coys to line in trenches & MG's in B.W.Q. to OB Headquarters near YZEEVILLE draft of 15 OR from 215 Bn.	

Army Form C. 2118.

WAR DIARY
or
INTELLIGENCE SUMMARY
(Erase heading not required.)

Place	Date	Hour	Summary of Events and Information	Remarks and references to Appendices
Meteren	7/8		39th Bde M.G.C.	
	8/8		Draft on given perform moves of which have now been in use being made.	
	9/8		Conference at 114 Bde. H.Q. Maps re reorganisation of bns in order to get 3 Lewis Gun sections M.G. and to continue training A + C. Casualties Wounded 2 O.R.	
	10/8			
	11/8		Pte 4/Lt A. COCKBURN joined Bde.	Pulm no 4 9
	14/8		1 section of A, B + C Coys relieved by 9/KOYLI. 1 coy 315 American M.G. Bn. 3 sections withdrawn to reserve in WELSH CAMP near B.H.Q.	

WAR DIARY or INTELLIGENCE SUMMARY

(Erase heading not required.)

Army Form C. 2118.

Place	Date	Hour	Summary of Events and Information	Remarks and references to Appendices
Iveuille	13/5		35th Bn. M.G.C. Casualties Wounded 1 O.R. A.C.A. Guns redistributed in sectors so as to allow 1 section per Coy to be withdrawn into Reserve for Training.	B.Orders No 50 96 in
	14/5		Received news that Germans are retiring in front of 112" Div. on our left.	O.O. No 51
	15/5		Issued orders for advance in event of enemy retiring. Redistribution of Bns with 2 Coys in line B & C Coy in Brown Line A Coy at Toutencourt. Relieved by Infantry 2nd Div of AMERE	O.O. No 52 O.O. 3.L.
	16/5		Two 2nd Lts attached Lt R.B. FLETCHER to GRANTHAM for Staff Course Lt N.P. HALL Coy Comdr to LEWIS Infantry for Course of duty with Distinguishing unit.	

WAR DIARY
INTELLIGENCE SUMMARY
(Erase heading not required.)

38th Bn. M.G.C.

Place	Date	Hour	Summary of Events and Information	Remarks and references to Appendices
Inconville	17/5		Nil	
	18/5		Arrangements made for relief of 3/5th American Infantry by a Coy of 314th B" (Amer.) Canadies & a L.D.R. Relief carried out at all the U.S. troops withdrawn. Major G. A.) Weiss reported from leave. One Company W-Scheme B- plan under orders with 3 days rate taken with a view to crossing ANCRE orders issued accordingly	Appx 53 Appx 54
	19/5		Orders for Coy. M.G. to form Canadies in N.W. Corps & 2/5 Div. tomorrow Div- to be formed. As crossing ANCRE of enemy resistance weakens	Appx 55
	20/5			

Signed [illegible] Lt Col
R.

Army Form C. 2118.

WAR DIARY or INTELLIGENCE SUMMARY

(Erase heading not required.)

Place	Date	Hour	Summary of Events and Information	Remarks and references to Appendices
Mesnil	21/8	9.30 a.m.	36th Bn M.G.C. "A" & "D" Coys ordered to rendezvous preparatory to B'ns to which they were attached crossing the river i.e. "A" to 115 "D" to 111. "A" Dispersed as follows. 1 section attached to 14/R.W.F. & 1 section to 2/R.W.F. Remaining two with Coy Hqrs. at Apr Bq. A.3.D. "D" remained concentrated in near MESNIL afterwards moving back to vicinity of ENGLEBELMER owing to hostile shelling.	
		1.30 p.m.	Notified of successful attack by Third Army this morning. Harassing fire ordered for tonight.	Order 56
		9.30 p.m. 10.0 p.m.	Orders reco to prepare to five evenings of Hare tomorrow "B" & "C" Coys ordered forward to cooperate at per M.R.B/5/551. Hostile plane passing very high dropped two bombs in on "D" Coy transport in valley near Hqrs. Great damage to men animals & limbers.	M.G.C. 5/71 5/77
			Casualties Killed Lieut C W PUGH 10 O.R. Wounded 11 O.R.	
			Vehicular damage 3 Limbers 1 Pack Saddle 5 sets wheel harness lost	Animals Killed 2 Riders 10 L.O. Wounded 3 Riders 9 L.O.

2449 Wt. W14957/M90 750,000 1/16 J.B.C. & A. Forms/C.2118/12.

WAR DIARY
or
INTELLIGENCE SUMMARY

Army Form C. 2118.

Place	Date	Hour	Summary of Events and Information	Remarks and references to Appendices
Inerville	24/5	10 a.m.	38th Bn. M.G.C. Return from Div. H.Q. 113 Bde. Stand by for word to attack in conjunction with 3rd Corps on line ALBERT – LA BOISSELLE – VILLERS. "B" less 2 sections ordered to report to 113 Bde H.Q. "C" Coy warned to stand by to follow up.	M/5 B/5 775 – 775
		9 a.m.	Action of "B" Coy. Moved into position in Brickfield N.W. of ALBERT to cover movings. Remaining Coys standing by.	
		11.0 p.m.	Orders from Div. for 113 Bde. to attack RUBBER LANE & CRUCIFIX CORNER. Arranged covering fire by 16 guns 5 "A" & 7 "B" under O.C. "A" Coy.	under O.C. Dunbar 5?
			Draft of 25 O.R. from base joined Bn.	
			Action of Coys.	
	23/5	4.45 a.m.	All guns "A" & 5 guns "B" engaged enemy with sweeps. Engaged many small parties of enemy with success. Two Sections B Battery were allowed to 14th & 15th R.W.F. & Crowd Atriole. One Platoon infantry attached to each section as carrying party.	

Army Form C. 2118.

"WAR" DIARY
or
INTELLIGENCE SUMMARY

(Erase heading not required.)

Instructions regarding War Diaries and Intelligence Summaries are contained in F.S. Regs., Part II. and the Staff Manual respectively. Title Pages will be prepared in manuscript.

Place	Date	Hour	Summary of Events and Information	Remarks and references to Appendices
Acheville	23/5	Noon	38th Bn M.G.C. Received orders from Div= for general attack. A B & D Coys to be attached to Bdes 'C' to be in reserve, concentrate at V.B.4.95 One Coy infantry to be attached to each M.G. Coy until Brigades as carrying parties. Brigades not yet available for Shelter, & possibly not for pack transport.	Order 58
		4.30pm	6 guns "D" Coy (1½ sections) attached 14/3 bdes gite 15/3 bdes. 1 section in B= Reserve. Major A.C. McCann joined as 2nd i/c vice Major J.H.J. Works to British mission to U.S. Army.	
	24/5	1.0 am	Action of Coys: "A" with 115 Bde. Sections att= infantry came into action after crossing rivers & got some useful targets. Remainder in B= Reserve crossed at 11.0 a.m. but did not come into action. Bivouac in Dupret for the night. "B" with 113 Bn. Had some opposition. The section got some from Tangu. Considerable casualties from shell & m.g. fire.	
		8pm	"C" Grand ANCRE & ALBERT & bivouacked on E. bank in reserve	

'WAR' DIARY or INTELLIGENCE SUMMARY

Army Form C. 2118.

Place	Date	Hour	Summary of Events and Information	Remarks and references to Appendices
Toutencourt	24/5	1 am	35th R. M.G.C. "B" with 119, 1,3 Lewis section crossed ANCRE by 5.30 a.m. were established on RED LINE	
		4.00	Reserve section crossed	
		12 midnight	Advance on POZIERES resumed.	
			Lieut HENSHALL attached an enemy M.G. which was holding up advance & captured gun & team. Many prisoners taken in THIEPVAL.	
			R.H.Q. remained at YPRESVILLE. Rec'd N. LANG "B" Coy — 2. O.R.	
			Casualties: Killed N. LANG "B" — Wounded S O R.	
			Lts Q.H. & MONKS joined "B"	
Toutencourt	25/5	1.30 am	Action of Corn.	
			"A" Resumed advance, on MAMETZ wood & BAZENTIN-LE-GRAND. Numerous small targets engaged. 2/Lt HANDS captured 6 prisoners. MG section attached to infantry	

Army Form C. 2118.

WAR DIARY
or
INTELLIGENCE SUMMARY
(Erase heading not required.)

Place	Date	Hour	Summary of Events and Information	Remarks and references to Appendices
Grenville	25/6		35th Bn. M.G.C.	
		10 a.m.	"B" continued in attack on CONTALMAISON which was successful. Casualties heavy. No 2 Section having to be pulled out to reconstitute. This Coy found the infantry carrying parties inadequate, as the men were not accustomed to the weight of such but was found one gun put out of action.	
		2.30 a.m.	"C" moved through LA BOISELLE to horizon W. of CONTALMAISON. 2/Lt Low with No 1 Section captured 22 prisoners & 2 m.g.	
		5.0 pm	Advanced to ridge E of MAMETZ WOOD. No 4 Sect. supported attack by 15th Divn on MONTAUBAN	
	25/6		"D" Halted at POZIERES. Received advance at dawn on HIGH WOOD. Advance held up by M.G.	
		10 a.m.	Casualties Wounds 5. O.R.	
			Lt. A.J.B. BANFORD & a draft of 30 O.R. mostly machine gunners, joined Bn.	

Army Form C. 2118.

"WAR DIARY"
or
INTELLIGENCE SUMMARY

(Erase heading not required.)

Instructions regarding War Diaries and Intelligence Summaries are contained in F.S. Regs., Part II. and the Staff Manual respectively. Title Pages will be prepared in manuscript.

Place	Date	Hour	Summary of Events and Information	Remarks and references to Appendices
CONTALMAISON	26/7		B⁽ᵈ⁾ Hqrs moved to CONTALMAISON & was established next to Div. Hqrs. Actions of Coys. "A" accompanied B⁽ᵗⁿ⁾ to Eastern edge of MAMETZ WOOD. Lt. SHAW wiped our hostile patrol	
		6.0 pm	Drove off enemy counter-attack killing some & taking remainder prisoner. B⁽ᵗⁿ⁾ BAZENTIN-LE-GRAND & PETIT FARM. More trouble experienced in getting hr forward & what with casualties & loss of kit only 2 guns were now in action. The advance of this B⁽ⁿ⁾ (12) seems to have been heard more than the others, & the attempt to get the Vickers guns forward with the infantry was not a success. No use was made of packs or limbers. "C" Move to ridge between BAZENTIN LE GRAND & LONGUEVAL to support attack on LUTEN. 2/Lt. WALLER hirs one lost at strong point holding up 13/R.W.F. & caused its surrender with 30 prisoners.	

Place	Date	Hour	Summary of Events and Information	Remarks and references to Appendices
Combles Maison	26/6		"B" Coy considerable opposition encountered, & no great advance made. Carrying parties in the other two Brigades rather more successful, but diminishing in numbers owing to casualties among infantry. Casualties 6 O.R. Killed Wounded - Lieut V.L. SWINNY & " " H.J. FOWLER "B" 15 O.R.	
"	27/6		Opposition considerably stiffer & units NE of Div- rather disorganised. No advance made. "B" Coy got some good targets in attempts [on] enemy counter-attack near LONGUEVAL "D" Coy Lieut STEWART got some good targets in berry off crossing high ground N. of GINCHY. Casualties. Killed 3 O.R. Wounded Lt. W.A. HENSMAN "B" 15 O.R. Strength of 10 O.R. joined Bn	

Place	Date	Hour	Summary of Events and Information	Remarks and references to Appendices
CONTALMAISON	25/5		38th Bn. M.G.C.

Situation
Germans returned to have dug trench in front of GINCHY. DELVILLE wood not yet cleared. 115 B⁰ only hold part of LONGUEVAL. Any stray reorganizing of units. Running runners made to R.H.A. for harassing fire on new trench "C & D" to carry this out. | |
| | | 4 P.M. | Received orders from Bde to co-operate in attack on DELVILLE WOOD & GINCHY, to take place at dawn tomorrow. Owing to short notice instructions & plan had to be issued Verbally. C & D Coys placed at disposal of O.C. B⁰ for barrage work.
Casualties Wounded 2Lt E.B. PROBERT "C" 5 O.R. | |
| | 26/5 | 5.30 a.m. | Action of Coys.
"A" accompanied 115 B⁰ in left attack.
"B"   "   113 " " Right "
"C" Barraged Sugar Refining S. of DELVILLE WOOD, Southern edge of Wood & Waterlot Corner of GINCHY. 34,000 rounds fired. Gun moved to offensive position W. of GINCHY | |

WAR DIARY
or
INTELLIGENCE SUMMARY

(Erase heading not required.)

Army Form C. 2118.

Place	Date	Hour	Summary of Events and Information	Remarks and references to Appendices
Contalmaison	29/5	5:30 a.m.	30th Bn. A.G.C. "D" Coy cleared trenches on left flank in T.2. T watch northern edge of DELVILLE WOOD. Attack met with opposition, & all objectives gained. An attempt to push on to MORVAL met m.g. fire. "A" Coy supported this advance by direct covering fire with 1 section. B Coy also got into action in the advance. Only three sections of the coy in action, A Coy being withdrawn into Reserve in DELVILLE WOOD to near the log hut. Remainder being exhausted. Casualties. Wounded Lieut J.T. RICHMOND "B" 30/5 of 25 O.R. joined "B".	
"	30/5		Germans reinforced by artillery & m.g. Troops of several different Divisions identified on our front. Prisoners taken more than half totals taken by V Corps. G.O.C. V Corps visited Div. Hq. to congratulate them on their success.	

Army Form C. 2118.

WAR DIARY
or
INTELLIGENCE SUMMARY

(Erase heading not required.)

Place	Date	Hour	Summary of Events and Information	Remarks and references to Appendices
Combles	30/9		35th Bde M.G.C. "D" Coy were to have accompanied advance on MORVAL. This "E" Coy was not formed & the Coys were located in their assembly positions - shells but very few casualties. Casualties. Wounded 4 O.R. Draft of 3 O.R. joined Bn.	
"	31/9		No advance made. Orders received in afternoon to attack MORVAL at Dawn Sept 1st. Verbal orders issued for "E" Coy to fire barrage in support as follows: All guns to two minutes rapid on MORVAL to support 114 Bde. "C" Coy thin to barrage high ground in T.5.c & D & trenches in T.12.A. B. in support of 115 Bde advancing on shirts left flank in T.S.a & b. "A" Coy in support of 115 Bde. "B" leading position T.9.6.1. T.3.D.13. Casualties Wounded 2/Lt MATTHEWS "A" Coy — 1 O.R.	[signature] 2/10/1916

2449 Wt. W14957/M90 750,000 1/16 J.B.C. & A. Forms/C.2118/12.

TABLE to accompany 58th BATTN. O. ORDER NO. 48.

1. Serial No.	2. Date August.	3. Unit.	4. From.	5. To	6. Relieving.	7. New H.Q.	8. Instructions.
1	5th	"A" Coy.	T.5.a.	VARENNES.	—	—	Clear Camp at 9-0 a.m.
2	5th	"B" Coy.	T.5.a.	VARENNES.	—	—	Clear Camp at 9-30 a.m.
3	5/6th	"D" Coy.	T.5.a.	Purple Line.	"A" Coy. 17th Bn.R..C.	V.18.a.1.9.	Details arranged by Coy. Commander.
4	5/6th	"C" Coy.	ACHEUX	Left Forward Coy.	"D" Coy. 17th Bn.R..C.	P.30.c.25.00.	
5	6/7th	"A" Coy.	VARENNES	Centre Forward Coy.	"B" Coy. 17th Bn.R..C.	V.6.d.9.9.	
6	6/7th	"B" Coy.	VARENNES	Right Forward Coy.	"C" Coy. 17th Bn.R..C.	V.18.a.1.9.	
7	6th	Rear H.Q.	T.5.a.	O.36.d.4.4.	Rear H.Q. 17th Bn.R..C.	O.36.d.4.4.	Clear Camp at 10-0 a.m.
8	6th	Adv.H.Q.	T.5.a.	P.27.b.1.2.	Adv.H.Q. 17th Bn.R..C.	P.27.b.1.2.	Clear Camp as 2-0 p.m.

Note. Administrative Instructions follow.

SECRET.

38th. BATTALION MACHINE GUN CORPS.

ORDER NO. 48.

3rd August, 1918.   Copy No. 23

Ref. Map Sheet 57.D., 1/40,000.

1. The 38th Battn.M.G.Corps will relieve the 17th Battn.M.G.Corps, in accordance with march and relief table overleaf.

2. All details will be arranged by Company Commanders concerned. R.Q.M.S. will act for Rear Bn.H.Q.

3. All Defence Schemes, present dispositions, aero-photos, details of work in hand, transport lines, tents and shelters, will be taken over and receipts passed. Copies will be sent to Bn.H.Q. by 12 Noon the day following relief.

4. Defence Schemes concerning the action of the Right Supporting Division will be sent to Bn.H.Q. by 9-0 a.m. 5th instant.

5. Command will pass on completion of relief. Bn.H.Q. will close at T.5.a.7.5. and re-open at P.27.b.1.2. at 6-0 p.m., 6th instant.

6. Completion of relief will be wired by Code Word "ARCHER".

7. Battle Surplus will move with Companies Transport and report to O.C., Battle Surplus, O.36.d.4.4.

W. Wright Capt. & Adjt.
38th Battn.M.G.C.

Issued at 3-0 p.m.

Copies to :-

Os.C.,
    A.B.C. & D. Coys)
    Battle Surplus.)
Capt.Smith.   )
Intl.Offr.   ) to
Sigl.Offr.   ) ACKNOWLEDGE.
Bn.T.O.   )
R.Q.M.S.   )
M.O.   )
Chaplain.   )
A/R.S.M.   )
17th Battn.M.G.C.   )

38th Divn. "G"   )
  "   "   "Q"   ) for
O.C., 38th Div.Train.)inform-
113th Brigade.   )ation.
114th Brigade.   )
115th Brigade.   )

File.
War Diary.

T A B L E to accompany 38th BATTN. M.G.C. ORDER NO. 49.

Serial No.	Date.	Unit.	Guns.	From.	To.	Relieved by.	Remarks.
1.	12/15th.	1 Section "A" Coy.	V.1. 1 & 2 V.2. 3 & 4	Lino	Bn.H.Q.	1 Platoon 314 American M.G.Battn.	
2.	12/15th.	1 Section "B" Coy.	V.13. 5 & 6 V.8. 1. V.14. 3.	"	"	"	
3.	12/15th.	1 Section "C" Coy.	Q.27. 1 & 2 Q.33. 5 & 6.	"	"	"	

SECRET:

38th. BATTALION MACHINE GUN CORPS.

ORDER NO.49.

11th August, 1918.   Copy No 15

Reference Map 57 D., 1/40,000.

1. Three Sections of the 38th Battn.M.G.Corps will be relieved by 3 Platoons (1 Company) of the 314 American M.G.Battn. on the night 12th/13th in accordance with table on reverse.

2. Company Commanders concerned will be responsible for Guides being at Bn.H.Q., P.27.b.1.2. at 7-30 p.m. These Guides will take platoons to respective Coy.H.Qrs, and return with empty limbers to Bn.H.Q.Transport to which this Company will be attached.

3. All other arrangements will be made by Company and Platoon Commanders on arrival of Platoons at Coy.H.Qrs. about 9-0 p.m.

4. Location of American M.G.Coy. Commander will be at "A" Coy. H.Q., V.6.d.9.9.

5. Company Commanders will arrange to leave one full rank N.C.O. and the Nos.1 of each gun team behind with the American Platoon for instructional purposes.

6. All Trench Stores will be handed over and receipts obtained. Copy of receipts to be forwarded to this Office by noon 13th instant.

                                            J.Smith Capt. & Adjt.
                                               38th Battn.M.G.C.

Issued at 9-0 p.m.

Copy to/
    Os.C.,
      A.B.C. & D.Coys.   )
    Bn.T.O.   ) to ACKNOWLEDGE.
    O.C., 314th American M.G.Battn.)

    38th Divn. "G")
      "   "   "Q")
    113th Brigade.)
    114th Brigade.) for information.
    115th Brigade.)
    O.C., Rear H.Q.)
    Q.M.   )

    File.
    War Diary.

SECRET.

38th. BATTALION MACHINE GUN CORPS.

ORDER NO.50.

12th August, 1918.   Copy No. _____

Reference Map : Sheet 57 D., S.E.

The following changes will take place on night of 13th/14th :-

1. "B" Coy.
   (i)   V.24.   1.& 2. relieved by guns of 18th Battn.
         W.13.   3.& 4.   "   "   "   " "D" Coy.
         W.13.   1.& 2)
         W.14.   1.& 2.)   abandoned
         W.8.   3.& 4.)
         W.9.   1.& 2.)

         and redistributed as follows - positions to be reconnoitred and
         fixed by O.C., "B" Coy :-

         2 guns W.15.d.98.10. to fire S.E.
         2 guns W.14.b.90.10.   "   "   S.
         2 guns W.10.a.50.70.   "   "   S.
         2 guns W.2.d.50.10.   "   "   S.

         remaining 4 guns to be withdrawn into reserve.

2. "A" Coy.
   (i) (a) The following guns will be relieved :-

         Q.32. 3.& 4. by 2 guns of "D" Coy.

       (b) The following positions will be abandoned :-

         W.2. 1.& 2.

         These guns will be disposed of as follows :-

         2 guns at W.15.b.6.8. (approx) to fire N.E. - position to be
            reconnoitred and fixed by O.C., "A" Coy.

         2 guns to relieve 2 guns of "C" Coy. at Q.33. 1.& 2.

   (ii) Guns in following positions will be withdrawn into reserve :-

         W.7. 1,2,3, & 4.

   (iii) W.2. 4. will be transferred to South side of Valley in
            neighbourhood of W.2. E.

3. "C" Coy.
   (i) The following positions will be relieved by guns of "D" Coy.

         Q.31. 5.& 7.
         Q.32. 5.& 6.

         these guns will be withdrawn into reserve.

   (ii) (a) The following will be relieved by 2 guns of "A" Coy.

         Q.33. 1.& 2.

         these guns will be disposed of as follows - positions to be
         reconnoitred and selected by O.C., "C" Coy :-

(P.T.O.)

3. "C" Coy. (continued) -

   (ii) (a) contd. -

   2 guns in Q.26.a. to fire N.E.
   2 guns will be pushed forward by day for sniping - O.C.,
   "C" Coy. will reconnoitre position about W.4.b.4.9. or
   Q.35.c.25.50.

4. "D" Coy.
   (i) will vacate the following positions :-

   V.18.   3,4,5, & 6.
   W.1.   3. & 4.
   Q.31.   1,2,3,4, & 5.
   Q.25.   1.

   These guns will be disposed of as follows :-

   2 guns to relieve 2 guns of "B" Coy...W.13. 3.&4.
   2 guns   "   "   "   "   " "A" Coy...Q.32. 3.&4.
   2   "   "   "   "   "   " "C" Coy...Q.32. 5.&6.
   2   "   "   "   "   "   " "C" Coy...Q.31. 6.&7.

   remaining 4 guns to be withdrawn into reserve.

5. Reserve Sections.
   The following will be reconnoitred and occupied by reserve
   Sections in event of alarm :-

   "B" Coy.   V.18.   3-4-5- & 6.
   "A" Coy.   W.7.   1-2-3- & 4.
   "D" Coy.   W.1.   3.& 4.
              Q.31.   1.&2.
   "C" Coy.   Q.31.   3-4-5-
              Q.25.   1.

   The following concrete emplacements completed, or under
   construction, are allotted to Coys. as alternative positions
   for reserve guns as follows :-

   "B" Coy.   W.13.a.5.1.) one gun in each.
              W.13.a.6.1.)
              V.12.c.9.3. ...2 guns.
   "A" Coy.   W.7.c.25.70...2 guns.
   "D" Coy.   V.6.b.2.3.....2 guns.

   ─────────────────────

                              A.G. Lyttelton. Lieut-Colonel.
                              Commanding, 38th Battn.M.G.C.

Copy to/
   Os.C.,
     A.B.C. & D.Coys. - to ACKNOWLEDGE.   38th Divn. "G".)
   O.C., Rear H.Q.   113th Brigade.) for
   Filo.   114th Brigade.)information
   War Diary.   115th Brigade.)

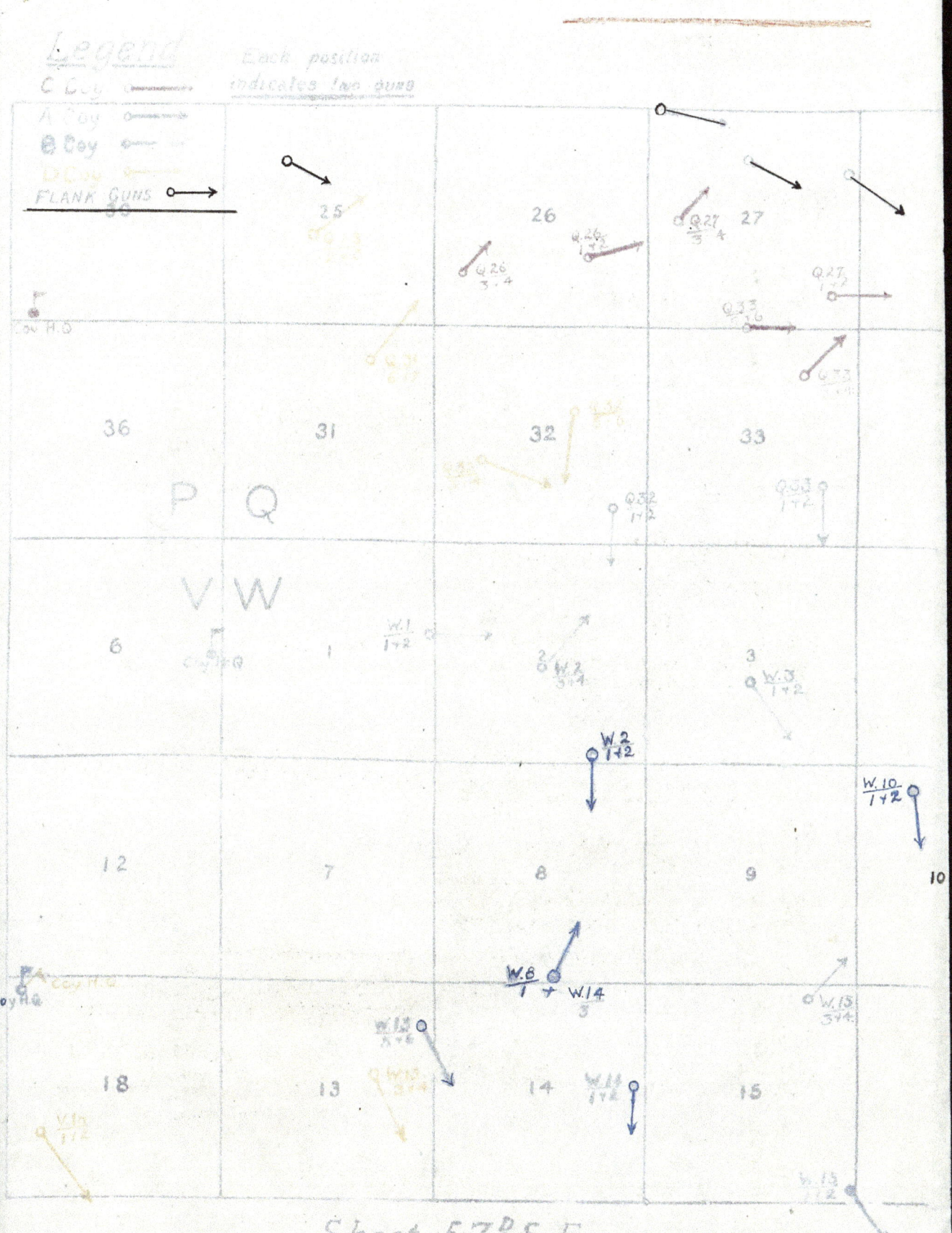

SECRET.

38th. BATTALION MACHINE GUN CORPS.

ORDER NO.51.

18th August, 1918.

Ref: Map Sheet 57 D. 1/40,000.

1. The enemy are reported to have withdrawn to the general line
   BUCQUOY - PUISIEUX - R.2.
   It is possible that the enemy may withdraw Eastwards from South
   of the R.ANCRE also.
   The Division on our left have reached the line - Q.6.Central -
   Q.12.a.central, and are pushing forward patrols to the spur in
   R.2. and towards the general line BATTERY VALLEY - THIEPVAL.
   A patrol of that Division crossed the R.ANCRE at Q.3.a.7.8.
   unopposed and is being followed by a Battalion whose objective
   is R.26.central.
   The enemy still hold a position round ALBERT Cathedral ; the
   Division on our right is operating against them from the South
   and have pushed patrols into W.24.

2. With a view to testing whether the enemy has withdrawn, 115th
   Infantry Brigade will send a Company via AUTHUILLE towards
   R.31.central and 115th Infantry Brigade a Company via AVELUY
   towards Cross Roads X.13.a.05.30.

3. If these Companies meet no opposition -

    (a) The 114th Infantry Brigade will then advance via AUTHUILLE
        and AVELUY towards the general line LA-BOISELLE - OVILLERS-
        LA-BOISELLE - THIEPVAL, and will make good the same. Bde.H.Q.
        will be at the old Battn.H.Q. Q.23.a.9.5.
    (b) The 115th Infantry Brigade will take over the whole present
        Divisional front and will have the 2nd/318 American Infantry
        Regiment attached to it in accordance with Warning Order
        (GS2.5/109/A).
    (c) The 113th Infantry Brigade will concentrate in the BROWN LINE
        ready to leapfrog through 114th Infantry Brigade to a general
        line - the cutting in X.17.a. - Windmill, POZIERES and ridge
        in R.26. West of COURCELETTE.

   A tracing over the 1/20,000 map is attached showing in RED the
   tactical points which must be occupied by the 114th Infantry Bde.
   and in BLUE the points to be occupied by 115th Infantry Brigade.

    (d) The Divisional Artillery (less the present advanced sections)
        will move into position in the PIONEER ROAD - MARTINSART -
        MESNIL VALLEY. 121st Bde.R.F.A. South of MARTINSART⊗; D.A.C.
        to HARPONVILLE.
        4 Sections 60-pdrs. and 4 Sections 6" Hows. will also move
        into position in the MARTINSART - MESNIL VALLEY.

4. "D" Company (Capt.GOLDSBROUGH) will be under the orders of 114th
   Infantry Brigade.
   The 114th Infantry Brigade will NOT wait for this Company to report
   before moving. The Company will come under the orders of 115th
   Infantry Brigade when that Bde. passes through 114th Brigade.

5. Dumps of ammunition, supplies and water will be formed in the
   MARTINSART VALLEY, W.S., W.O.

6. Battn.H.Q. will not move.

Issued at 4-15 a.m.

Lieut-Colonel.
Commanding 38th Battn.M.G.C.

P.T.O.

⊗ 122nd. Bde.R.F.A. NORTH of MARTINSART.

Copy to/
    Os.C.,) to acknowledge.
    D. Coy.)

    A. Coy.
    B. Coy.
    C. Coy.
    Bn.T.O.
    O.C., Rear H.Q.
    File.
    War Diary.

Identification Trace for use with Artillery Maps.

	19	20	21	22	23	24	
	21st Div: 25	26	27	28	29	30	
R	31	32	33	34	35	R 36	
X	1	2	3	4	5	X 6	
	7	8	9	10	11	12	
	13	14	15	16	17	18	
	Sheet - 57d SE		Scale - 1/20,000.				

NOTE.—(1). These traces are intended to facilitate the communication of information as to the position of targets, which have been located on a squared map.
(2). The squares on this trace are 500 yards in length on the 1/10,000 scale, 1,000 yards in length on the 1/20,000 scale, and 2,000 yards in length on the 1/40,000 scale.
(3). The squares on the trace are fitted to the squares of the map showing the targets, which are then drawn on the trace. Sufficient letters and numbers must also be added to enable the recipient to place the trace in the correct position on his own map. A little detail may also be traced, but this is not essential. The name and scale of the map to which the trace refers must be always given. The trace can be used for the 1/10,000, 1/20,000, or 1/40,000 scale.

G.S.G.S. 3083.

Tracing taken from Sheet ....
of the 1 .... map of ....
Signature .... Date ....

SECRET.

38th. BATTALION MACHINE GUN CORPS

ORDER NO.52.   Copy No. 14

15th August 1918.

Ref: Map Sheet 57 D. 1/40,000

1. 113th Inf.Bde. will be relieved in the Line by 115th Inf.Bde. to-morrow 16th Inst, and will move to TOUTENCOURT on relief.

2. 114th Inf.Bde. is in the BROWN LINE.

3. The Battalion will be re-disposed as follows -:-

   "B" & "C" Coys in the Line.(Tracing attached).
   "D" Coy on the BROWN LINE.
   "A" Coy at TOUTENCOURT.

4. The Dividing Line between Companies in the Line will be the Grid Line East and West between squares W.1. and W.7. with the position W.2. 1 & 2 inclusive to the Right Company

   (a) "B" Coy will occupy the Right Sub-Sector with 3 Sections and 1 Platoon 318th American Machine Gun Company.
       O.C., "B" Coy will take over
           V.18. 1 & 2.)
           W.13. 3 & 4.) from "D" Coy.

           W.15.b. (2 guns) from "A" Coy.

   The position for 2 guns at W.15.d.9.2. will be vacated.
   The fourth Section will remain in present position - WELSH CAMP.
   Coy.H.Q. will not move.

   (b) "C" Coy will occupy the Left Sub-Sector with 2 Sections and 2 Platoons 318th American Machine Gun Company.
       O.C.,"C" Coy will take over :-
           Q.32. 5 & 6.)
           Q.32. 3 & 4.) from "D" Coy.

           Q.32. 1 & 2.)
           Q.33. 1 & 2.) from "A" Coy.
           W.2. 3 & 4.)

       The following positions will be vacated :-
           Q.27. 3 + 4
           Q.27. 1 & 2.
           Q.33. 3 & 4.
           Q.25. 2 & 3.
           Q.31. 6 & 7.
           W.1. 1 & 2.
           W.3. 1 & 2.

       Two Sections "C" Coy will be in Reserve at WELSH CAMP.
       Coy.H.Q. will not change.

5. "A" Coy on relief will march to TOUTENCOURT with its Transport. Billets will be arranged by 113th Bde.
   2nd Lt.HANDS will send advance party to report to Town Major's Office TOUTENCOURT, at 9-30 a.m., the 16th instant.

P.T.O.

6. "D" Coy will on relief march to WELSH CAMP.
   In event of a forward move they will accompany 114th Bde.

7. All details not herein mentioned will be arranged between
   Officers Commanding Companies concerned.

8. Relief to be complete by 12 midnight 16th/17th and to be
   reported to Bn.H.Q. by Code Word "GEOFFREY".

Issued at 11-45 p.m.

                                            Smith Capt for Lieut-Colonel.
                                     Commanding 38th Battn.M.G.C.

Copies to/
    O&.C.,
      A. B. C & D Coys. } to ACKNOWLEDGE.
    Q.M.
    Bn.T.O.
    O.C.,
      Rear H.Q.
    113th Bde.
    114th Bde. } For information.
    115th Bde.
    38th Div. "G".
    38th Div. "Q".
    File.
    War Diary.

SECRET.

38th BATTALION MACHINE GUN CORPS.

ORDER NO.53.

16th August, 1918.   Copy No 14

1. One Company of 314th American Machine Gun Battalion will relieve the 318th American Machine Gun Company in the line on the night 18th/19th instant.

2. Company Commander of 314th M.G.Battn. will meet Os.C. "B" and "C" Coys. 38th Battn.M.G.C., and O.C., 318th M.G.Coy. at 318th M.G.Coy. H.Q. (V.6.d.9.9). at 10-45 a.m., 17th, to arrange all details.

3. Company Commanders of 38th Battn.M.G.C. will relieve their F.C.Os. and Nos.1; at the same time.

                                                             Adamson Maj.
                                            for Lieut-Colonel.
                              Commanding, 38th Battn.M.G.Corps.

Copy to/
    Os.C.,
      "B" & "C" Coys.   )
    314th American M.G.Battn.) to ACKNOWLEDGE.
    318th   "   M.G.Coy.)

    115th Brigade.)
    Os.C.,   )
      "A" & "D" Coys.)
    Rear H.Q.   ) for information.
    Bn.T.O.   )
    Q.M.   )
    File.   )
    War Diary.

SECRET.
****

38th BATTALION MACHINE GUN CORPS.

ORDER NO.54.

18th August, 1918.   Copy No 17

1. Order No.53 is cancelled.

2. The 318th American M.G.Company will be withdrawn from the line to-night 18th/19th August. *and proceed to VARENNES*

3. 2 Sections of "C" Coy. 38th Battn.M.G.C. at Welsh Camp will relieve guns of 318th American M.G.Coy. at -

    Q.33. 5 & 6.
    Q.33. 1 & 2.
    Q.32. 1 & 2.

and will re-occupy Q.33. 3 & 4.
W.2. 3 & 4 will not be occupied.

4. The Section of "B" Coy. 38th Battn.M.G.C. in Welsh Camp will relieve the Platoon of American M.G.Coy. attached to "D" Coy.

5. Relief complete will be reported to Bn.H.Q. by code word "JAMES".

                                                            Lieut-Colonel.
Issued at 4-15 p.m.   Commanding, 38th Battn.M.G.Corps.

Copy to/
    Os.C.
        "B" & "C" Coys.   )
        318th M.G.Coy.   ) to ACKNOWLEDGE.
        Reserve Sectns. "B" & "C" Coys.)

        "A" & "D" Coys.   38th Divn. "G".)
        Rear H.Q.   115th Brigade.)
        Bn.T.O.   ) for information.
        Q.M.   )
        File.   )
        War Diary.

SECRET.

38th BATTALION MACHINE GUN CORPS.

ORDER NO.55.

19th August, 1918.   Copy No. 16

1. One Company 17th Battn.M.G.C. is placed under the orders of the 38th Division.
   On the night 20/21st this Company will relieve "C" Coy. 38th Battn.M.G.C. in the line, and also the guns of 21st Battn.M.G.C. which cover the front of 110th Brigade.
   No movement to take place before 9-0 p.m.

2. On relief, "C" Company will occupy Billets near Bn.H.Q. P.27.b.1.2. O.C., "C" Coy. will arrange billetting party to be at Bn.H.Q. at 3-0 p.m. to-morrow, 20th.

3. O.C., "C" Coy. will meet Os.C. 17th & 21st Battns.M.G.C. at 21st Battn.H.Q., ACHEUX at 9-30 a.m. to-morrow, 20th to arrange details.

4. Trench tracings, trench stores, Defence schemes, aero-photos, work in hand, will be handed over and receipts taken. Copy of receipts to reach this Office by 12 noon, 21st instant.

5. "A" Company, 38th Battn.M.G.C. will move from TOUTENCOURT to "Welsh Camp" near Bn.H.Q. on the night 20/21st August. No movement to take place before 9-0 p.m.

6. Certificates of cleanliness in respect of Billets and Transport lines at TOUTENCOURT vacated by "A" Coy. will be rendered to this Office.

7. Relief complete will be wired to Bn.H.Q. by Code Word "ARTHUR".

                                            Smith. Capt. & Adjt.
                                                 38th Battn.M.G.C.

Issued at 10-30 p.m.

Copy to/
    Os.C.
      "C" Coy,   )
      "A" Coy,   ) to ACKNOWLEDGE.
    17th Battn.M.G.C.)
    21st Battn.M.G.C.)

    Os.C.
      "B" & "D" Coys.   38th Div. "G",)
      Bn.T.O,   "   " "Q"   )
      Q.M,   "   " Train.) for information.
      File,   115th Brigade.)
      War Diary,   114th Brigade.)
                         113th Brigade.)

SECRET.   M.G.B./S.845.
****

AMENDMENT to 38th BATTN.M.G.C.ORDER NO.55.

1. Paras.1 to 4 (inclusive) are cancelled, and the following
    substituted :-
    To-night, 20/21st August, "C" Company 38th Battn.M.G.C.
    will take over from 21st Battn.M.G.C. the following M.G.
    positions :-

            Q.27. 2.
            Q.21. 3.
            Q.21. 2.

    The following positions at present occupied by "C" Coy. will
    be vacated :-

            W.32. 3. & 4.
            Q.32. 5. & 6.
            Q.36. 1. & 2.

2. Trench tracings, trench stores, Defence Schemes, aero-photos,
    details of work in hand, etc. will be taken over, and lists
    forwarded to this Office by 12 noon, 21st instant.

3. Relief complete will be wired to Bn.H.Q. by Code Word "LAURENCE".

                                              Smith. Capt. & Adjt.
                                                     38th Battn.M.G.C.
Issued at 3-15 p.m.

Copy to all recipients of Order No.55.
    O.C., "C" Coy. to acknowledge.

S E C R E T.

38th. BATTALION MACHINE GUN CORPS

ORDER NO. 56.

Copy No. 13

Ref. Maps, Sheet 57D. 1/40,000.
Sheet 57D. S.E., 1/20,000.

1. The remainder of Third Army attacked this morning on a front of about seven miles and drove the enemy back three miles on a front of five miles ; at 7-30 this morning our troops were reported on the line COURCELLES - ACHIET -le-PETIT with Cavalry and Tanks in advance. 21st Division took BEAUCOURT and advanced to the line R.2.b., R.3.a., R.3.c., taking prisoner 2 Officers and 120 O.Rs. The enemy still appears to hold his position East of the ANCRE, South of MIRAMOUNT.

    Our patrols encountered opposition along the whole Division front this morning.

2. Patrolling will be carried out vigorously by the Brigades in the line to-night and under cover of any mist that there may be to-morrow morning with the object of ascertaining any alteration in the enemy's dispositions.

3. Harassing fire by Artillery and Machine Guns will be carried out to-night, but not against any targets nearer than 1,000 yards East of the Eastern branches of the ANCRE.

4. If the enemy appears to be withdrawing, Machine Gun Companies will act as ordered in M.G.B./S.851, dated 20th instant.

5. Addressees marked * to ACKNOWLEDGE.

21st Augt '18
Issued at 5-45 p.m.

Lieut-Colonel,
Commanding, 38th Battn.M.G.C.

Copy to/
Os.C.,
A.B.C. & D.Coys.
Rear H.Q.
Bn.T.O.
Q.M.
Int.Offr.
Sigl.Offr.
File.
War Diary.

SECRET & URGENT.   M.G.B./.S.871.

O's.C.,
  B. & C. Coys.

  Reference M.G.B./S.851 of yesterday.

  Para.2.   These guns will move forward to-night and be in
position by dawn ready to open fire to cover the crossing.
  One Section "A" and "D" Coys. have been detailed by Brigades
for same duty. Orders for move forward by your Company as before,
vide para.5.

                              (Sgd.) A.G.LYTTELTON.   Lieut-Colonel.
                                      Commanding, 38th Battn.M.G.C.
21st August, 1918.
  9-30 p.m.

M.G.B./S.877.

SECRET & URGENT.

Os.C.
"B" & "C" Coys.

1. Brigades will be prepared on receipt of orders from Div.H.Q. to force the crossings over the ANCRE and seize ground on the far side in the following manner,:-

   (a) Force to be employed by each Brigade will be

        4 Stokes Mortars.
        4 Companies.

   (b) Battle patrols composed of one platoon from each Company will cross the ANCRE covered by fire from the Stokes Mortars where necessary.
      As soon as these patrols have effected a crossing and formed a bridgehead, they will be reinforced by the remainder of their Companies.

2. Guns mentioned in M.G.B./S.871 (issued at 9-30 p.m.) will support the crossing by direct overhead fire should any target present itself.

3. ACKNOWLEDGE.

                            (Sgd.) A.G.LYTTELTON.
                                    Lieut-Colonel,
22nd August, 1918.   Commanding, 38th Battn.M.G.C.
  2-35 a.m.

SECRET & URGENT.   M.G.B./S.875.

O.C.,
"B" Coy.

     "B" Company, less two Sections, will report to 113th Brigade H.Qrs. V.4. Central at 7-0 a.m. ready to move. H.Q. and fighting limbers of these Sections will report to you at 5-0 a.m. Senior Subaltern will take command of 2 remaining Sections, and establish himself at your present H.Qrs. Orders already issued will hold good for the two latter Sections.
Two S.A.A. limbers for the Sections accompanying you will be held ready to join 113th Brigade Transport on receipt of instructions from you.

                              (Sgd.) J. SMITH, Capt. & Adjt.
                                    for Lieut-Colonel.
                        Commanding, 38th Battn.M.G.C.

22nd August, 1918.
12-45 a.m.

SECRET & URGENT.   M.G.B./S.878.

O.C.,
 "C" Coy.

1. In the event of the attack of the 18th Division to-day being successful, 113th Inf. Brigade may be called upon to co-operate by passing through ALBERT and attacking towards OVILLERS.

2. 8 Guns of "B" Coy. will support above attack from positions :-

  (i) W.22.b. & d.
  (ii) W.24.a. and W.23.b.
  (iii) neighbourhood of ROUTON LANE & RANCH TRENCH.

moves from one position to another being made by alternate Sections.

3. It is possible that your Company may be required to follow 113th Brigade and come under orders of that Brigade for purposes of consolidation.

4. The following information has been received as to the crossings North of ALBERT :-

Road Bridge over Rly. W.22.d.7.5. destroyed. (deep cutting here).
River bridge W.23.c.2.4. gap of 20 feet.
Footbridge in-tact at W.23.a.6.9. but difficult of approach from the west owing to floods.

5. ACKNOWLEDGE.

        (Sgd.) J.SMITH, Capt. & Adjt.
          for Lieut-Colonel.
       Commanding, 38th Battn.M.G.C.

22nd August, 1918.
 9-0 a.m.

38th BATTALION MACHINE GUN CORPS.

ORDER NO. 57.

22nd August, 1918.   Copy No. _____

Map Ref: Sheet 57D., S.E. 1/20,000.

1. The Third Corps is renewing the attack at 4-45 a.m. to-morrow.

2. The 115th Brigade is attacking at the same time and is to seize and consolidate RUBBER LANE. After this objective has been gained the hostile post at CRUCIFIX CORNER about W.12.c.0.1. is to be seized.

3. 8 Guns "A" Coy. and 8 guns "B" Coy. under command of Capt. GODDING "A" Company will come into action in squares W.10. and W.16. to-night and will open at Zero with direct over-head fire on such portions of the first objectives as are within range. Fire will be lifted off targets when Infantry approach it. If weather conditions render it impossible to see target from Batteries, this target will not be engaged at all. After lifting, or if target be not engaged, fire will be directed on to trenches in W.18.b. and maintained until Zero plus 1½ hours (CRUCIFIX CORNER will only be engaged if fire be asked for by Infantry). 2 Guns will search AUTHUILLE WOOD from Zero up to Zero plus 1½ hours. Should Infantry meet with opposition from here in their advance on CRUCIFIX CORNER more guns will be employed.

4. Visual Signal Stations will be established about W.15.b.8.0. and W.10.a.5.1.

5. 5,000 rounds per gun in belts will be dumped at gun positions by dawn 23rd instant.

6. On completion of operation, all guns will remain in position pending further orders.

7. 115th Infantry Brigade H.Q. will be at W.25.b.0.7. O.C., "A" Coy. will establish his headquarters at HEATHCOTES BANK (near 115th Bde. adv H.Q.)

8. ACKNOWLEDGE.

                                                                        Lieut-Colonel.
Issued at 11-0 p.m.   Commanding 38th Battn. M.G.C.

Copies to/
    Os.C.,
    A.Coy. (2 copies).
    Divn. "G" (map attached).
    115th Inf. Brigade (map attached).
    File.
    War Diary.

SECRET.   M.G.B/S.895

38th. BATTALION MACHINE GUN CORPS.

WARNING ORDER.

23rd August, 1918.

Probable attack by 5th Corps and 18th Division tonight, 23/24th August, at 1-0 a.m.

1. Right attack 113th and 115th Brigades and right Centre attack 114th Brigade.

2. Machine Gun Companies allotted Brigades as follows :-

    "A" Coy....115th Brigade.
    "B" Coy....113th Brigade.
    "D" Coy....114th Brigade.
    "C" Coy....in Reserve.

3. Fighting limbers & Coy. H.Q. will report to Company H.Q. at once. Remainder of Transport of A.B. & D.Coys. will be held in readiness to join Transport of Brigades to which Coys. are allotted.

4. Os.C. A.B.D.Coys. will report to Brigade Commanders forthwith to receive instructions as to concentration of Coys. in preparation for advance.
   O.C., "C" Coy. will withdraw all guns and all kit from present positions and concentrate Company at V.6.d.9.9. and report concentration complete to Bn.H.Q. by Code Word "BEN".

5. One Company of Infantry is to be at the disposal of each of A.B. & D.Coys. for carrying parties as it is uncertain to what extent pack or wheel transport will be able to cross the ANCRE.

6. At least half the guns of each Coy. going forward with Brigades are to be employed on the final objective.

7. ACKNOWLEDGE.

Issued at 1-45 p.m.

                                    Lieut-Colonel.
                        Commanding, 38th Battn.M.G.C.

Copy to/
    Os.C., A.B.C. & D.Coys.
    Transport Officers, A.B.C. & D.Coys.
    O.C., Rear H.Q.   R.S.M.
    Q.M.   Chaplain.
    Bn.T.O.
    Sigl.Offr.
    M.O.

7. (contd).   The bridges made by 151 and 123 Field Coys.R.E. are allotted for use to 115th and 114th Brigades respectively. 113th Brigade are using the crossings in ALBERT.

8. Machine Gun Companies are allotted to Brigades as follows :-

   "A" Coy........115th Brigade.
   "B" Coy........113th Brigade.(remaining 2 Sectns. to report
   "B" Coy........114th Brigade.   to Bde. at once).
   "C" Coy........in Reserve.

9. For this attack each Brigade are detailing one Infantry Coy. as carrying party for its own M.G.Coy, until bridges are suitable for pack or wheeled transport.
   Guns now in position in the line will be withdrawn from position at once.

10. Advanced Headquarters are moving as under before Zero.

    114th Brigade to Q.28.a.9.4.
    115th Brigade to W.3.d.8.5.

11. O.C., "C" Company will send an Officer to Bn.H.Q. at 7-0 p.m. to-day for the purposes of synchronising watches.

12. Until further orders, the aeroplane signal to denote the assembly of hostile troops for counter-attack is to be a red smoke bomb dropped in the direction of their place of assembly.

13. S.A.A. for A.B. & D. Coys. will be drawn through Brigades to which they are attached. "C" Coy. through Bn.H.Q.
    Rations from to-morrow will be drawn by Coys. from Brigades to which they are attached. "C" Coy. as usual.

14. Addressees marked * to ACKNOWLEDGE.

                                              Lieut-Colonel.
Issued at 6-30 p.m.   Commanding, 38th Battn.M.G.C.

Copy to/
*Os.C., A.B.C. & D.Coys.   38th Divn. "G".
* Rear H.Q.   "   "   "Q".
 *Bn.T.O.   "   "   Train.
 *Q.M.   113th Brigade.
  Sigl.Offr.   114th Brigade.
  Intl.Offr.   115th Brigade.
  M.O.   File.
  Chaplain.   War Diary.
  R.S.M.

SECRET.
****

38th. BATTALION MACHINE GUN CORPS.

ORDER NO. 58.

23rd August, 1918.   Copy No. 20

1. H.G.B./S.851, dated 20th August is cancelled.

2. Six Armies (British and French) are attacking to-day between ARRAS and SOISSONS.
   The Corps on our left is attacking IRLES and ACHIET le GRAND to-day. GOMIECOURT has been taken by us to-day.

3. The V Corps is attacking to-night, 23rd/24th at 1-0 a.m. Objectives and boundaries are shown on the attached map.
   The 18th Division on our right is attacking at the same hour with the object of seizing the line X.25.a. - X.20.a.9.9.

4. The Left attack is being carried out by the 21st Divn.
   The Centre attack is being carried out by the 17th and 38th Divns.
   The Right attacks is being carried out by the 38th Divn.

5. The Right attack is being carried out by the 113th Brigade on the right and the 115th Brigade on the left, the boundary between the two being the road X.13.a.3.5. - OVILLERS (inclusive to 115th Bde.) - point X.8.b.9.3. where the track cuts the red line.
   115th Brigade is attacking with one Battalion in front closely supported by another and one in Reserve. The support Battalion is being employed in forming a left defensive flank and taking and occupying the trench system in the apex of the triangle (made by the boundary lines) in X.2 ; The Reserve Battalion is being employed in mopping up the remainder of the country between the left boundary of the right attack and the right boundary of the centre attack, paying special attention to any posts which fire on to the crossings of the ANCRE.
   Both Brigades are forming up for attack on RUBBER LANE, the dividing line being the sunken road W.18.d.2.7.

6. The right half of the centre attack as shewn on the attached map is being carried out by 114th Brigade who are forming a defensive flank along the right boundary of their attack.

7. Bridges are being taken in hand by Field Coys. as under :-

   By 151 Fld.Coy....W.17.c.8.6. footbridge; at once.
   "   "   "   " ...W.11.d.4.6. for all arms.   ) immediately that
   " 123   "   " ... C.36.c.1.3. & 1.7. for all arms.) those crossings
   "   "   "   " ... C.29.d.8.5. footbridge.   ) can be approached
   "   "   "   " ... C.24.c.5.0.   "   "   ) without drawing
                                                       fire.

                                                P.T.O.

SECRET

Identification Trace for use with Artillery Maps.

16	17	18	13	14	15
				LEFT ATTACK	
22	23	24	19	20	21
28	29	30	25	26	27
			CENTRE ATTACK		
34	35	36	31	32	33
		Q	R		
4	5	W	X	2	3
10	11	12	7	8	9
			INTER-BRIGADE BOUNDARY		
16	17	18	13 RIGHT ATTACK	14	15
22	23	24	19	20	

NOTE.—(1). These traces are intended to facilitate the communication of information as to the position of targets, which have been located on a squared map.
(2). The squares on this trace are 500 yards in length on the 1/10,000 scale, 1,000 yards in length on the 1/20,000 scale, and 2,000 yards in length on the 1/40,000 scale.
(3). The squares on the trace are fitted to the squares of the map showing the targets, which are then drawn on the trace. Sufficient letters and numbers must also be added to enable the recipient to place the trace in the correct position on his own map. A little detail may also be traced, but this is not essential. The name and scale of the map to which the trace refers must be always given. The trace can be used for the 1/10,000, 1/20,000, or 1/40,000 scale.

G.S.G.S. 3025.

Tracing taken from Sheet 57 D S E
of the 1: 20,000 map of
Signature   Date

SECRET.

38 DIV
IV SS141
20/8/18

H.A.B./S.851.

38th. BATTALION MACHINE GUN CORPS

INSTRUCTIONS for MACHINE GUN COMPANIES in the LINE in the event of the Division being ordered to cross the ANCRE.

FIRST BOUND.

1. On receipt of the order "Advance", Bn.T.O. will send H.Qrs. and fighting limbers to Company H.Qrs. All guns, belt boxes, and kit (with the exception of the guns mentioned in para.2,) will be collected under Company arrangements. Guns will be moved forward to prepared positions - the Right Company in W.10. and W.16; the Left Company in Q.35, & W.5.

2. The following guns will not wait for orders from Battn.H.Q., but will move forward to prepared positions, vide para.1 as soon as the O.C., Infantry Battn. notifies the Section Officer that the Infantry are about to cross the ANCRE.

   Right Coy.   Left Coy.
   W.15.   1 & 2.   Q.33.   1 & 2.
   W.16.   1 & 2.   Q.33.   3 & 4.
   W.10.   1 & 2.

   Teams will carry forward as many belt boxes as they can carry; the remainder will be collected vide para.1.

3. As soon as guns are in position, Coys. will send an Officer to report to Bn.H.Q.
   Fighting limbers will be kept as near the guns as the situation allows.

4. Bn.H.Q. will be with Left Brigade H.Qrs. at HESNEL, Q.28.a.

5. On receipt of orders from Bn.H.Qrs., Coys. will cross the ANCRE - the Right Coy. at AVELUY and the Left Coy. at AUTHUILLE. If bridges are not passable for wheels, the two leading sections will cross on pack transport, and will move :-

   Right Coy. to DONNET POST, W.12.d.9.1.
   Left Coy. to Q.36.b.8.2.

   Pack mules will be off loaded and sent back :-

   Right Coy. to 1st "C" in CRUCIFIX CORNER, W.12.c.1.1.
   Left Coy. to "C" in CAMPBELL AVENUE, Q.36.c.9.1.

   Remaining two Sections will meantime be manhandled across. They will then be loaded on pack mules and proceed to join leading Sections.

SECOND BOUND.

6. On the second objective being reached, Coys will move forward on receipt of orders from Bn.H.Q. to the general line X.15, R.27, using limbers or pack transport.
   The dividing line between Coys. will be E. & W. Grid line between Q.36 and W.6.
   Right Coy. will rendezvous at Road junction, X.9.c.8.9.
   Left Coy.   "   "   at HOUQUET FARM, R.23.b.3.9.
   Os.C. Coys. will report personally to 113th Inf.Bde.Hqrs. in R.32.

7. Bn.H.Q. will move to 113th Bde.H.Qrs., R.32.

A.G. Lyttelton Lieut-Colonel.
Commanding, 38th Battn.M.G.C.

20th August, 1918.

38th BATTALION MACHINE GUN CORPS:

ORDER NO. 57.

22nd August, 1918.

Copy No. 3

Map Ref: Sheet 57D., S.E. 1/20,000.

[Stamp: GENERAL STAFF, 38TH (WELSH) DIVISION]

1. The Third Corps is renewing the attack at 4-45 a.m. to-morrow.

2. The 113th Brigade is attacking at the same time and is to seize and consolidate RUBBER LANE. After this objective has been gained the hostile post at CRUCIFIX CORNER about W.12.c.0.1. is to be seized.

3. 8 Guns "A" Coy. and 8 guns "B" Coy. under command of Capt. GODDING "A" Company will come into action in squares W.10. and W.16. to-night and will open at Zero with direct over-head fire on such portions of the first objectives as are within range. Fire will be lifted off targets when Infantry approach it. If weather conditions render it impossible to see target from Batteries, this target will not be engaged at all. After lifting, or if target be not engaged, fire will be directed on to trenches in W.18.b. and maintained until Zero plus 1½ hours (CRUCIFIX CORNER will only be engaged if fire be asked for by Infantry). 2 Guns will search AUTHUILLE WOOD from Zero up to Zero plus 1½ hours. Should Infantry meet with opposition from here in their advance on CRUCIFIX CORNER more guns will be employed.

4. Visual Signal Stations will be established about W.15.b.8.0. and W.10.a.5.1.

5. 5,000 rounds per gun in belts will be dumped at gun positions by dawn 23rd instant.

6. On completion of operation, all guns will remain in position pending further orders.

7. 113th Infantry Brigade H.Q. will be at W.25.b.0.7. O.C., "A" Coy. will establish his headquarters at HEATHCOTES BANK (near 115th Bde. adv. H.Q.)

8. ACKNOWLEDGE.

Issued at 11-0 p.m.

[Signed] Major
for Lieut-Colonel.
Commanding 38th Battn. M.G.C.

Copies to/
    Os.C.,
    A.Coy. (2 copies).
    Divn. "G" (map attached).
    113th Inf. Brigade (map attached).
    File.
    War Diary.

SECRET.
****

38th. BATTALION MACHINE GUN CORPS.

ORDER NO.58.

23rd August, 1918.   Copy No. 13

1. M.G.B./S.851, dated 20th August is cancelled.

2. Six Armies (British and French) are attacking to-day between ARRAS and SOISSONS.
   The Corps on our left is attacking IRLES and ACHIET le GRAND, to-day.
   GOMIECOURT has been taken by us to-day.

3. The V Corps is attacking to-night, 23rd/24th at 1-0 a.m.
   Objectives and boundaries are shown on the attached map. (to M.G Coys)
   The 18th Division on our right is attacking at the same hour with the object of seizing the line X.25.a. - X.20.a.9.9.

4. The Left attack is being carried out by the 21st Divn.
   The Centre attack is being carried out by the 17th and 38th Divns.
   The Right attacks is being carried out by the 38th Divn.

5. The Right attack is being carried out by the 113th Brigade on the right and the 115th Brigade on the left, the boundary between the two being the road X.13.a.3.5. - OVILLERS (inclusive to 115th Bde.) - point X.8.b.9.3. where the track cuts the red line.
   115th Brigade is attacking with one Battalion in front closely supported by another and one in Reserve. The support Battalion is being employed in forming a left defensive flank and taking and occupying the trench system in the apex of the triangle (made by the boundary lines) in X.2 ; The Reserve Battalion is being employed in mopping up the remainder of the country between the left boundary of the right attack and the right boundary of the centre attack, paying special attention to any posts which fire on to the crossings of the ANCRE.
   Both Brigades are forming up for attack on RUBBER LANE, the dividing line being the sunken road W.18.d.2.7.

6. The right half of the centre attack as shewn on the attached map is being carried out by 114th Brigade who are forming a defensive flank along the right boundary of their attack.

7. Bridges are being taken in hand by Field Coys. as under :-

   By 151 Fld.Coy....W.17.c.8.6. footbridge; at once.
      "   "   " ....W.11.d.4.6. for all arms.   ) immediately that
      "   123   " " ...Q.36.c.1.5. & 1.7. for all arms.) those crossings
      "   "   " " ...Q.29.d.8.3. footbridge.   ) can be approached
      "   "   " " ...Q.34.c.5.0.   "   "   ) without drawing
) fire.

                                                P.T.O.

7. (contd). The bridges made by 151 and 123 Field Coys.R.E. are allotted for use to 115th and 114th Brigades respectively. 113th Brigade are using the crossings in ALBERT.

8. Machine Gun Companies are allotted to Brigades as follows :-

   "A" Coy........115th Brigade.
   "B" Coy........113th Brigade.(remaining 2 Sectns. to report
   "D" Coy........114th Brigade.   to Bde. at once).
   "C" Coy........in Reserve.

9. For this attack each Brigade are detailing one Infantry Coy. as carrying party for its own M.G.Coy, until bridges are suitable for pack or wheeled transport.
   Guns now in position in the line will be withdrawn from position at once.

10. Advanced Headquarters are moving as under before Zero.

    114th Brigade to Q.28.a.9.4.
    115th Brigade to W.3.d.8.5.

11. O.C., "C" Company will send an Officer to Bn.H.Q. at 7-0 p.m. to-day for the purposes of synchronising watches.

12. Until further orders, the aeroplane signal to denote the assembly of hostile troops for counter-attack is to be a red smoke bomb dropped in the direction of their place of assembly.

13. S.A.A. for A.B. & D. Coys. will be drawn through Brigades to which they are attached. "C" Coy. through Bn.H.Q.
    Rations from to-morrow will be drawn by Coys. from Brigades to which they are attached. "C" Coy. as usual.

14. Addressees marked * to ACKNOWLEDGE.

Issued at 6-30 p.m.

A.G. Lyttelton, Lieut-Colonel.
Commanding, 38th Battn.M.G.C.

Copy to/
Os.C., A.B.C. & D.Coys.   38th Divn. "G".
*Rear H.Q.   "   "   "Q".
*Bn.T.O.   "   "   Train.
*Q.M.   113th Brigade.
 Sigl.Offr.   114th Brigade.
 Intl.Offr.   115th Brigade.
 M.O.   File.
 Chaplain.   War Diary.
 R.S.M.

S E C R E T .   M.G.B./S.733.

Herewith Tracing to accompany Order No.50.

                                        Lieut-Colonel.
12th August, 1918.   Commanding, 38th Battn. M.G.C.

Copy to all recipients of Order No.50.

Confidential

1918

WAR DIARY
~ of ~
38th Battⁿ M.G. Corps
from 1st to 30th September 1918

Vol: 7

Army Form C. 2118.

WAR DIARY
or
INTELLIGENCE SUMMARY
(Erase heading not required.)

Instructions regarding War Diaries and Intelligence Summaries are contained in F. S. Regs., Part II. and the Staff Manual respectively. Title Pages will be prepared in manuscript.

Place	Date	Hour	Summary of Events and Information	Remarks and references to Appendices
35th Bn. M.G.C.	1/9/18	4:45am 5:40 a.m.	Attack on MORVAL was quite successful, but the further advance on SAILLY SAILLISEL only partly so. Action of Coys. "A" Two sections accompanied leading Bns. of 115 Bde. & engaged enemy retiring from MORVAL	
			"B" Took up positions covering rally between BOULEAUX WOOD & MORVAL. An attack proceeded. Guns limbered up & moved to T.10.a & T.17.a & 2 E of MORVAL. After firing barrage moved up E. of MORVAL.	
			"C" Remained in position on conclusion of barrage.	
			"D" Inspection of the areas engaged during this barrage a few days later revealed several graves & much German equipment lying about.	
	6:30 p.m.		"C" Coy covered advance of 113 Bde. on SAILLY SAILLISEL using direct fire on to WOOD E. of village. 15,000 rounds fired.	
	7.0 p.m		"B" advanced with 113 Bde. & on the capture of the village was forward Guns were disposed in U.1.d - U.5.a & U.14.b.	

Army Form C. 2118.

WAR DIARY
or
INTELLIGENCE SUMMARY
(Erase heading not required.)

Instructions regarding War Diaries and Intelligence Summaries are contained in F. S. Regs., Part II. and the Staff Manual respectively. Title Pages will be prepared in manuscript.

Place	Date 1918	Hour	Summary of Events and Information	Remarks and references to Appendices
			36th Bn. M.G.C.	
	2/9	5:0 a.m.	No advance during morning 115th, 13th attacked MESNIL-EN-ARROUAISE. C Coy barraged wood in U.3.c.+d & cross roads in U.10.c+d. Attack did not succeed.	
		12.0 midnight	Enemy Divns ordered to take up defensive positions owing to 4th Army rumour of forthcoming counter attack. Dispositions as follows: SAILLY-SAILLISEL & two coy flanks of SAILLY-SAILLISEL & two A Coy Two sections in reserve. B Coy U.1.D - U.5.a & U.14.b C Coy J.5.c & T.17.a & e D Coy T.12.b+d & J.12.a & e For the defence of an entrenched line in open fighting it seems best to place the majority of guns forward as above.	
	3/9		No counter-attack. Enemy retires & Divn advances to bn hi of canal du NORD. A Coy Two sections moved to trenches in U.11.a & e + U.17.a. B Coy Two sections remained in reserve.	

Army Form C. 2118.

WAR DIARY
or
INTELLIGENCE SUMMARY
(Erase heading not required.)

Instructions regarding War Diaries and Intelligence Summaries are contained in F. S. Regs., Part II. and the Staff Manual respectively. Title Pages will be prepared in manuscript.

Place	Date 1916	Hour	Summary of Events and Information	Remarks and references to Appendices
30th B- M.G.C.	3/9		B Coy USA & U11b C " Mga & e D " Accompanied 114 Bde as advance guard to the spurs west of MANANCOURT & ETRICOURT. Limbers and most of the men, & guns were carried the whole way.	
	4/9.	5.0 p	114 Bde crossed the Canal. "D" Coy covered the crossing & got some good targets. One of the Machine sections was ordered up to support; the section went on & the guns were taken up over the open in the limbers at a gallop, arriving without any casualties, in time to catch a hostile counter attack, with very good results, the attack being completely stopped. Remaining Coy guns not moved.	
	5/9		Three sections "B" Coy crossed canal to ems/that. Forth section employed long range fire from W bank.	

2449   Wt. W14957/M90 750,000 1/16 J.B.C. & A. Forms/C.2118/12.

WAR DIARY
or
INTELLIGENCE SUMMARY.

Army Form C. 2118.

Place	Date	Hour	Summary of Events and Information	Remarks and references to Appendices
LES BOEUFS	5/9		38th Bn. M.G.C. Bn. relieved by 21st Bn. & concentrated at LES BOEUFS. Bn. surplus came up early from CONTAL MAISON & packed and accumulated in comp. With tents & material from German Dug-outs	
	6.7 & 8.9		Casualties 3 O.R. Wounded. Bn. rested & refitted. Lt. W.A. HENSHALL rejoined from hospital. 2/Lt. E.A. CLARK B" } P.H. WOODS B" } joined Bn. 2/Lt. HARRISON B" } & T.H. POTTIE E" } when 21 O.R. & O Transport Waggon Capt. WRIGHT returned from leave	
Lechelle	10/9	2.15 p.m.	Move to L'ECHELLE as a battalion. Weather very bad & considerable difficulty was experienced in getting transport out of camp. Assembly Station very bad, in old huts which had been used by Germans on horse lines	Order No 59
Etricourt	11/9		Relieved 17th Bn. in line opposite GOUZEAUCOURT. A & C Coys attached 115 Bn. B " " " 113 " D " " " 114 " 115 Bn. " in left subsection 113 Bn. in right subsection. Disposition of M.G. better shown on a better chart	Order No 60

WAR DIARY
INTELLIGENCE SUMMARY

Army Form C. 2118.

Place	Date	Hour	Summary of Events and Information	Remarks and references to Appendices
Thiepval	11/9		38th Bde M.G.C.	
			Bde Hqrs established alongside Div. H.Q.	
"	12/9		115 Bde covered by A + C Coys attempted to advance left of line in support of N.Z. Div. on our left. Attempt unsuccessful owing to heavy m.g. fire from left flank.	
"	13/9		Arranged redistribution of guns in depth. A Coy in front system covering AFRICAN SUPPORT TRENCH. B + C Coys on main line of resistance in rear of BESSART WOOD. S Coy in close support just N. of FINS–GOUZEAUCOURT Road.	M.G.O. S-9.19
			All coys to use vigorous harassing fire, especially by night. S.O.S. lines worked out for all available guns.	Table Harass-ing etc
			Lt A.J. POWELL 15 (period B)?	
			53 O.R. Killed	
			Casualties 2 O.R. " Wounded	
"	14/9		Nil	

WAR DIARY
INTELLIGENCE SUMMARY

Place: Etricourt

Date	Hour	Summary of Events and Information	Remarks
13/9 14/9		38th Bn M.G.C. Completed redistribution of guns following casualties reported on 14.5. Casualties: Lt. A.J.R. BAMFORD, H.J. TOBIN, 2/Lt. J.H. MATHESON wounded (gassed). O.R. 15 wounded O.R. 1	
17/9	4.0 p.m.	Plan Hqrs moved back to Rocquigny — moving to provisional Brigade Hqrs. H.V. guns forward Hqrs established along C. Bde. Hqn prior E. of BESSART WOOD. Coys redistributed in preparation for forthcoming attack. Casualties 3 O.R. wounded	M.G.B. 5.975 Order No 52
18/9	5.20 a.m.	Div.-attacks in conjunction with rest of IV Corps & Fourth Army. Action of Corps. A. Barrage under O.C. B." B. Predatory Under orders 113 B.de. Two sections went forward with infantry Two sections advanced with of GOUZEAUCOURT. leading War of O.C. B." Barrage under O.C. B."	Fourth Army Order No 51

Army Form C. 2118.

WAR DIARY
or
INTELLIGENCE SUMMARY.
(Erase heading not required.)

Place	Date	Hour	Summary of Events and Information	Remarks and references to Appendices
BESSART WOOD	15/9		"38th Bn. M.G.C."	
			"B" Coy. Under orders 114 Bde. Three sections advanced with infantry to assist in consolidation of final objective. One section barrage.	
			Barrage of all guns was co-ordinated by O.C. "B". Attack my higher. (114 Bde.) was successful. Lieut NEILL with one of the forward sections beat off an attempted counter attack from GOUZEAUCOURT. Lieut WHITE with another forward section accounted for 2 m.g. posts, & greatly assisted infantry in consolidation.	
			Attack on left only partly successful, in extreme left - could not get on.	
			A & C Coys fired two phone barrages during the day to cover attempts to get the left flank forward.	
	9.0 p.m.		A & C Coys fired a barrage on southern edge of GOUZEAUCOURT to cover attempt by 114 Bde. to advance from	

WAR DIARY
INTELLIGENCE SUMMARY

Place	Date	Hour	Summary of Events and Information	Remarks and references to Appendices
			35th Bn M.G.C.	
Bumar Wood	19/9		Final objective to the outskirts of the village. This is noted a Change of direction half left, & it is proved to be unfavorable to reorganize the infantry in time for it.	
			Total rounds fired in barrages 258,000	
			Casualties Killed 1/Lt O.R. Wounded 2/Lt K.R.T. LOW — E.L. HARRISON — H. NELLIS Wounded O.R. 25 Gassed O.R. 15	
	19/20		No change in situation. B & D Coys returned to 175 Bn & moved to Gumcapt lines (near 115)	F.14
			A? Coys disposed to cover front of S.O.S. line for all arms. Casualties Wounded 2/Lt L.V. WHEELER O.R. 4	
Lexain Wood	20/9		B. No change in situation. B & D Coys move back to vicinity of ROEQUIGNY	
	20/21		Remainder of Bn relieved by 17 Bn & moved to Tamhor lines. B Coy joining Bn writ 10 O.R.	F.23
			2/Lt. J.H. WARD & 2/Lt F. WATKINS	

Army Form C. 2118.

WAR DIARY
or
INTELLIGENCE SUMMARY

(Erase heading not required.)

38th Bn M.G.C.

Place	Date	Hour	Summary of Events and Information	Remarks and references to Appendices
BEAULEN- COURT	21/9		Bn Concentrated in Bns Reception Camp. C.O. attend Divs Army Conference of Bn Commanders at BOULLENS. 30 O.R. joined Bn	
"	22/9 (Sunday)		Day spent in making accommodation. Bn Forage team driven Horses etc., & in cleaning up 2/Lt M. FAIRBAIRN } joined Bn 33 O.R.	
"	23/9		Ditto.	
"	24/9		Training - Close Order Drill, Range Practice, gun drill in morning. Recreation - games in afternoon. Officers Baths & rides in evening. Lt-Col A.G. LYTTELTON to U.K. on leave. Major AG return took command of Battalion. 2Lt P. GRAZEBROOK, C.T. } joined Battalion " GLENDENING, V.H. }	
"	25/9		Training as on 24th.	

WAR DIARY or INTELLIGENCE SUMMARY

Army Form C. 2118.

Place	Date	Hour	Summary of Events and Information	Remarks and references to Appendices
BEUVREQUIN	26/9		Training: Range practices, Physical training, simple tactical schemes. Lt. T.R.H. SMYTH 2Lt. W. PROSSER 2Lt. G.L. DURANT } + 45 O.R's joined Battalion. Gassed. O.R. 1.	
	27/9		Training as on 26th. Lt. P.H. JENRICK 2Lt. G.T. VEEK } joined Battalion	
	28/9		Moved to SOREL-LEGRAND as a Battalion 140/m arriving at N.19.G. 7pm. Accommodated in billets hut & tents. Battalion at ordinary notice. Gassed. O.R. 1.	Order No. 613
	29/9 30/9		Day spent in preparation for action, inspections, cleaning etc. do	P.T.O.

Hawkins
Major
Commanding
38th Battn. M.G. Corps

SECRET & URGENT.

38th BATTALION MACHINE GUN CORPS.

ORDER NO.62.

17th September, 1918.

1. Bn.H.Q. closes present H.Q. at 6-30 p.m. today.
   Advanced H.Q. ("G") opens at W.3.a.3.1. same hour.
   Rear H.Q. ("A" & "Q" Branches) opens at O.36.c.5.6. (approx)
   at the same hour.
   All communications other than "G" Branch will be sent to
   Rear H.Q.

2. One cyclist runner per Company will report to rear H.Q.
   this evening and will be attached to Bn.H.Q. until further
   notice.

Issued at 4-30 p.m.

Wright Capt. & Adjt.
38th Battn.M.G.C.

Copy to/
    All M.G.Coys.
    Bn.T.O.
    Q.M.
    Sigl.Offr.
    Intl.Offr.
    R.S.M.
    File.
    War Diary.

G.S.O.1	
G.S.O.2	
G.S.O.3	
G.S.O.4	

WAR DIARY
or
INTELLIGENCE SUMMARY.
(Erase heading not required.)

Instructions regarding War Diaries and Intelligence Summaries are contained in F. S. Regs., Part II. and the Staff Manual respectively. Title pages will be prepared in manuscript.

Place	Date	Hour	Summary of Events and Information	
SCRELLE GRAND	1/10/18		Training carried on – Clock drill, Arms Drill, Rangepractice, Tactical exercise, Pt. Instr.	FRANCE 62c NE
EPEHY	2/10/18		do	do
	3/10/18		Draft of 19 O.R. joined Battalion. Advanced Battn. HQrs established in Railway Cutting S.E. of EPEHY. A & B Companies moved to Gunners in N of PEIZIERES	62 & NW & S.W.
	4/10/18		A Company attacked tactically to 115 Brigade & moved 1700 hrs to BONY	
			B " " " " 113 " 1430 " N. of LEMPIRE.	
			C & D Companies moved to bivouacs W. of PEIZIERES	
			C Company moved 1900 to TOMBOIS FARM (SW. of VENDHUILE) and took up positions in MACQUINCOURT & HIDDEN TRENCHES on ridge in A2 to deal with expected enemy counter attack down rally running NE from RICHMOND QUARRY & COPSE & to deal with any enemy movement in this neighbourhood. Fire not required.	
	5/10/18		115 Brigade relieved Brigade of 50th Div. N of LECATELET "A" Coy. relieved "A" Coy 50th Battn.	
			"D" Company came under orders of 114 Brigade and moved to 520 D. "C" Company (reserve) moved to 520 B. "B" Company moved into line with 113 Brigade which relieved Brigade of 50th on L.of 114 Brigade at AUNZENCHEUR	
			Casualties 1 OR accidentally wounded. 5th Inverness 10R reported from CCS 2Lt E. T. Jones (B) & Sgt Martin (D) to 3rd Army Inf School course	
			Casualties. Killed OR 1 Wd (gas) OR 1	
			Wounded OR 3 Rejoined from CCS OR 1	
	6/10/18			
VENDHUILE	7/10/18		Battn. relvd HBn moved to RICHMOND QUARRY (S28 A). A & C Coys of 33rd Batn. placed under orders of Battn. for coming operation. Casualties. Wounded OR 1	

WAR DIARY
or
INTELLIGENCE SUMMARY.
(Erase heading not required.)

Army Form C. 2118.

Place	Date	Hour	Summary of Events and Information	Remarks and references to Appendices
AUBENCHEUL	8/10/18	01.00	115 Brigade — on right and 113 Bgde — on left — attacked MASNIERES — BEAUREVOIR LINE and moved by S. + N. respectively of VILLERS OUTREAUX to objective E. of village. 'A','B', + 'C' Companies and 'A'+'C' Companies of 38" B attn. covered attack by fire on enemy front + support line, roads, buildings +c. in and around village, ANGELUS ORCHARD + Trenches N.E. thereof + on objective (Road from T.3.a.8.9. — MARLICHE FARM). 'A' + 'B' Companies — when objective gained — took up consolidation positions.	FRANCE 62.B.S.rt. 1/20,000.
		11.00	114 Brigade continued advance to E. of MALINCOURT. half Company of 'D' attached to each Battalion of 114 Bgde (under orders of 114 Bgde) 'C' Company followed and organised defence in depth of objective. 'A' + 'B' Companies covered advance by fire on village + surroundings. Casualties: Killed O.R. 1. Wounded: 2nd Lt. W.A. WHITE " W. PROSSER O.R. 10.	
	9/10/18		33rd Division moved through 114 Bgde + continued advance, meeting with little opposition 'A' Company (115 Bgde) in billets at VILLERS OUTREAUX. B (113 Bgde) moved to billets at MALINCOURT.	

Army Form C. 2118.

WAR DIARY
or
INTELLIGENCE SUMMARY.
(Erase heading not required.)

Instructions regarding War Diaries and Intelligence Summaries are contained in F. S. Regs., Part II. and the Staff Manual respectively. Title pages will be prepared in manuscript.

Place	Date	Hour	Summary of Events and Information	Remarks and references to Appendices
AUBENCHEUL	9/10/18		"C" Company returned to orders of Battalion + were billeted in MALINCOURT. "D" (with 114 Bgde) marched to billets at CLARY. Casualties Killed O.R. 6. 2 Lt. COCKBURN Wounded 18. O.Rs	
BERTRY VILLERS OUTREAUX	10/10/18	Noon	'A' Company proceeded to BERTRY with 115 Bgde. Battn. HQrs moved to VILLERS OUTREAUX. Lt. Col. A.G. LYTTELTON (home leave to U.K.) resumed command of Battalion. Casualties: Wounded O.R. 1 Missing O.R. 2. N.Y.D.(gas) O.R. 2	Order No 64
CLARY	11/10/18	1030	Battn. HQrs. moved to billets at CLARY. Casualties Wounded O.R. 2. Gassed O.R. 2. N.Y.D.N. O.R. 1.	Order No 65
BERTRY	12.10.18		Bn. H.R. marched to BERTRY. Arranged to relief 33rd Bn. on high ground west of SELLE River with "A" C o. but relief postponed 24 hours during the afternoon. B + C Coys to BERTRY 1. O.R. rejoined from hospital	
BERTRY	13.10 /18		A Coy relieved 2 Coys of 33rd Bn. in line. B Coy to TROISVILLES with 114 Bgde. Lt BENSON (A) W/C B: for tour of duty at PENGELLY (B) GRANTHAM	

D. D. & L., London, B.C. (A8001) Wt.W1777/M2031 750,000 5/17 Sch. 83 Forms/C2118/14

Army Form C. 2118.

WAR DIARY
or
INTELLIGENCE SUMMARY.
(Erase heading not required.)

Place	Date	Hour	Summary of Events and Information	Remarks and references to Appendices
BERTRY	19/7/18		8th B". M.G.C.	
			Casualties. Wounded 2 O.R. A Co".	
			1 O.R. injured.	
	15/10/18		2 sections "C" Co" placed in line under orders O.C. "A" Co".	
			Casualties. Wounded 1 O.R. } A. Co.	
			gassed 3 O.R. }	
			2/Lt J. HOWELLS & H.A. POTTER joined B". Posted to "b" & "C"	
	16/10/18		Reconnaissance of battery positions for cooperation in attack of 66th Div.	
			east of LE CATEAU.	
			Casualties. Killed 2 O.R. C.	
			gassed 9 O.R. C.	
	17/10/18		A Co" fired barrage in support of attack of 66th Div.	
			2 sections "C" relieved A & 2 sections "C" in line.	
	18/10/18		B Co" & 2 sections "C" Co" + GRAZEBROOK "A"	
			Casualties. Wounded 2/Lt "A"	
			1 O.R. C Co".	
			gassed 3 O.R.	
			1/Lt G.W. RADFORD # Coy joined B". Draft of 30 O.Rs joined B".	Order to 66
			2/Lt F.C. MILNER }	

E.J. JONES

Army Form C. 2118.

WAR DIARY
or
INTELLIGENCE SUMMARY.
(Erase heading not required.)

Place	Date	Hour	Summary of Events and Information	Remarks and references to Appendices
Bertry	18/10/18		Preparations for forcing the line of the SELLE R. Two Coys 38" B". placed under command of O.C. 38th B". for initial barrage. Casualties 1 O.R. Gassed.	Order No. 67
"	19/10/18		Adv. B" Hqrs. moved to dug-out K.15.a.5.4 under CAMBRAI – LE CATEAU R⁵. "A" & "C" Coys to battery positions "113 B⁹⁵ & "114 B⁹⁵" on right. "B" Coy accompanied "113 B⁹⁵" on right r "114 B⁹⁵". "B" Coy accompanied W⁸ of attack. Assembly positions in valley of SELLE R. Casualties wounded O.R. 1 "B" Coy.	
"	20/10/18		Attack began at 2.0 a.m. M.G. barrage should have started with the Artillery barrage, but owing to the vigorous action of the heavy artillery during the last five minutes before Zero, it began about 20 seconds early & overshadowing. Complete silence before Zero went much matters easier. All objectives reached by 5.50 a.m. about 250 prisoners taken & the same number of dead counted. A & C Coys carried the SELLE Ends in the afternoon & took up barrage positions in Each flank. B & D Coys jogged in defeat for [illegible] Coys 38 B" were in the [illegible]	

Army Form C. 2118.

WAR DIARY
or
INTELLIGENCE SUMMARY.
(Erase heading not required.)

Instructions regarding War Diaries and Intelligence Summaries are contained in F.S. Regs., Part II. and the Staff Manual respectively. Title pages will be prepared in manuscript.

Place	Date	Hour	Summary of Events and Information	Remarks and references to Appendices
K5 a5 4	20/10/18		38th Bn. M.G.C. Casualties Gassed 2 O.R. & a lot of mind. Vigorous harassing fire by all coys.	
"	21/10/18		No cessation. Casualties (A) wounded 2/Lt. M. FAIRBAIRN (A) O.R. 16. "A" 1 "B" 2 "C" 6 "D" 9 Gassed O.R. 4	
	24/10/18	7.0 p.m.	"A" "C" & "D" Coys relieved by 33rd Bn. "B" Coy less two sections remained in action east of SELLE to cover the advance of 15th Div. from LE CATEAU. Remaining 2 sections in Livenne aj. of river. Casualties Killed 2 O.R. "B" "C" Adv. B.H.Q. to BERTRY Wounded 2 O.R. " " "B" " " " 3 O.R. " " "D" " "	W/17 G/24×.15 - W/20 G/22.10.15
"	25/10/18		Attack by 33rd Divn. 38th Bn. in Support. Adv. B.H.Q. at LE CATEAU Rd. as before. A. C & AMERVAL RIDGE with 115 Bde. B Wounded in Guenard on Riv. Rouelle G Coy to FOREST with I 113 Bde B Coy TROISVILLES with 114 Bde.	

WAR DIARY
or
INTELLIGENCE SUMMARY.
(Erase heading not required.)

Army Form C. 2118.

Place	Date	Hour	Summary of Events and Information	Remarks and references to Appendices
K25a&4	23/10/15		35th Bn. M.G.C. Casualties Killed 1 O.R. 1 O.R. Gand 1 O.R. D °	
MONTAY	24/10/15		Bn. remained in support to 35th Bde. Adv. B.H.Q. moved to MONTAY with Div. HQ. "A" Coy moved to CROIX with 115 Bde. Remaining Coys did not move. Rear B.H.Q. TROISVILLES. "A" Coy Killed O.R. 2 "A" Casualties Wounded O.R. 2 "B" Draft of 35 O.R. joined Bn.	
"	25/10/15		"B" Coy moved to RICHEMONT KBEUSE Rear B.H.Q. to MONTAY.	
HERPIES 1914	26/10/15		Bn. relieved 33rd Bde. "A" Coy to line (left) HAM POIX DU NORD "B" " " " (right) " PAUL JACQUES FM "C" " Support " " D " " " Rest Rear B.H.R to " CROIX	

WAR DIARY or INTELLIGENCE SUMMARY

Army Form C. 2118.

Place	Date	Hour	Summary of Events and Information	Remarks and references to Appendices
POIX DU NORD	27/10/15		38th B'n M.G.C. Adv. B.H.Q. moved to POIX DU NORD. Reconnaissance arrangements for Coy's buses & light Railways of fire. Casualties Wounded 3 O.R.	
"	28/10/15		Draft of 25 O.R. joined B'n. RHQ. Nil. Casualties Wounded Major C.A.M. Jackson, 2/Lt C.M. Hawes. Killed 3 O.R. 5 O.R.	
"	29/10/15		Co-operated in raid by 17/R.W.F. 12 guns "A" Coy under Capt. GODDING fire barrage in support of infantry. 6 forward guns "B" Coy engaged any hostile harassment. Return of raid & tracing 15 prisoners & large number of enemy killed. Casualties Wounded Capt. J. Wilkinson 5 O.R.	W.21 2/25.10.15

Army Form C. 2118.

WAR DIARY
~~INTELLIGENCE~~ SUMMARY.
(Erase heading not required.)

Instructions regarding War Diaries and Intelligence Summaries are contained in F. S. Regs., Part II. and the Staff Manual respectively. Title pages will be prepared in manuscript.

38th Bn. M.G.C.

Place	Date	Hour	Summary of Events and Information	Remarks and references to Appendices
Pont Du Nord	30/10/18		Nil. Casualties Killed 4 O.R. Wounded 3 O.R.	
"	31/10/18		Nil. Casualties Wounded 4 O.R. owing to absence of trenches & dugouts & in exposure to proper hostile shelling.	A.G. Littleton Lt Col 38th Bn. M.G.C.

38th. BATTALION MACHINE GUN CORPS.

ORDER No. 64.

1. Bn.H.Q. will move to CLARY to-morrow at 10.30 hours.
   Parade outside Bn.H.Q. at 1025 hours.
2. R.S.M. will detail 2 O.Rs to report to Lieut. GRIFFITH at 09.00 hrs. and will act as billeting party.
3. Officers kits will be dumped at Q.M. Stores by 09.30 hours to-morrow.

W. Knight Capt. & Adjt.
38th Battn. M.G.C.

10th October 1918.
23.20. hours.

Copies to/
All Coys.
H.Q. Officers.   R.S.M.
38th Div. "G".
"   "   "Q".
38th Div. Train.

38th BATTALION MACHINE GUN CORPS.

ORDER No. 65.

1. Bn.H.Q. move to BEUVRY to-morrow. Parade on ground opposite Bn.H.Q. at 10.15 hours.

2. R.S.M. will detail 2 O.Rs on cycles to report to Lieut. GRIFFITH at 09.00 hours and will act as billeting party.

3. Officers kits will be ready at Mess for loading on G.S.Wagon at 09.15 hours.

                                                             Capt. & Adjt.
11th October 1918.   38th Battn.M.G.C.
22.45 hours.

Copy to/
    H.Q.Officers.   R.S.M.
    All Coys.
    38th Div."G".
      "   " "A" & "Q".
      "   " Train.

38th BATTALION MACHINE GUN CORPS.
****

ORDER NO.66.

18th October, 1918.

1. To-morrow night, 17th/18th instant, "B" Coy. 38th Battn. M.G.C. will relieve "A" Coy. 38th Battn. M.G.C.
   Details to be arranged between Company Commanders concerned.
   Note: "B" Coy. will occupy "A" Coy's dispositions as on morning of 16th instant, not the Battery positions.

2. "C" Coy. will arrange to relieve their two Sections at present in the line – relieving two Sections "C" Coy. to be attached to "B" Coy. for duty and discipline only.

3. Relief to be complete by 8-0 p.m. Completion will be wired to Bn.H.Q. by Code Word "CYNTHIA".

4. Os.C., A.B. & C. Coys. to acknowledge.

                                      Capt. & Adjt.
16.00 hrs.   38th Battn.M.G.Corps.

Copy to/
   Os.C.
     A.B.C. & D.Coys.
     Bn.T.O.   38th Divn. "G".   )
     Q.M.   113th Brigade.   )
     File.   114th   "   ) for
     War Diary.   115th   "   ) information.
                  38th Divn. "Q" %)
                  "   " Train.   )

SECRET.

38th BATTALION MACHINE GUN CORPS

ORDER NO. 67.

19th October, 1918.   Copy No. 15

Reference Map, 57.B.,N.E. 1/20,000.

1. The Third Army is attacking on the night 19th/20th instant.

    The 38th Division is attacking with objectives and boundaries as shown on the attached map.
    113th Brigade is attacking on the right, 114th Brigade on the left.
    Fourth Army is not attacking.
    Zero hour will be notified later.

2. 38th Battalion Machine Gun Corps (less 2 Companies) and two Coys. 33rd Battn.M.G.Corps will cover the advance as follows :-

Group	No. of guns	1st Target Co-ordinate	Time	2nd Target Co-ordinate	Time	Rate of fire
No. 1(a)	4 guns "C" Coy. 33rd Battn.M.G.C.	K.17.c.3.7.				
	4 guns "C" Coy. 33rd Battn.M.G.C.	K.9.d.90.75. K.16.b.7.5		K.17.a.3.7.		
1(b)	8 guns "C" Coy. 33rd Battn.M.G.C.	K.16.d.8.5.		K.17.b.2.8.		
2(a)	4 guns "A" Coy. 33rd Battn.M.G.C.	K.16.b.7.5.				
	4 guns "A" Coy. 33rd Battn.M.G.C.	K.16.b.2.9.		K.10.d.5.6.		
2(b)	8 guns "A" Coy. 33rd Battn.M.G.C.	K.10.c.1.5.		K.10.b.5.6.		
3(a)	8 guns "A" Coy. 38th Battn.M.G.C.	K.16.d.85.	.50.	NIL		
3(b)	8 guns "A" Coy. 38th Battn.M.G.C.	K.17.c.1.3.				
4(a)	8 guns "C" Coy. 38th Battn.M.G.C.	K.16.b.1.3.				
4(b)	8 guns "C" Coy. 38th Battn.M.G.C.	K.9.d.9.6.				
5(a)	3 guns "B" Coy. 38th Battn.M.G.C.	K.23.a.4.5.				
(b)	3 guns "B" Coy. 38th Battn.M.G.C.	K.23.a.7.9.		K.17.b.1.5.		

NOTE: Reference columns a & b co-ordinates given represent centre of area to be covered evenly ; 30 yards of front per gun on area shown on attached tracing.

1.

2.

3. When the final objective is reached, "A" & "C" Companies, 38th Battn.M.G.Corps will advance to positions about K.17.c.1.4. and K.10.d.2.8. respectively to barrage a line -
"A" Coy....K.12.b.9.6. - L.7.c.5.5.
"C" Coy....K.6.d.5.7. - K.12.b.9.6.

Companies 33rd Battn.M.G.C. will remain in position and will be prepared to open fire against any attack directed against flanks of 38th Division.
Guns of 25th Battn.M.G.C. (attached 66th Division) are co-operating by maintaining a slow rate of fire on the ravines North of RICHMONT HILL.

4. Twelve foot-bridges over the SELLE River are allotted to each attacking Brigade ; their positions and markings have been communicated to all concerned.
Artillery bridges will be constructed at K.16.c.0.5. and K.15.d.7.7. and the track will be marked to these bridges from the road junction K.25.a.6.0. through K.21.c. & a.

5. One tank is co-operating with each Brigade and will cross the river at the bridge K.16.c.0.5.

6. After the final objective is reached, Brigades, after 06.00 hrs. are establishing an outpost line in advance thereof and exploiting forward by means of strong patrols and cyclists as far as the line - K.12.d.9.0. - Road Junction K.6.c.2.2. - Road RICHMONT K.5.b.
Artillery and Machine Guns will not fire West of this line except in the case of observed fire.

7. The action of our aircraft will be as usual ; a red smoke bomb denotes assembly for counter-attack.

8. Battn.Headquarters will be established at K.25.d.7.4. at 17.00 hrs. 19th October.
Group H.Qrs. 1....K.26.c.8.4.
"   "   2....
"   "   3....K.20.d.5.1.
"   "   4....K.19.d.3.9.
"   "   5....K.27.c.3.8.

Signal Officer will connect Battn.H.Qrs. with Group Headquarters by wire. Two runners per Group will report to K.25.d.7.4. at 17-30 hrs. 19th October. Watches - 1 per battery - will be synchronised at Battn. H.Qrs. at 18-30 hrs. 19th Octr.

9. Addressees marked * to ACKNOWLEDGE by wire.

Lieut-Colonel,
Commanding, 38th Battn.M.G.Corps.

Issued at 11-00 hrs.

Copies to/
    ?s.C.,
    * A,B, & C. Coys.38th Battn.M.G.C.   38th Divn, "G",)
    * A + C   Coys.33rd Battn.M.G.C.   "   "   "Q",) for
                                                        33rd Battn.M.G.C.) infn.
    File.   113th Brigade,   )
    War Diary.   114th Brigade,   )
                                           25th Battn MGC.

SECRET
M.G.C./B.208.

38th BATTALION MACHINE GUN CORPS.

Reference Order No.67. - para.2 :-

Times and rates of fire will be as follows :-

Group.	Time.	Rate of fire.
FIRST TARGET.		
All Groups. *(except 5(a) ... Z to Z+15 ; 5(b) ... Z to Z+20)*	Zero to Zero plus 3 mins.	250 rounds per minute. *250 RPM. for 1st 3 mins / 100 " Remainder*
SECOND TARGET.		
No.1(a)	Z. plus 3 mins. to Z. plus 35 "	100 rounds per minute.
No.1(b)	Z. plus 5 mins. to Z. plus 45 "	100 rounds per minute.
No.2(a)	Z. plus 5 mins. to Z. plus 35 "	100 rounds per minute.
No.2(b)	Z. plus 5 mins. to Z. plus 35 "	100 rounds per minute.
No.5(a)	Z. plus 5 *(20)* mins. to Z. plus 45 "	100 rounds per minute.

19th Octr.1918,
11-30 hrs.

Lieut-Colonel
Commanding, 38th Battn. M.G. Corps.

Copy to all recipients of Order No.67.

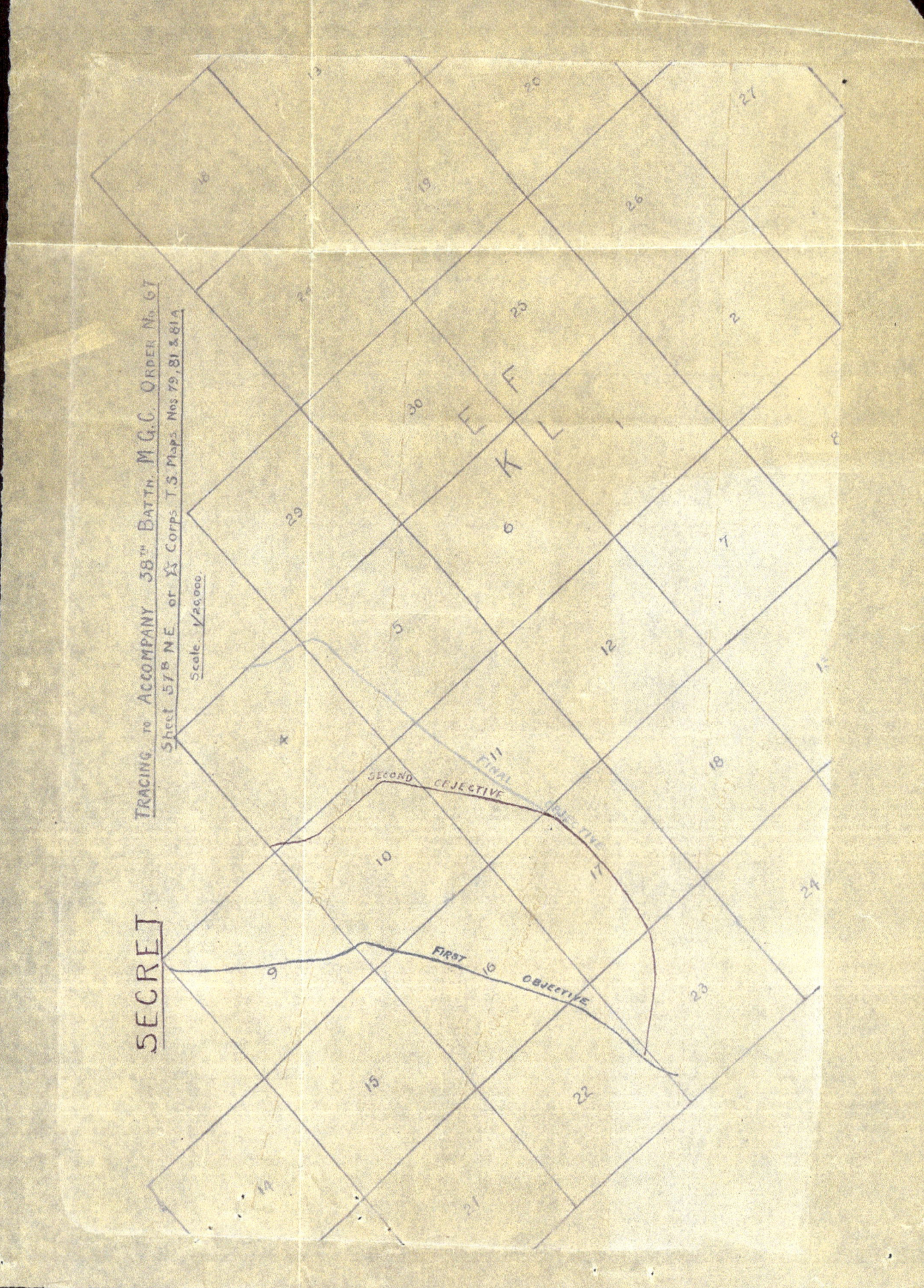

Secret   A, B, C, D Coys, Aus B.H.Q.
                                   N 17
                                   21.10.15

1. The 33rd Division are assembling on this Bde
frontage tomorrow night to continue the attack.
2. Place of assy to be notified later. B. & Q.
it and C Coys will move to TROISVILLES
O.C. New B.H.Q. will detail an officer to
arrange billets with Town Major (who lives at
BERTRY) and will notify billeting parties of
all concerned. If possible new B.H.Q's & H.Q.
will be accommodated in TROISVILLES
tomorrow.
Communication. C.H.Q. will connect with 113 Inf.
Bde which moves to TROISVILLES tomorrow.
3. A and D Coys will be under orders of O.C.
33rd Bn att'd tomorrow night to form a covering
barrage. Details later.
4. At 0500 hours 23rd inst 33 Bn att'd will
be at our disposal to move forward. The
following is to be given to which 105 Inf Bde,
113 Inf Bde, & 1st B.K.B. to which attached
respectively. Still no orders.

Secret. 22.10.18 W 20

1. Reference W 17 dated 21.10.18
   cancel para. 3: remainder holds good.

2. D Coy 38 Bn MGC will pull out
   when relieved by 33 Bn MGC to
   Irouvilles
   # 2 Sections B Coy 38 Bn MGC will also
   move to Irouvilles when relieved
   by 33 Bn MGC.
   Lt Stewart D Coy will arrange
   coy billets (evacuated by 2 MG Coys
   33 Bn MGC or there vacated by 19th
   Bde at 16.00 hrs today).
   He will allot sufficient accomod
   for 2 Sections B Coy. (Rear HQ.
   B Coy. J 35 c 2.0)

3. 8 Guns B Coy will remain at
   K 13 a 4.5 and fire barrage
   to support attack by 18 Bn.
   (issued separately) and will
   remain in position until

Page 2

4. Adv. H.Q. B Coy will be K.25.d.7.4 from 18.15 hours onwards & will be in telephonic communication with 115 Adv. Exchange K.25.d.7.4

5. Acknowledge.

Copies to/
B Coy } 38 Bn H.Q.C
D Coy }

15.40 hours

W Wright Capt & Adjt
38 Bn Inf C

SECRET.

W.21.

38th BATTALION MACHINE GUN CORPS.

28-10-18.

Reference Maps. - 51.A. N.W., 57.A. N.E., 51.S.W., & 57.A. N.W.

1. At 08.00 hours to-morrow, infantry of the 115th Brigade are forming up on line as per attached tracing, and are raiding as far as objective shown. The raid will be covered by machine guns of "A" Coy as detailed below.

2.

No. of Task.	No. of Guns.	Position.	Target.	Time of Fire.	Rate.
1.	4 8	I) II)	A	Z to Z plus 2	250 r.p.m.
2	4	I	A2	Z plus 2 to Z plus 60.	100 r.p.m. Z plus 2 to Z plus 12.
	2	II	B	Z plus 2 to Z plus 12.	50 r.p.m. Z plus 2 to Z plus 30.
	6	II	C	Z plus 2 to Z plus 60.	100 rpm. Z plus 30 to Z plus 33.
3	2	II	C	Z plus 12 to Z plus 60.	50 rpm. Z plus 33 to Z plus 60.

3. The six forward guns in S.25.a., S.9.d., S.26.a. will fire on any hostile movement clear of friendly troops.

4. Capt.A.C.GODDING M.C. will be Group Commander H.Q. X.29.d.3.4. One runner will be ~~detailed~~ sent to Bn.H.Q.(Adv.) for any messages.

5. M.G's will take Zero time from the opening of the Artillery barrage.

6. "A" Coy.M.G.C. to acknowledge.

(sd) W.WRIGHT. Capt. & Adjt.
38th Bn.M.G.C.

Issued to runners 20.00 hours.

Copies to/
1. "A" Coy.M.G.C.
2. 115th Inf.Bde.
3. "B" Coy.M.G.C.
4 & 5. File.

Date .... Signature ....

of the 1: .... map of ....

Tracing taken from Sheet ....

	Sheet 51 SE (A)	Sheet 51 SW	
			Target C
			Target B / Target A2 / Objective / Target A1
	24	19	20
8 guns A Coy Position 2		2 guns	Forming Up Line / 2 guns
4 guns Position 1	30 X	25 S	26
			Scale 1:20,000 Date 28.10.18

SECRET.
****

38th BATTALION MACHINE GUN CORPS.

ORDER NO.67.

19th October, 1918.

Copy No. 6

[Stamp: GENERAL STAFF, 38th (WELSH) DIVISION. M.V. 146 Date 19.10.18]

Reference Map, 57.B., N.E. 1/20,000.

1. The Third Army is attacking on the night 19th/20th instant.

    The 38th Division is attacking with objectives and boundaries as shown on the attached map.
    113th Brigade is attacking on the right; 114th Brigade on the left.
    Fourth Army is not attacking.
    Zero hour will be notified later.

2. 38th Battalion Machine Gun Corps (less 2 Companies) and two Coys. 33rd Battn.M.G.Corps will cover the advance as follows :-

Group.	No. of guns.	1st Target Co-ordinate	Time	2nd Target Co-ordinate	Time	Rate of Fire.
No. 1(a)	4 guns "C" Coy.33rd Battn.M.G.C.	K.17.c.3.7.				
	4 guns "C" Coy.33rd Battn.M.G.C.	K.9.d.90.75. K.16.b.75		K.17.a.3.7.		
1(b)	8 guns "C" Coy.33rd Battn.M.G.C.	K.16.d.8.5.		K.17.b.2.8.		
2(a)	4 guns "A" Coy.33rd Battn.M.G.C.	K.16.b.7.5.				
	4 guns "A" Coy.33rd Battn.M.G.C.	K.16.b.2.9.		K.10.d.5.6.		
2(b)	8 guns "A" Coy.33rd Battn.M.G.C.	K.10.c.1.5.		K.10.b.5.6.		
3(a)	8 guns "A" Coy.38th Battn.M.G.C.	K.16.d.85.50.		NIL		
3(b)	8 guns "A" Coy.38th Battn.M.G.C.	K.17.c.1.3.				
4(a)	8 guns "C" Coy.38th Battn.M.G.C.	K.16.b.1.9.				
4(b)	8 guns "C" Coy.38th Battn.M.G.C.	K.9.d.9.6.				
5(a)	3 guns "B" Coy.38th Battn.M.G.C.	K.23.a.4.5.				
	5 guns "B" Coy.38th Battn.M.G.C.	K.23.a.7.9.		K.17.b.1.5.		

[Stamps: G.S.O.1 / G.S.O.2 / G.S.O.3 / G.S.O.4]

Note : Reference columns 3 & 5 co-ordinates given represent centre of area to be covered evenly ; 30 yards of front per gun on area shown on attached tracing.

1.

3. When the final objective is reached, "A" & "C" Companies, 38th Battn.M.G.Corps will advance to positions about K.17.c.1.4. and K.10.d.2.8. respectively to barrage a line –
"A" Coy.....K.12.b.9.6. – L.7.c.5.5.
"C" Coy.....K.6.d.5.7. – K.12.b.9.6.

Companies 33rd Battn.M.G.C. will remain in position and will be prepared to open fire against any attack directed against flanks of 38th Division.
Guns of 25th Battn.M.G.C. (attached 66th Division) are co-operating by maintaining a slow rate of fire on the ravines North of RICHMONT HILL.

4. Twelve foot-bridges over the SELLE River are allotted to each attacking Brigade ; their positions and markings have been communicated to all concerned.
Artillery bridges will be constructed at K.16.c.0.5. and K.15.d.7.7. and the track will be marked to these bridges from the road junction K.25.a.6.0. through K.21.c. & a.

5. One tank is co-operating with each Brigade and will cross the River at the bridge K.16.c.0.5.

6. After the final objective is reached, Brigades, after 06.00 hrs. are establishing an outpost line in advance thereof and exploiting forward by means of strong patrols and cyclists as far as the line – K.12.d.0.0. – Road Junction K.6.c.2.2. – Road RICHMONT K.5.b.
Artillery and Machine Guns will not fire West of this line except in the case of observed fire.

7. The action of our aircraft will be as usual ; a <u>red</u> smoke bomb denotes assembly for counter-attack.

8. Battn.Headquarters will be established at K.25.d.7.4. at 17.00 hrs.19th October.
Group H.Qrs. 1....
" " 2....K 26 C 8 4
" " 3....K.20.d.5.1.
" " 4....K.19.d.5.9.
" " 5....K 27 C 3 8

Signal Officer will connect Battn.H.Qrs. with Group Headquarters by wire. Two runners per Group will report to K.25.d.7.4. at 17-30 hrs. 19th October. Watches – 1 per battery – will be synchronised at Battn. H.Qrs. at 18-30 hrs. 19th Octr.

9. Addressees marked * to ACKNOWLEDGE by wire.

Lieut-Colonel.
Commanding, 38th Battn.M.G.Corps.

Issued at 11-00 hrs.

Copies to/
    ?s.C.,
    * A,B. & C. Coys.38th Battn.M.G.C.   38th Divn. "G".)
    * A + C   Coys.33rd Battn.M.G.C.   " " "Q".)for
                                         33rd Battn.M.G.C.)infn.
    File.   113th Brigade.
    War Diary.   114th Brigade.
                                        25th Battn MGC.

SECRET.
****

M.G.B./S.208.

38th BATTALION MACHINE GUN CORPS.

Reference Order No.87. - para.2 :-

G.S. 146
19/10/18

Times and rates of fire will be as follows :-

Group.	Time.	Rate of fire.

FIRST TARGET.

All Groups.	Zero to Zero plus 3 mins.	250 rounds per minute.
5(a)	Z to Z+15	250 RPM for 1st 3 mins
5(b)	Z to Z+20	100 " " Remainder

SECOND TARGET.

No.1(a)	Z. plus 3 mins. to Z. plus 35 "	100 rounds per minute.
No.1(b)	Z. plus 5 mins. to Z. plus 45 "	100 rounds per minute.
No.2(a)	Z. plus 5 mins. to Z. plus 35 "	100 rounds per minute.
No.2(b)	Z. plus 5 mins. to Z. plus 35 "	100 rounds per minute.
No.5(a)	Z. plus 20 mins. to Z. plus 45 "	100 rounds per minute.

19th Octr.1918.
11-30 hrs.

Lieut-Colonel
Commanding, 38th Battn.M.G.Corps.

Copy to all recipients of Order No.87.

38th BATTALION MACHINE GUN CORPS.

ORDER NO. 68.

11th November 1918.

1. To-morrow the 12th inst. "A" & "D" Coys will move to AULNOYE area. "D" Coy will clear Cross Roads D.3.c.8.0. at 11.00 hours. "A" Coy will clear the same point at 13.30 hours.

2. Billeting parties of 1 Officer & 4 O.Rs will report to Lieut. F.S. GRIFFITH at Bn.H.Q. at 11.30 hours to-morrow. Lieut. CULHANE will allot Transport areas for the above companies.

Issued at 16.00 hours.

[signature]
Capt. & Adjt.
38th Battn.M.G.C.

Copy to/

O.C., "A" Coy.   R.Sgt.
"   "D" "   File.
2.C.   War Diary.
Lieut. Griffith.
"   Culhane.
O.M.

989

CONFIDENTIAL

WAR DIARY
of 38th. Battn. M.G.Corps
From 1st. to 30th. November. 1918

Vol: 9

Despatched 7.11.18

Army Form C. 2118.

WAR DIARY
or
INTELLIGENCE SUMMARY.

(Erase heading not required.)

Place	Date	Hour	Summary of Events and Information	Remarks and references to Appendices
Poix du Nord	Nov 1st		35th Bn M.G.C. Conference at Bde Hqs attended by C.O. Subject: forthcoming attacks on FORET de MORMAL Casualties Wounded 2 O.R. (1 at duty) 2/Lt. E.G. HORNE joined Bn, posted to "A" Coy	
"	2nd		Casualties Gased 2 O.R. "C" Wounded 1 O.R. "B" Preparation of battery positions in connection with forthcoming attack.	
"	3rd	4.0 pm	B.H.Q. moved to ENGLE FONTAINE All coys moved to battery positions at dusk Casualties Wounded O.R. 2 "B" & R&Q Gased O.R. 11 "C"	W 24 W 24/1 By 4 W 24/1 9/3/11/15

D. D. & L., London, E.C. (AF001) Wt. W1771/M2031 750,000 5/17 Sch. 52 Forms/C2118/4

Army Form C. 2118.

WAR DIARY
or
INTELLIGENCE SUMMARY.
(Erase heading not required.)

Place	Date	Hour	Summary of Events and Information	Remarks and references to Appendices
FORET DE MORMAL	4/11	5:30	39 B.M.G.C. Attack opened on left of 38th Divn. Counter-barrage put down on our front.	W 24 1/3/11/15
		6:15	Our attack launched. All core fired barrage as ordered. It was not possible to support infantry very closely owing to the trees & the danger of bullets ricochetting. Counter-barrage heavy especially on night's casualties in "C" & "D" positions heavy. This is the first time since the Bn was formed that a battery has been badly shelled while firing a barrage. 115 Bde. captured 1st objective, the Blue line. 115 " accompanied by "C" Coy. leapfrogged through 115 Bde. & took 2nd objective the Red line, 4 guns only of "C" were able to get forward, remainder being out of action from casualties to teams. 114 Bde. accompanied by "A" Coy. (12 guns only in action) captured 3rd + 4th Objectives, Brown & Green lines. All above moves were completed according to time table. B & D Coys remained in position ready to move forward to consolidate Final objective in Japan.	

WAR DIARY or INTELLIGENCE SUMMARY

Army Form C. 2118.

Place	Date	Hour	Summary of Events and Information	Remarks and references to Appendices
FORET de MORMAL	4th Nov.	1.0 a.m.	38th Bde M.G.C.	

"B" & "D" Coys tried to limber up & advance. Some delay was caused by casualties to officers & the "B" Coy O.iD was sent for some hour. "D" Coy were established in battery positions covering green line by 4.30 a.m. Getting limbers through the forest presented some difficulties on the by roads & paths were blocked by trees felled by shell fire, & the main roads had been mined by the enemy. "D" Coy with only 1 officer left bivouacked near the ROUTE DU CHÊNE CUPLET.

B.H.Q. established with 114 Bde Hgrs on R. du Chêne CUPLET.

Firing a barrage in support of the initial attack & then advancing to consolidate the line of 4 objective is a big job for a Coy to undertake.

Casualties: Killed D.R 4 (3 "C", 1 "B") O.R 40 (33 "C", 7 "B")

        Wounded Lt Gwawr A)
                       2nd Lt Back)
                       2nd Lt G.L DURANT)
                       Lt POWELL) B
                       2nd Lt JONES)

WAR DIARY
INTELLIGENCE SUMMARY

Army Form C. 2118.

Place	Date	Hour	Summary of Events and Information	Remarks and references to Appendices
FORET DE MORMAL	Nov 5th 1918	4.30 a.m.	35th = Bⁿ M.G.C. 33rd Divⁿ passed through to continue the advance. Bⁿ moved as follows: H^q + B + D Coy's with 115 B^{de} to bivouac near CROISILLES INN with 114 + 115 B^{de}. A + C Coy remained in Henry Farm. All ranks spent a poor day + night. Casualties Wounded 5 O.R. "B"	Heavy rain
	Nov 6th		A few tents used for accommodation of men but orders to move forward were received soon after noon	
		13.15	B.H.Q. marched to billets at SARTRARAS "B" + D Coys to RIBAUMET + BERLAIMONT A + C as above all in billets Casualties. Killed 1 O.R. "B" Gassed 1 O.R. "C"	

Army Form C. 2118.

WAR DIARY
or
INTELLIGENCE SUMMARY.
(Erase heading not required.)

Place	Date	Hour	Summary of Events and Information	Remarks and references to Appendices
SART BARAS to AULNOYE	Nov 7	1400	35th Bn M.G.C. Received orders to move across SAMBRE with whole Bn less 2 sections A & C Coys which were to accompany 114 B^{de} & 115 B^{de} on pack transport. Owing to the orders being very clear not being accompanying them. Crossed SAMBRE without any guns accompanying them. Arrangements altered accordingly, but owing to lack of bridges over river & congested state of roads movements were not completed till early following morning. Dispositions as follows:- B.H.Q. AULNOYE A Coy to AVESNES - MAUBEUGE Rd with 113 B^{de} B " AULNOYE C " 1 sec^n AULNOYE (attached 115 B^{de}) 2 sec^n BERLAIMONT D " ECUELIN with 114 B^{de} Casualties. Killed O.R. 1 "B" 1 Wounded O.R. 13 "B" 13 Gassed O.R. 1 "B" 2 Capt. J. SMITH rejoined from leave, took over command of "B" Coy. 2/Lt E.T. JONES joined Coy.	

Army Form C. 2118.

WAR DIARY
or
INTELLIGENCE SUMMARY.
(Erase heading not required.)

Place	Date	Hour	Summary of Events and Information	Remarks and references to Appendices
AULNOYE	8/11/18		35th Bn M.G.C. Stay spent reorganizing, moving up new echelons of transport & 2 reserve sections "C" & "D" Coy. "A" Coy with 113 Bde made an advance to high ground west of MAUBEUGE - AVESNES Road. Capt R.H. Jones joined B & took over "B" Coy & L. Smith took over "D" Coy. Major H. Williamson transferred for town of July at home on expiration of leave.	
	9/11/18		German retreated. 113 Bde & "A" Coy moved to WATTIGNIES. Further advance of Div impossible till communications improved. Major A.C. McCann rejoined from CAHIERS Casualties Killed 1 O.R. "A" Coy wounded 1 O.R. "D" Coy Major J.H.S. Gibson Instructional Staff CAHIERS attached to B"	

Army Form C. 2118.

WAR DIARY
or
INTELLIGENCE SUMMARY.
(Erase heading not required.)

Instructions regarding War Diaries and Intelligence Summaries are contained in F.S. Regs., Part II. and the Staff Manual respectively. Title pages will be prepared in manuscript.

Place	Date	Hour	Summary of Events and Information	Remarks and references to Appendices
AULNOYE	10/11/18		35th Bn - M.G.C. Nil. Casualties Wounded 1 O.R. "A" Draft of 6 officers + 73 O.R. joining Bn. at B.R. EDWARDS } to "A" Coy LISCOMBE } 2/Lt H.J. WHEELOCK } to "B" F.G. RITCHIE } 2/Lt J.F. DEVEREUX } to "C" L. HOUSTON }	
"	11/11/18	11.0	Hostilities ceased. L.O.R. rejoining from C.C.S.	
"	12/11/18		Bn concentrated at AULNOYE Major W.L. ANDERSON rejoined from leave.	App. No 39

WAR DIARY
~~INTELLIGENCE SUMMARY~~

Army Form C. 2118.

Place	Date	Hour	Summary of Events and Information	Remarks and references to Appendices
HuNOYE	13/11/18		38th Bn M.G.C. Major F.M.S. GIBSON returned to CAMIERS. 1 Signaller joined Bn.	
	14/11/18		Major C.A.M. JACKSON rejoined Bn & took on command of "A" Coy. Organisation of games, recreation, improvement of billets & refitting generally begun.	
	15/11/18		2/Lt W.A.A. WHITE "D" Coy awarded V.C. Major F.C. W.TAYLOR to England on 1 month's leave.	
	16/11/18		Draft of 1 off: 2/Lt H MAKIN ("B" Coy) & draft of 72 O.R. joined Bn. Lt MEESON to Home establishment for tour of duty.	
	17/11/18		Draft of 9 O.Rs joined Bn. Thanksgiving Church Parade Service	

Army Form C. 2118.

WAR DIARY
or
INTELLIGENCE SUMMARY.
(Erase heading not required.)

Place	Date	Hour	Summary of Events and Information	Remarks and references to Appendices
Ambros	19/11/18 20 21		38th Bn M.G.C. Nil. Training such as ceremonial drill, route-marches in morning training in afternoon.	
	22/11/18		Draft of 3 officers & 25 O.R. joined Bn 2/Lt S. ANDREWS " A.J. Jones	
	23/11/18		Major A.E. McCANN to England on leave. Major W.C. ATKINSON took over 2 i/c. Capt. J. SMITH took over command of "B" Coy Ceremonial parade for presentation of medals by G.O.C. Div.	
	24/11/18		Nil.	
	25/11/18		Bn played 1st round in Rugby football competition v Div. Signals Won 1 try to nil	
	26/11/18		Nil.	

Army Form C. 2118.

WAR DIARY
or
INTELLIGENCE SUMMARY.
(Erase heading not required.)

Place	Date	Hour	Summary of Events and Information	Remarks and references to Appendices
Belvoir	27/4/18		Guns found & attached 2nd & 13th R.W.T. for instruction.	
	28/4/18		Nil	
	29/4/18		Capt. G.J. Norris to 9th Staff course Grantham. Draft of 12 O.R. joined Bn	
	30/4/18		Grant Cross Country Run v. 130 Field Ambulance. Tied for 1st place	

A.G. Lyttelton Lt-Col
38th Bn M.G.C.

Secret   38 Bn M.G.C.   Copy No W.24

Reference: Maps 51A S.E. 51 S.W. and attached
            57A N.E 57A N.W. tracing X.

1. At a time and date to be notified later
the 38 Div. is attacking on a one Brigade
Front. The 115 Bde ␣␣ capturing the
Blue Line, the 113 Bde the Red Line and
the 114 Bde the Brown & the Green Lines.

2. 38 Bn M.G.C. will support the attack with
First task overhead fire as follows:

Coy.	No of guns	Battery Posⁿ	Target	Time of fire	Rate
A	16	F12a 25.95 to " 25.45	A₁	Z+45 to +47	250 R.P.M
B	16	S25 b 0.3 S25 b 0.0	B₁	do.	do
C	16	F12a 15.30 to F12a 15.00	C₁	do.	do.
D	16	S29 d 6.0 to S29 d 45.75	D₁	do	do

Second Task.

Each Company will fire on its second

Page 2

(2.g. A Coy. Target A₂) from plus 47 to plus 65 at 100 R.P.M.

Time for opening fire will be taken from the watch with no reference to the opening of the artillery barrage.

Note Company Commanders will picquet the danger area in front of their guns.

3. Synchronisation. One officer per Coy will be at BHQ adv. to synchronise watches at 17.00 hours and 21.00 hours on Y day.

4. Rendezvous. On completion of the barrage A and C Coys. will come under the orders of 114 and 115 Inf Bdes respectively.

A Coy. A Coy will send (a) 2 sections forward with 15 Bn Welsh Regt, along line Route defileg. one of these will be detailed to support (direct) advance of 14 Bn Welsh Regt in A.5.b. Both sections will finally assist consolidation of the Green Line.

(b) One section to consolidate XRoads S 30 d 3.4

Page 3.

One section will be kept in Reserve in vicinity of A 6 d 0.3.

C Coy. O.C. C Coy will send one section to consolidate X roads S29 a 15.25. and 3 sections to support 118 Inf Bde advance from Blue line to Route du Chene Cuplet: 2 sections to positions in Blue line in A 3 d; and one section in A 9 b.
  Afterwards they will move to consolidate Red line.

B and D Coys. O's C B and D Coys will be prepared to move forward at a moment's notice by 10.30 hours (wheels as far as possible) pack transport afterwards.)
  Probable moves ① To A 10 a
                  ② To vicinity of Green line, to assist in consolidation.

Officers commanding companies attached to Inf Bdes will ensure that closest co-operation is maintained.

Page 4

Machine guns Bttn. H.Q. will close at F 4 c 7.4
and reopen at A1 d 6 2 at [crossed out]
14.30 hours on Y day
D Coy adv. will move to Dickens X 29
[illegible] and B Coy also to [illegible]
(H.Q. to be [illegible] as soon as possible)
be the same hours

6   M.G. Coys to acknowledge

6.   to [illegible]
                             left rest
Casualty   3 [illegible]

[illegible list on left:]
5-6   [illegible]
7   [illegible]
8   [illegible]
9-10 [illegible]
11-12 [illegible]

Secret 38 Dn M.G.C. W 24/1
          Addendum to W 24 of 2.11.18   3 Nov 18

All Companies will move to Battery
Positions at dusk 3/day. In case
of an S.O.S. signal each Battery
will open rapid fire on
the lines of final target for 5
minutes and gradually reduce
fire with the artillery. Acknowledge
                                    (M.G. Corps only)
Copies to recipients of W 24.

Issued at 10.45 hours.   W.M.G[?]
                              Capt. & Adjt
                            38 Dn M.G.C

Secret   38 Bn M.G.C.   Copy No. 10

Reference: Maps 51B SE 51B NE and attached
57A NE 57D NW tracing X

1. At a time and date to be notified later the 38 Div.
is attacking on a one Bde. Front. The 115 Bde is
capturing the Blue Line, the 113 Bde the Red Line and
the 114 Bde the Brown & the Green Lines

2. 38 Bn M.G.C. will support the attack with over-
head fire as follows:

First Task

Coy	No of Guns	Battery Posn	Target	Range of Elev	Rate
A	16	F12a 35.95 to " 25.45	A1	Z+45 to +47	250 R.P.M
B	16	S25 b 0.3 S25 b 0.0	B1	do	do
C	16	F12a 15.30 to F12a 15.00	C1	do	do
D	16	S29 d 6.0 to S29 d 45.75	D1	do	do

Second Task

Each Company will fire on its second target

Page 2

(B.J. A Coy Target A2) from plus 47 to plus 65 at 100 R.P.M.

Time for opening fire will be taken from the watch with no reference to the opening of the Artillery barrage

NOTE Company Commanders will picquet the danger area in front of their guns

3. Synchronization One officer per Coy will be at B.H.Q. add to synchronise watches at 17.00 hrs and 21 hrs on Y day.

4. The Advance On completion of the barrage A & C. Coys will come under the orders of 114 & 115 Inf Bdes respectively.

A. Coy. B. Coy will send (a) 2 Sections forward with 15 Bn. Welsh Regt along line ROUTE dE HECQ: one of them will be detailed to support direct advance of 14 Bn Welsh Regt in A5.b. Both sections will finally assist consolidation of the Gun line.

(b) One Section to consolidate X Roads 580 d 3.4

One Section will be kept in Reserve in vicinity of A6d03

Page 3

6. O.C. C Coy will send one section to consolidate X roads S.29.a.15.25 and 3 sections to support 113 Inf Bde advance from Blue line to ROUTE on their Objet,
2 sections to positions in Blue line in A.3.d and one section in A.9.b.
Afterwards they will move to consolidate Red line
B and D Coys O.C. B & D Coys will be prepared to move forward at a moment's notice by 12.30hrs (wheels as far as possible) pack transport afterwards
  Probable move (1) To A.10.a
                 2. To vicinity of Green line
                 to assist in consolidation
Officers Commanding Companies attached to Inf Bdes will ensure that closest co-operation is maintained

5 Headquarters Adv. H.Q. will close at F.4.c.7.4 and reopen at A.8.6.2 at 14.30 hours on Y day
D Coy Adv will move to TUILERIES X.29.d and B. Coy Adv to ENGLEFONTAINE
B.H.Q to be notified as soon as possible by the same hour

Page 2

B & G Companies to acknowledge

W Wright Capt. & Adjt.
38th Batt. C.E.F.

Copies to:
1-4 All Coys
5-7 Inf Bdes
8 Rear B.H.Q.
9-10 Div G.
11-12 File & H.Q.

G.S.O. 1
G.S.O. 2
G.S.O. 3
G.S.O. 4

Secret. 38 Bn M.G. No. M 149 W 24/1
Date. 3-11-18 3-XI-18
19r
1Q

Addendum to W24 of 2.XI.18.
M.G. Companies will move to Battery Positions
at dusk Y day. In case of S.O.S.
signal Each Battery will open
rapid fire on the lines of its first
target for 5 minutes: and gradually
reduce fire with the Artillery.
M.G. Coys to acknowledge.
Copies to recipients of W24.   Colonel etc
                                         38 Bn M.G. Capt & Adjt

Issued 10.45 hrs.

38th Battn. M.C.C.
Scale 1: 20,000

Identification Trace for use with Artillery Maps.

22	23	24	19
28	29	30	25
		S	T Sheet 51 S.W.
		A	B Sheet 57 A.N.W
	5	6	1
10	11	12	7

Date: 2.11.18

Identification Trace for use with Artillery Maps.

19	24	23	22
25 Sheet 51 S.W.	30	29	28
1 Sheet 57 N.W.	6	5	4
7	12	11	10

S T
A B

Date: 21.11.18

27 D2 B2 3 A2 C2 9

26 D1 A1 B1 C1 2

38th Batt: M.G.C.
Scale: 1-20,000

CONFIDENTIAL

War Diary
of
38th Batt'n M.G. Corps
From 1st to 31st December 1918

Vol. 10

Vol. 10

Army Form C. 2118.

WAR DIARY
~~INTELLIGENCE SUMMARY~~
(Erase heading not required.)

Instructions regarding War Diaries and Intelligence Summaries are contained in F.S. Regs., Part II. and the Staff Manual respectively. Title pages will be prepared in manuscript.

38ᵗʰ Bⁿ M.G.C.

Place	Date	Hour	Summary of Events and Information	Remarks and references to Appendices
Aulnoye	1/12/18		Nil.	
	2/12/18		Bⁿ lost to R.A.M.C. in Rugby Football Comp⁺	
	3/12/18		Visit of H.M. The King. Bⁿ lost to 19ᵗʰ Welsh in Asso⁺. Football Comp⁺	M.G. B 49
	4/12/18		Nil.	
	5/12/18		Brank Cross Country Run. Bⁿ beat R.A.M.C.	
	6/12/18		Capᵗ. Ag⁺ Wright on leave to U.K. Capᵗ. Goldsbrough 2ⁱ⁄c took over duties of Adj⁺.	
	7/12/18		Nil.	
	8/12/18			
	9/12/18		2/L⁺ W.G. Coutts joined Bⁿ posted to "A" Cº	

Army Form C. 2118.

WAR DIARY
or
INTELLIGENCE SUMMARY.
(Erase heading not required.)

38th Bn M.G.C.

Place	Date	Hour	Summary of Events and Information	Remarks and references to Appendices
Aubigny	10 11 12		Nil. Very bad weather	
	13/12		Major A.E. McCann returned from leave	
	14/12		Lieuts G.E. WALLER & H.J. TOBIN rejoined Bn from hospital. To "A" Coy	
	15/12		Nil.	
	16/12		Draft of 14 O.R. joined Bn. Formed Bn Glee Party	
	17/12		Nil.	
	18/12		2 O.R. joined Bn	
	19 20 21 22 23		Nil. Bad weather interfered with training & sport Lt HORNE rejoined from hospital. Posted to "A" Coy	
	24/12		13 O.R. joined Bn from Base. "A" Coy Sergts Christmas Dinner	

WAR DIARY
or
INTELLIGENCE SUMMARY.

(Erase heading not required.)

Army Form C. 2118.

Place	Date	Hour	Summary of Events and Information 5th Bn. M.G.C.	Remarks and references to Appendices
Amerval	25/12		C & D Coys Bn Xmas dinner & concerts. Part of the food & rations etc. had arrived from England, & supply of turkeys fowls, there was plenty of pork, beefetc, & everyone seemed satisfied, however	
	26/12		Officers Xmas/old Bn. got 2nd prize in 16-voice Glee, Pte Parry (HQrs) 2nd prize in Baritone Solo. C & D Coys songs. Dinner	
	27/12		A & B Coys Dinners Deferred from 25th. All s'own arrivals in time. Concerts after Dinners.	
	28/12 29/12 30/12		Nil	
	31/12		Bn. marched to ENGLEFONTAINE (12 miles) en route to BEAUCOURT. Transport marched to MONTAY	Order no 69

A.G. Lyttelton
5th Bn M.G.C.

M.G.B.49.

O's.C.,
  A, B, C & D Coys.
H.Q.Officers.
Q.M.
Bn.T.O.
R.S.M.
_____

1.   His Majesty the King will be passing by car through AULNOYE between 11.00 hours and 11.15 hours on December 3rd.

2.   Probable route U.23.d. - concrete bridge U.29.a. - C.5.a.- PETIT MAUBEUGE - C.11.

3.   Battalion will parade as strong as possible (less Transport and 50% employed). 50% Headquarters will parade with Companies. The Sergeant Major will arrange details. Battn. Association Football Team will not parade: Cross Country Runners will parade to-morrow.

4.   Battalion will fall in in mass on Field U.28.b. at 09.00 hrs

         <u>Dress.</u>
         <u>Officers.</u>   Kid Gloves - no canes - puttees - spurs.

                 <u>O.Rs.</u>   Belt and Side-Arms - Woollen Gloves - any mounted men, bandoliers and spurs.

5.   Commanding Officer - Second-in-Command - Adjutant - Company Commanders will be mounted.

6.   Battalion will move away after his Majesty has passed, following Divisional Headquarters personnel.

                                       (sd) W.WRIGHT. Capt. & Adjt.
                                                     38th Battn.M.G.C.

2nd December 1918.

TABLE showing STAGING PLACES, ROUTES, ACCOMMODATION and DESTINATIONS to accompany 38th Bn.M.G.C. ORDER No.69.

Column.	31st/1st.	1st/2nd.	2nd/3rd.	3rd/4th.	4th/5th.
114th Bde. GROUP					
Dismounted Troops.	ENGLEFONTAINE, HECQ & VENDEGIES Area - via LOCQUIGNOL. (Billets)	INCHY - via MONTAY. (Billets)	Embus for BEAUCOURT - via CAMBRAI BAPAUME ALBERT HEDAUVILLE VARLOY.		
Transport.	NEUVILLE or MONTAY - via LOCQUIGNOL & ENGLEFONTAINE. (Men in billets - horses under cover)	LASNIERES - via NEUVILLY, INCHY, AUDENCOURT, CAUDRY STA., HAUCOURT & LESDAIN. (Huts)	HANANCOURT & ETRICOURT - via FINS. (Huts - Horses under cover)	ALBERT or MEAULTE - via MOISLAINS & CLERY. (Tent Camps between ALBERT & BOUZINCOURT or Tent Camps HEAULTE).	BEAUCOURT. BAVELINCOURT. AMIENCOURT.

38th BATTALION MACHINE GUN CORPS.

ORDER No. 89.

28th December 1918.

Copy No. 16

Ref. Maps. VALENCIENNES. 12. 1/100,000
        LENS. 11.   "
        AMIENS. 17.   "

1. The Battalion will move to BEAUCOURT Area with the 114th Bde. Group on the 31st inst. Time of parade later.

2. The Battalion will move in two portions – mounted and dismounted – the former by march the whole way, and the latter by march to INCHY and thence by bus.

3. Dates, routes, staging places, accommodation and destination as per table overleaf.

4. Strict attention will be paid to march discipline, and smartness in getting in and out of billets. Staging areas must be left scrupulously clean.

5. <u>Distances</u> to be maintained are :-

    Between Battalions   - 500^x
       "   Companies   - 100^x
      "   Transport of
                  Units   - 100^x

6. EMBUSSING. G.R.O. 3159 will be strictly adhered to, except that 25 Officers and Men is the load for each Bus.
Bus columns will halt for ½ hr. after the first hour and a half, and for ¼ hr. after every subsequent 2½ hrs.
The rate will be 7 m.p.h. and the journey will probably take about 8 hours.

7. Administrative instructions will be issued separately.

8. ACKNOWLEDGE. *(only recipients marked x)*

                                    R.W. Goldsbrough Capt. & A/Adjt.
                                             38th Battn. M.G.C.

Issued at   hours.

Copy to/
    Os.C.,
  X A. B. C & D Coys.   R.S.M.
  X Bn. T.O.   Chaplain.
  X R.Q.M.S.   38th Div. "G".
    M.O.   "   "   "Q".
    Sig.O.   File.
    B.I.O.   War Diary.
    114th Inf. Bde.

WAR DIARY.
~ of ~
38th Batty M.G. Corps
from 1st Jan '19 to 31st Jan '19

Vol: 11

CONFIDENTIAL.

Army Form C. 2118.

WAR DIARY
or
INTELLIGENCE SUMMARY.
(Erase heading not required.)

35th Bn M.G.C.

Place	Date	Hour	Summary of Events and Information	Remarks and references to Appendices
Inchy	1/19		Left ENGLEFONTAINE at 9.10 a.m. fine weather. Arrived INCHY for dinner 12 mdy. Good billets. Transport marched from MONTAY to MAISNIÈRES. 19 miles	
Beaucourt	2/19		Entrained at D30. Arrangements not too good, & the battalion got split up at the start. C.O's being Jup. Arrived BEAUCOURT 4 p.m. Several lorries broke down, & did not arrive till 10 p.m. These included the lorries with cooks & rations. Transport to MANANCOURT. Reinforcements 4 N.C.Os. 14 miles	
"	3/19		All hands busy arranging billets. Advance party's efforts have been much impeded by difficulty of getting material & there is a lot to be done. Transport marched to MEAULTE across devastated area. Accommodation very bad both for men & animals. Distance 24 miles.	
"	4/19		Transport joined Bn. 15 miles march. All animals in good condition. Very little difficulty on the march. Reinforcements 2 O.R.	

Army Form C. 2118.

WAR DIARY
or
INTELLIGENCE SUMMARY.
(Erase heading not required.)

Place	Date	Hour	Summary of Events and Information	Remarks and references to Appendices
Beaumont	5/1/19		38th F.A. Here	
	6/1		Nil. Capt. Wright rejoined from leave	
	7/1			
	8/1/19		Nil	
	9/1			
	10/1		Reinforcements 1 O.R.	
	11/1		Demobilised Lt A. Stewart M.C.	
			" G.W. Radford M.C.	
			15 O.R.	
	12/1		" Lt J.E. Culhane	
			21 O.R.	
			" 11 O.R.	
	13/1		Reinforcements 16 O.R.	

Army Form C. 2118.

WAR DIARY
or
INTELLIGENCE SUMMARY.
(Erase heading not required.)

Place	Date	Hour	Summary of Events and Information	Remarks and references to Appendices
Beaucourt	14/1		38th Bn. M.G.C. Capt. T. F. DAVIES Lt. R.L. THOMPSON 3 O.R. Demobilised	
	15/1		B" year 19/wish in hop-of-war 2 falls to 1. Demobilised 15 O.R. Reinforcement 1 O.R.	
	16/1 17/1		Nil.	
	18/1		Demobilised Lt. F.S. GRIFFITH 18 O.R. Reinforcement 1 O.R. Major Jackson returned from leave	
	19/1		Demobilised 14 O.R.	

WAR DIARY
or
INTELLIGENCE SUMMARY.
(Erase heading not required.)

Army Form C. 2118.

Place	Date	Hour	Summary of Events and Information	Remarks and references to Appendices
Beauvoir	20/1		38th Bn HQ. Demobilizs Lieut - A.J. Jones 2/Lt A+Allan 21 O.R.	
	21/1		Rifle meeting. Prize list. M.G. Comp. 1st C.Co 2nd D. 3rd A. China Plate 1st A Co 2nd D. 3rd B. Rifle Team Comp. 1st B Co 2nd A. Individual 1st 2/Lt Watkins 2nd Capt Smith 3rd Lt Andrews	Revolver Team 1st B Co 2nd B. Individual 1st Capt Smith 2nd Lt Wheelock 3rd 2/Lt Beaver Rifle Pool 1st Lt Wheelock 2nd Lt Shaw 3rd Pt Mobley Revolver Pool 1st Lt Wheelock 2nd Major McCrum 3rd Capt Smith Rifle S.A.S Prelim. 1st Shaw 2nd 2/Lt Discombe Revolver " 2/Lt Beaver Sgt Trimble Pt Blow Brown
	22/2		Rifle meeting cont. Demobilizd 1. J.H.I. Holwill 16 O.R.	

WAR DIARY
or
INTELLIGENCE SUMMARY.

Army Form C. 2118.

(Erase heading not required.)

Place	Date	Hour	Summary of Events and Information	Remarks and references to Appendices
Beaumont	23/2		38th Bn. M.G.C. Nil	
	24/2		Semi final of Tug of war. Lost to 19/R.W.F.	
	25/2		Demobilised 19 O.R.	
	26/2		Demobilised Major C.A.M. Jackson Lieut H.S. Newton 17 O.R.	
	27/2		Demobilised 22 O.R.	
	28/2		Final of Bn. Cross Country. B Co finishes 3rd Lt E.T. Jones Demobilised. 17 O.R.	

WAR DIARY
or
INTELLIGENCE SUMMARY

Army Form C. 2118.

Place	Date	Hour	Summary of Events and Information	Remarks and references to Appendices
Beaucourt	29/1		38th Bn M.G.C. Lecture on Poor Person among by Lt Col Parkinson 15/West Regt	
			Strength Major R.H. Jones 13 O.R.	
	30/1		terms (ilig) (Repatriation) 2 O.R.	
	31/1		Reinforcement 1 Junior S.O.	

A.G. Lyttelton Lt=Col
38th Bn M.G.C.

W 12

CONFIDENTIAL.

War Diary
~ of ~
38th Battn M.G. Corps
from 1st to 28th Feb 1919.
(Vol: 12.)

Army Form C. 2118.

WAR DIARY
or
INTELLIGENCE SUMMARY.
(Erase heading not required.)

Instructions regarding War Diaries and Intelligence Summaries are contained in F. S. Regs., Part II. and the Staff Manual respectively. Title pages will be prepared in manuscript.

Place	Date	Hour	Summary of Events and Information	Remarks and references to Appendices
Beaumont	1/2/19		3rd B⁻ M.G.C. Demobilised Lieut J.N.SHAW M.C. 2/Lieut J.H. POTTIE 25 O.Rs	
	2/2/19		Football officers v. sergeants. Officers won 5-0 (five love) Demobilised Lieut V.H. GLENDENING 19 O.R.	
	3/2/19		Demobilised Lieut H.A. POTTER 2/Lieut T.W. LISCOMBE 15 O.R.	
	4/2/19		Bⁿ won Divisional Bicycle Race.	
	5/2/19		Nil.	
	6/2/19		Bⁿ visited by H.R.H. The Prince of Wales Demobilised 12. O.R.	
	7/2/19		Demobilised 10. O.R.	

Army Form C. 2118.

WAR DIARY
or
INTELLIGENCE SUMMARY.

(Erase heading not required.)

35th B. M.G.C.

Place	Date	Hour	Summary of Events and Information	Remarks and references to Appendices
Beaucourt	8/2/19		Demobilized 10 O.R.	
	9/2/19		" " 4 O.R.	
	10/2/19		Lieut. D. ANDREW RUF won 3-1.	
	11/2/19		Leaves 38 Por. 16 Rm RWF RUF	
			Lieut McMychillan left for Conference at War Office, London	
			26 O.R.	
	13/2/19		Demobilized 20 R's Major H.C. McLaren assumed command.	
	14/2/19		Demobilized 20 R's	
			" 30 R's	
			" 20 R's. Leave Party with Major Adamson had to Portsmouth, Hrs.	
	15/2/19		" 20 R's. Arleville.	
	18/2/19		Proceeded to the Evaluators. Bordeaux leave to UK Capt. Jannik left unit (Regulars)	
	19/2/19		Lt Col McLachlan granted 7 D.R's Capt 2Rth Amyth left unit (Regulars)	
	19/2/19		Demobilized 7 OR's	
	20/2/19		Demobilized 1 OR.	
	21/2/19		8 OR's	
	23/2/19		Major T. McClean ordered to Etaples (23-27th): Major W. Adamson had assumed command.	

Army Form C. 2118.

WAR DIARY
or
INTELLIGENCE SUMMARY.
(Erase heading not required.)

February 1915.

Place	Date	Hour	Summary of Events and Information	Remarks and references to Appendices
Beaucourt	24th		38 Bn M.G.C. 38th v 385th. Association Football. Bac won 3-1.	
	26th		Rumoured 3 O.R.s.. Lt Col Williams on leave to U.K. 26-1st March. Officers return match with NCOs knelt. NCOs won 6-4.	
	27th		13.8.287 Sergt. S.E. Bryant married mademoiselle Marie Depontal of Fleurbaix. Service was conducted by Father Hughes R.C. The whole Battalion was present. Wedding breakfast for sergeants followed. Regimental concert was held in the evening. Major McClean returned from leave. Lt McDarby leaves to U.K. 28 – 13th March Sergt Bryant went 7 days leave to Headins.	
	28th			

A McLean
Major
Commanding 38th Bn.
Machine Gun Corps

1/3/19

CONFIDENTIAL

M 13

War Diary

of the

38th Battⁿ M.G. Corps

From 1st to 31st March 1919

Volume 13

Army Form C. 2118.

WAR DIARY
or
INTELLIGENCE SUMMARY.

(Erase heading not required.)

Instructions regarding War Diaries and Intelligence Summaries are contained in F. S. Regs., Part II. and the Staff Manual respectively. Title pages will be prepared in manuscript.

38th Bn. M.G.C.

Place	Date	Hour	Summary of Events and Information	Remarks and references to Appendices
BEAUCOURT	1/3/19		Association Football v 121 Brigade R.F.A. Lost 3 nil.	
	2/3/19		Demotilyca 1 O.R.	
	3/3/19		Nil	
	4/3/19		"	
			Regimental Concert held in evening.	
	5/3/19		Demotilyca O.R. 9.	
	6/3/19		Nil	
	7/3/19		Demotilyzed Major F.C.W. Taylor O.R. 10	
	8/3/19		Demotilyzed O.R. 12.	
	9/3/19		} nil	
	10/3/19			
	11/3/19		Nil	
	12/3/19		Demotilyzed O.R. 20	
	13/3/19		Instructions received to form Cadre B - eventually to proceed to U.K. for home service.	
	14/3/19		Major General T. Astley Cubitt C.B, C.M.G, D.S.O. paid farewell visit prior to proceeding to Rhine Army	
	15/3/19		nil	
	16/3/19			

Army Form C. 2118.

WAR DIARY
or
INTELLIGENCE SUMMARY.
(Erase heading not required.)

38th Bn. M.G.C.

Place	Date	Hour	Summary of Events and Information	Remarks and references to Appendices
BEAUCOURT	17.3.19		Nil	
	18.3.19		Lt. Col. O.C. Lyttelton rejoined from leave	
	19.3.19		Nil	
	20.3.19		Nil	
	21.3.19		Lt. Col. O.C. Lyttelton went to U.K. M.G.T.C. Major M.C. Milani took command of the Corps.	
	22.3.19		Nil	
	23.3.19			
	24.3.19			
	25.3.19		1 Man killed and 1 wounded in an accident at ELISY.	
			1 Officer and 33 O.R. return to 61st Batt. M.G.C.	
	26.3.19		Lt. R.W. Janvier with H.T. Wheeler went to 61st Batt. M.G.C.	
	27.3.19		Nil	
	28.3.19		Major W.L. Adamson, Lt. B.R. Edwards, Lt. E.G. Howe to 61st Batt. M.G.C.	
	29.3.19		Nil	
	30.3.19		Nil	
	31.3.19	10.30 hr	Battn. moved from BEAUCOURT to PONT NOYELLES (motor coach)	

A.M. Lawry Major
Commdg 38th Batt. M.Gun.Corps

www.ingramcontent.com/pod-product-compliance
Lightning Source LLC
Chambersburg PA
CBHW080858230426
43663CB00013B/2575